Information Management: Support Systems & Multimedia Technology

edited by

George Ditsa
University of Wollongong, Australia

IRM Press
Publisher of innovative scholarly and professional
information technology titles in the cyberage

Hershey • London • Melbourne • Singapore • Beijing

Acquisitions Editor:	Mehdi Khosrow-Pour
Senior Managing Editor:	Jan Travers
Managing Editor:	Amanda Appicello
Copy Editor:	Michelle Wilgenburg
Typesetter:	Jennifer Wetzel
Cover Design:	Michelle Waters
Printed at:	Integrated Book Technology

Published in the United States of America by
    IRM Press (an imprint of Idea Group Inc.)
    701 E. Chocolate Avenue, Suite 200
    Hershey PA 17033-1240
    Tel: 717-533-8845
    Fax: 717-533-8661
    E-mail: cust@idea-group.com
    Web site: http://www.irm-press.com

and in the United Kingdom by
    IRM Press (an imprint of Idea Group Inc.)
    3 Henrietta Street
    Covent Garden
    London WC2E 8LU
    Tel: 44 20 7240 0856
    Fax: 44 20 7379 3313
    Web site: http://www.eurospan.co.uk

Library of Congress Cataloging-in-Publication Data

Ditsa, George.
  Information management : support systems & multimedia technology /
George Ditsa.
     p. cm.
Issued also as an e-book.
  ISBN 1-931777-41-1 (soft-cover) -- ISBN 1-931777-57-8 (e-book)
  1. Electronic data processing. 2. Management information systems. I.
Title.
  QA76.D59 2003
  658.4'038'011--dc21

                                    2002156227

British Cataloguing in Publication Data
A Cataloguing in Publication record for this book is available from the British Library.

New Releases from IRM Press

- **Multimedia and Interactive Digital TV: Managing the Opportunities Created by Digital Convergence**/Margherita Pagani
  ISBN: 1-931777-38-1; eISBN: 1-931777-54-3 / US$59.95 / © 2003
- **Virtual Education: Cases in Learning & Teaching Technologies**/ Fawzi Albalooshi (Ed.),
  ISBN: 1-931777-39-X; eISBN: 1-931777-55-1 / US$59.95 / © 2003
- **Managing IT in Government, Business & Communities**/Gerry Gingrich (Ed.)
  ISBN: 1-931777-40-3; eISBN: 1-931777-56-X / US$59.95 / © 2003
- **Information Management: Support Systems & Multimedia Technology**/ George Ditsa
  (Ed.), ISBN: 1-931777-41-1; eISBN: 1-931777-57-8 / US$59.95 / © 2003
- **Managing Globally with Information Technology**/Sherif Kamel (Ed.)
  ISBN: 42-X; eISBN: 1-931777-58-6 / US$59.95 / © 2003
- **Current Security Management & Ethical Issues of Information Technology**/Rasool Azari
  (Ed.), ISBN: 1-931777-43-8; eISBN: 1-931777-59-4 / US$59.95 / © 2003
- **UML and the Unified Process**/Liliana Favre (Ed.)
  ISBN: 1-931777-44-6; eISBN: 1-931777-60-8 / US$59.95 / © 2003
- **Business Strategies for Information Technology Management**/Kalle Kangas (Ed.)
  ISBN: 1-931777-45-4; eISBN: 1-931777-61-6 / US$59.95 / © 2003
- **Managing E-Commerce and Mobile Computing Technologies**/Julie Mariga (Ed.)
  ISBN: 1-931777-46-2; eISBN: 1-931777-62-4 / US$59.95 / © 2003
- **Effective Databases for Text & Document Management**/Shirley A. Becker (Ed.)
  ISBN: 1-931777-47-0; eISBN: 1-931777-63-2 / US$59.95 / © 2003
- **Technologies & Methodologies for Evaluating Information Technology in Business**/Charles
  K. Davis (Ed.), ISBN: 1-931777-48-9; eISBN: 1-931777-64-0 / US$59.95 / © 2003
- **ERP & Data Warehousing in Organizations: Issues and Challenges**/Gerald Grant (Ed.),
  ISBN: 1-931777-49-7; eISBN: 1-931777-65-9 / US$59.95 / © 2003
- **Practicing Software Engineering in the 21st Century**/Joan Peckham (Ed.)
  ISBN: 1-931777-50-0; eISBN: 1-931777-66-7 / US$59.95 / © 2003
- **Knowledge Management: Current Issues and Challenges**/Elayne Coakes (Ed.)
  ISBN: 1-931777-51-9; eISBN: 1-931777-67-5 / US$59.95 / © 2003
- **Computing Information Technology: The Human Side**/Steven Gordon (Ed.)
  ISBN: 1-931777-52-7; eISBN: 1-931777-68-3 / US$59.95 / © 2003
- **Current Issues in IT Education**/Tanya McGill (Ed.)
  ISBN: 1-931777-53-5; eISBN: 1-931777-69-1 / US$59.95 / © 2003

Excellent additions to your institution's library!
Recommend these titles to your Librarian!

To receive a copy of the IRM Press catalog, please contact
(toll free) 1/800-345-4332, fax 1/717-533-8661,
or visit the IRM Press Online Bookstore at: [http://www.irm-press.com]!

Note: All IRM Press books are also available as ebooks on netlibrary.com as well as
other ebook sources. Contact Ms. Carrie Skovrinskie at [cskovrinskie@idea-group.com] to receive
a complete list of sources where you can obtain ebook information or
IRM Press titles.

Information Management: Support Systems & Multimedia Technology

Table of Contents

Preface

Advances in computer technology and information systems have created new opportunities as well as challenges to the management of information resources. In the past two decades or so, information management has become a key issue of interest to both researchers and practitioners since the advent of computers. The issue has become more of a concern and a challenge to both communities with the tremendous advances in computer technology and information systems in recent times. The heightened concern and challenge is, in part, due to the tremendous amount of information generated with the advancement of computer technology and information systems.

Information support systems are designed in a way to help solve some of the concerns and challenges of managing information resources. These systems provide the tools and means of managing information resources on persons, groups, and organizations. Without doubt, support systems are key topics for current and future research efforts aimed at maximizing the management of information resources.

Multimedia technology has drastically changed the way we view, interact with, and use computers. Multimedia technology succeeded in transforming computers to the real "second person." Like never before, multimedia technology has made it possible for us to see, hear, read, feel, and talk to computers. Multimedia technology has transformed and further deepened our understanding and use of computers in a more meaningful way. Without doubt, multimedia technology is a key topic for current and future application of information technology.

John Waterworth, in an attempt to draw our attention to the significance of multimedia technology, states:

The widespread application of technology that combines photographic images, graphics, text, motion video and audio material in a well-integrated way is bound to have a major impact on the development of information systems that are more than word processors, computational number crunchers, or a combination of the two. This impact will be seen in business, in science, in education, in the home, and in public places. It will reach people at almost all levels of society, and will have significant, but as yet unknown, societal impacts. This makes multimedia a uniquely exciting field to be working at the moment (1991, p. 20).

Sheu and Ismail (1998) have further stated how multimedia technology has pervaded our lives and "has forever changed the way we live, work, entertain, and learn. With wide access to the Internet, kids can spend more time online experimenting with and learning from computers through the Information Super-highway than on the TV. Once the power of image, video, and graphic through high-speed fiber-optics transmission or wireless communication is enjoyed, the old-fashioned approach of using plain text as a main source of information will be a thing of the past" (p. xxi).

Multimedia technology has also offered the means and ways of managing information resources.

This book uniquely combines both issues of support systems and multimedia technology in information management today. The book has been arranged and organized having in mind both practitioners and researchers and is, therefore, suitable for both communities. The book is also suitable for graduates and under-graduates in support systems and multimedia technology.

ORGANIZATION OF THIS BOOK

This book is organized into 15 chapters. The first chapter, by Li Yao and Weiming Zhang, presents a Basic Organization Structure (BOS) model for building a large and complex distributed cooperative information system in large mutual networks. The chapter argues that a large and complex cooperative information system and its subsystems in a LAN can be modeled by multi-agent organization and basic organization respectively; and that with the BOS model, such a cooperative information system can be developed easily and is more manageable, effectively supporting the complicated cooperative methods under certain conditions.

Chapter II presents a novel method for software personalization by which a set of mechanisms tailored to a particular end user and his or her task can be achieved. This chapter, by Tamara Babaian, used the proposed method in a collaborative system called Writer's Aid. The method relies on a declarative specification of preconditions and effects of the system's actions and applies artificial intelligence, automated reasoning, and planning framework and techniques to dynamically recognize the lack or availability of the personal information at the precise time when it affects a system action and initiates an interaction with a user aimed at eliciting this information in case it has not yet been specified.

Chapter III, by Fiona Y. Chan and William K. Cheung, further deals with the concept of personalization, which edges improvement of stickiness of on-line stores. The chapter describes in detail how to implement a knowledge-based recommender system for supporting an adaptive store. The chapter proposed a conceptual framework, which is characterized by a user profiling and product characterization module, a matching engine, an intelligent gift finder, and a backend subsystem for content management.

Chapter IV presents a Compliance Flow Workflow for managing processes. This chapter, by Larry Y.C. Cheung, Paul W.H. Chung, and Ray J. Dawson, used model-based reasoning to identify the compliance errors of a process by matching it against the model of standards used. Some examples, drawn on a draft version of IEC61508, are used to illustrate the mechanism of modeling compliance checks.

Chapter V analyzes the role of users in enacting Intelligent Transport Systems functions and services. In this chapter, Thomas A. Horan reviews preliminary evidence from recent demonstrations and market research studies with a focus on the role of travelers in producing and using information about traffic conditions and traveler options. The potential for systems development is then considered with specific regard to alternative modes of travel, flexible travel, and emergency and commercial services.

Chapter VI addresses the issue of multimedia in computer supported collaborative work (CSCW). In this chapter, Dirk Trossen and Erik Molenaar present the realization of an application sharing service based on the paradigm of application's evolving state, which is mostly suited for closed development or teaching scenarios.

In Chapter VII, Steven Walczak, Irena Yegorova, and Bruce H. Andrews present the effect of training set distributions for supervised learning artificial neural networks on classification accuracy. The chapter examines the effect of changing the population distribution within training sets for estimated distributed density functions, in particular for a credit risk assessment problem.

Chapter VIII presents research into users' behavior in using a support system in an organizational setting. This chapter, written by George Ditsa, used a model from organizational behavior to investigate factors that explain users' behavior towards using executive information systems (EIS) and identifies the relative importance of those factors that determine the use of EIS. The chapter discusses the results of the study and its implications for research and practice.

Chapter IX is on culture and anonymity in group support systems (GSS) meetings. In this chapter, Moez Limayem, Mohamed Khalifa, and John Coombes used social psychology and Hofstede's model of cultural differentiation to explain the different effects of anonymity on the behavior of Hong Kong and Canadian groups during GSS sessions. This chapter hopes that understanding the effects of anonymity in different cultural contexts will better inform the design and facilitation of GSS in the increasingly diverse global settings.

Chapter X presents a detailed model for designing a Web-based Multi-Criteria Group Support Systems (MCGSS). The model is based on AHP and uses the intensity of preferences of group members rather than simple voting procedures. This chapter, by Sajjad Zahir and Brian Dobing, points out the advantages offered by this approach.

Chapter XI presents the basic concepts of the Activity Theory and its potential as a theoretical foundation for information systems research. This chapter, written by George Ditsa, argues that the set of philosophical concepts presented by the Activity Theory makes it possible to marry the human and the technological aspects of information systems into a more holistic research approach in information systems.

Chapter XII, by Roberto Paiano, Leonardo Mangia, and Vito Perrone, defines a publishing model for Web applications starting from the analysis of the most well-known modeling methodology, such as hypermedia design models (HDM), OOHDM, WebML, Conallen's method and others. The analysis focuses on verifying the state of the art about the modeling of Web application pages; in particular, the different types of elements that compose the Web page in the models considered.

Chapter XIII presents LEZI, an experimental software tool oriented to the production of indexed videos enriched with hypertextual and multimedia elements for distance learning applications. Written by Mario A. Bochicchio and Nicola Fiore, this chapter shows how a traditional lesson or a conference can be effectively transformed into a powerful multimedia product based on a very simple and regular structure.

Chapter XIV, by Antonio Díaz-Andrade and Martín Santana, introduces electronic journalism as a new trend in the news services that have recently been boosted by Internet diffusion. Using the Peruvian information media, this chapter presents electronic media pioneers in the world and the challenges they faced to deliver news to their traditional and Internet-based customers.

Finally, Chapter XV, authored by Dongming Cui and Jairo A. Gutiérrez, looks at an integrated network management framework using CORBA, mobile agents, and Web-based technologies. This chapter proposes a new Web-based network framework management, which combines the strengths of the above named technologies.

REFERENCES

Sheu, B.J. & Ismail, M. (Eds.)(1998). *Multimedia Technology for Application.* IEEE Press.

Waterworth, J. (Ed.)(1991). *Multimedia: Technology and Application.* Ellis Horwood.

Acknowledgments

Many people deserve my sincere thanks for their contribution to this book. The chapter authors did a remarkable job, not only in putting together high quality chapters, but also in submitting the chapters in a timely fashion to meet the tight schedule within which this book was published. Their insights and excellent contributions make this book what it is. My special thanks go to all these hardworking chapter authors. I would also like to thank all the chapter reviewers without whom we would not be able come out with this high quality book.

My sincere and special thanks go to IRM Press, Inc., whose contributions throughout the whole process from inception of the initial idea to the final publication have been invaluable. My special thanks go to the publishing team at the IRM Press, Inc. — in particular Amanda Appicello, managing editor, who continuously prodded via e-mail for keeping the project on schedule; Mehdi Khosrow-Pour, acquisitions editor, whose enthusiasm and professionalism motivated me to initially accept his invitation for taking on this project; and Jan Travers, senior managing editor, for professionally managing the team for this project.

Finally, I want to thank my family and friends for their love and support throughout the project, and my institution for creating the necessary environment for this project.

George Ditsa
University of Wollongong, Australia

Chapter I

An Intelligent Agent-Based Cooperative Information Processing Model

Li Yao
National University of Defense Technology, China

Weiming Zhang
National University of Defense Technology, China

ABSTRACT

This chapter presents a Basic Organization Structure (BOS) model for building the large and complex distributed cooperative information system in large mutual networks. It argues that a large and complex cooperative information system and its subsystems in a LAN can be modeled by multi-agent organization and basic organization respectively. With the BOS model, such a cooperative information system can be developed easily and it is more manageable, effectively supporting the complicated cooperative methods under uncertain conditions. BOS is mainly used to support the cooperative problem solving among the coarse-grained, loosely coupled, and groups of semiautonomous agents. The essential characteristics, knowledge representations, and computational models of the BOS model are illuminated in this chapter. As an application example, we use the BOS model to realize the distributed Assumption-based Cooperative Problem Solving (ACPS) in the Distributed Traveling Information Management System prototype.

INTRODUCTION

With the rapid development of new and high information technologies, such as distributed artificial intelligence, data ware, data mining, and computer supported cooperating work, the cooperative information systems appear more and more in various aspects in man's work and management. Establishing a cooperative information system on the Internet or Intranet can unify the different organizations, personnel, cultures, and machines on a virtual platform; therefore, it plays an important role for modern business enterprises to manage their information and knowledge.

However, constructing the cooperative information system on large network is a very sophisticated and difficult work. First, a system of such kind, involving hundreds, perhaps thousands of parts interacting with each other, is so complex that the work to implement and manage it is very hard. Second, the cooperative information system may include various kinds of information sources that often vary constantly over time in a dynamically changing environment. Such a system must dynamically and effectively process a great deal of complicated, incomplete, and inaccurate rude data from different information sources in order to generate information of reliability with good quality for the users. Thus, there is a pressing need for new models and techniques to support the developing and managing processes of such complex information systems.

Agent and agent-based computing provide the natural and valid means for building complex cooperative information systems (Mike, 1991) and are becoming a powerful paradigm for designing and developing complex software systems (Jennings, 2000; Zambonelli, 2001). However, although agent and agent-based computing have been an active research area for many years, it is only now that agent technologies are beginning to be applied to the development of large-scale and complex commercial, industrial, military, educational, and medical treatment information systems. So knowing how to build actual agent-based applications or multi-agent systems is still in its infancy.

To solve the information-processing problems by multi-agent systems cooperatively and efficiently, we present the Basic Organization Structure (BOS) model, which can support the complicated cooperative methods under uncertain conditions. We have used the BOS model as an organization framework to realize the

Assumption-Based Cooperative Problem Solving (ACPS) model (Yao, 1997a), which is a complicated cooperative method. By accumulating the evidences and eliminating the contradictions in the cooperation dynamically, ACPS is used to support the continuous cooperative problem solving among multiple agents under uncertain conditions. The research target is to develop a basic organizational structure for the distributed cooperative information system so as to build such large and complex information system rapidly and effectively. And the key issue in research is how to organize the local agents and problem solving within the network, so that in the fixed period and under the condition of limited bandwidth, the agent can effectively cooperate and process the incomplete, inaccurate, and complicated data information to get the user-satisfied solution.

In this chapter we show, with the aid of an application example, that a large and complex cooperative information system and its subsystems in a LAN can be modeled by organization and basic organization respectively. With the BOS model, such a cooperative information system can be developed easily and it is more manageable, effectively supporting the complicated cooperative methods under uncertain conditions. Specifically, the chapter is organized as follows. First, we introduce and discuss related work in this area briefly. Then, we introduce the basic concepts, knowledge representations, and the computing model of BOS. After this, we introduce the ACPS model and use an application example to show how to realize the ACPS method by BOS. Finally, we conclude by outlining some related issues and the future research directions.

BACKGROUND

The purpose of establishing organizations is to make the members in an organization cooperate effectively to realize goals. Nowadays, many DAI researchers believe that when designing a multi-agent system, an organization layer should be considered carefully and added to the system structure. This organization layer should include at least the organization knowledge, the problem solving strategies, and the corresponding mechanisms to control and monitor the cooperative procedures, etc. (Kirn, 1996).

As early as 1981, Fox had studied the relationship between organization theory and distributed systems, and argued that by viewing distributed systems as analogues to human organizations, concepts and theories germane to the management science field of organization can be applied (1981). In 1981, Wesson and other men studied the cooperative problem solving in the "Committee Organization" with the military situation assessment tasks (1981). In 1987, Huber proposed a new idea to research "Intelligent Organization" at the Hawaii International

Conference on System Science (HICSS) (Kirn, 1996). In 1995, Decker et al. established the MACRON system used in the Internet Cooperative Information Gathering (CIG) by using the idea of matrix organization in modern society (Decker, 1995). And in 1996, Stefan Kirn (1996) analyzed in an article the relations between the distributed artificial intelligence technology and the organizational intelligence (Matsuda, 1992). He pointed out that the organizational layer and the corresponding functional concepts played an important role in the inner structure designing of the MAS and the system implementations.

In recent years, more and more research works are about agent-oriented software engineering (Ciancarini, 2001; Jennings, 2000). Much of them are associated with concepts and theories from the management science field of organization (Zambonelli, Jennings & Wooldridge, 2001; Wooldridge, Jennings & Kinny, 2000). For example, Gaia (Wooldridge et al., 2000) suggests defining the structure of a MAS in terms of a role model. This model identifies the roles that agents have to play within the MAS and the interaction protocols in which the different roles are involved. Although the methods like Gaia are very useful for the analysis and design of MAS, they can not solve how to deploy MAS on a LAN or manage knowledge within MAS and the interrelationships between the various problem-solving components or subsystems in order to cooperate effectively.

In the early 1990s, we put forward a micro organizational structure (MOS) framework with the agents constrained by the organizations (Yao, 1995), and ACPS was also studied experimentally. Based on the MOS framework, the BOS model introduced in this chapter is designed according to the cooperative problem solving within the current LAN architecture and hierarchy organization. So it is a cooperative knowledge representation framework, which is mainly used to support the cooperative problem solving among coarse-grained, loosely coupled, and groups of semiautonomous intelligent agents. Our current research work is to apply the BOS model and the ACPS methods to the Distributed Traveling Information Management System and to establish a practical cooperative information processing system.

BASIC ORGANIZATION STRUCTURE (BOS) MODEL

Introduction to BOS

Generally speaking, complexity frequently takes the form of a hierarchy (Jennings, 2001). So we can organize the large and complex cooperative information system as a hierarchy multi-agent system. Because multi-agent systems are viewed as computational organization very naturally (Zambonelli, Jennings & Wooldridge, 2001), we can obtain some characteristics from analyzing organizational structure and functions (Yao, 1997b; Yao et al., 1999).

A social organization is generally composed of several smaller basic organizations. So, the cooperation exists both among these basic organizations and within each of them. For example, a university consists of many departments, and a department is divided into several teaching and researching sections or administrative sections. If a section is regarded as a basic organization, the organization is then composed of a chief of the section, several staff members, and the public facilities.

From a structural analysis viewpoint, large and complex computing organization in a LAN can be modeled by some smaller basic groups of agents, which is called BOS. From a function analysis viewpoint, BOS also has six main functions in an organization, such as representational function, organizational function, cognitive or decision function, interaction function, productive or operative function, vegetative or preservative function (Ferber & Gutknecht, 1998). Besides above properties, BOS at different abstract levels have some other commonness. The commonness is as follows: (1) Each BOS has a sole manager that administers the problem solving in a whole BOS. (2) Some shared knowledge, information or data can be stored on the server and managed by the special full time agent, which can cooperate with the agent playing same role in other BOS in order to utilize various resources in overall organization effectively. (3) Although an agent may play more than one role in an organization, sometimes it is necessary for the management of a BOS to divide the agents playing managing roles from agents playing productive roles. (4) BOS can be viewed as a distributed computer system that is situated in some environment, and that is capable of autonomous action in this environment in order to play the role in the organization and meet the local goal.

For example, Figure 1 is a part of organizational Chart of Distributed Traveling Information Management System (DTIMS) (Yao et al., 2002). In the vertical, it shows the authority and accountability relations, and in the lateral, it shows the divided work and cooperation relations. This hierarchical, multi-agent system can be modeled by three basic groups of agents, i.e., BOS.

From functional analysis and structural analysis above, we propose the BOS model. In this model, BOS can be considered as a basic block of an organization, in which the tight interrelations among several agents or among groups of agents can be represented, between blocks the loose interrelations among several agents or among groups of agents can be represented. By this way, the interrelations among several agents or among groups of agents can be controlled more effectively; thus, the system will run effectively and cooperatively as a whole and implement the corresponding global and local goals.

Figure 1. A Part of Organizational Chart of DTMIS

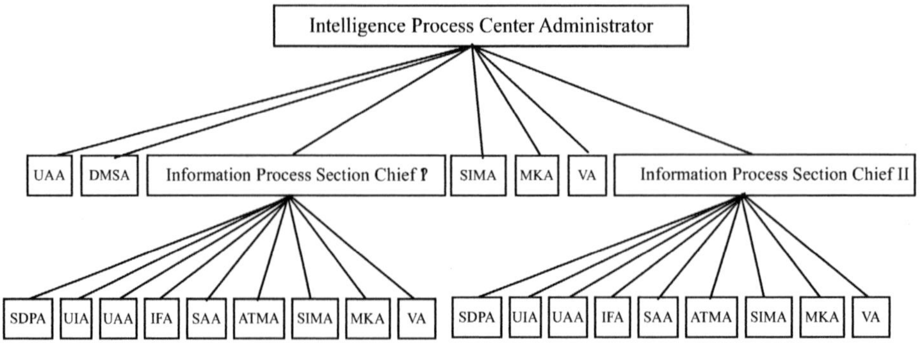

SDPA: Sensor Data Process Agent.
UIA: User's Information inputting Agent
SAA : Situation Accessing Agent
UAA : User Assistant Agent
MKA: Meta-Knowledge management Agent

VA : Visualizing Agent
IFA: Information Fusing Agent
ATMA: distributed Assumption-based Truth Maintenance Agent
SIMA: Sharing Information Management Agent
DMSA : Decision-Making Support Agent

The Characteristics of an Agent in a Basic Organizational Structure

If we want to view the multi-agent system as analogous to human organization, and apply the concepts and theories germane to the management science field of organization into this computing organization, we should ensure agents consisted in a MAS have some properties that are analogues to that the man has. So, in order to undertake organizational roles, we consider an agent as a computer system that is situated in some environment, and that capable of autonomous and flexible action in this environment under abiding by the organizational rules condition.

We can also define this type of agent as a semi-autonomous agent. This agent enjoys at least the following properties (Wooldridge, 2001):

- Autonomous: agents encapsulate some state that is not accessible to other agents, and make decisions about what to do based on this state, without the direct intervention of humans or others
- Reactivity: agents are situated in an environment, are able to perceive this environment, and are able to respond in a timely fashion to changes that occur in it
- Pro-activeness: agents do not simply act in response to their environment, they are able to exhibit goal-directed behavior by taking the initiative
- Social ability: agents interact with other agents (and possibly humans) via some kind of agent-communication language, such as KQML, ACL (Bradshaw, 1997), and typically have the ability to engage in social activities (such as cooperative problem solving or negotiation) in order to achieve their goals

In the DTIMS, we design and implement an agent with Belief-Desire-Intention structure, which is called CSA (Constrained-by-organization Semi-autonomic Agent), where the semi-autonomic primarily refers to being capable of autonomous and flexible action under the organizational rules. The architecture of CSA is presented in Figure 2.

Knowledge Representations in a Basic Organizational Structure

In the BOS model, a cooperatively information-processing system and their subsystems are modeled by organization and basic organization respectively. The system organization is an organic community, which is linked by the BOS according to the organizational structures and rules defined by the organizational model. All the BOSs in an organization have independent computing and cooperating abilities,

Figure 2. CSA Architecture

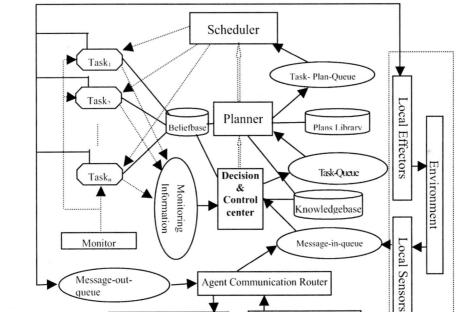

In the figure, the dashes stand for control flow and the real lines stand for information flow

and they are distributed in a LAN at different locations and interact with each other through high speed communication nets.

The BOS is a community, which is composed of agents and some agent can be a representative of a BOS. The agents here are semiautonomous intelligent agents, such as CSA in Figure 2, constrained by the organizational rules (i.e., commitments); and in the system implementations, they are defined as an active computing entity (i.e., programmable computing entity) with their data, knowledge, and operation sets encapsulated together. The cooperative actions within the BOS are cooperated and completed by various types of agents.

Five types of agents that play different roles are generally defined within BOS (see Figure 3). They are as follows.
1. Head Agent (HA)

   HA is the representative of a BOS. It is responsible for cooperating with other BOSs and scheduling the operations of various types of agents within the BOS. HA also takes charge of increasing new agents in a system or adding new functions to an agent and supervising the work state and progress within the BOS. HA is unique. It usually includes many modules, such as planner, task-distributor, scheduler, coordinator, monitor, and configurator in order to realize the functions mentioned above.
2. Maintenance and Management Agent (MA)

   The main task of MA is to assistant HA to maintain the normal run of the BOS and undertake the routine transaction management. MA usually includes visualizing, monitor, mediator, broker, coordinator, and so on.

Figure 3. The Basic Framework of a BOS

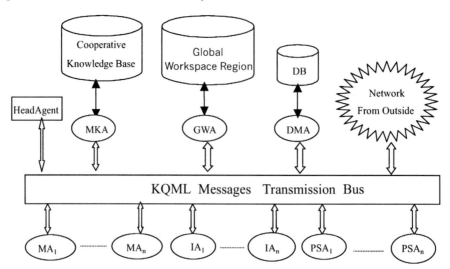

3.   Interaction Agent (IA)

Interaction Agent (IA) is in charge of the interaction activities between the BOS and its environment, as well as all interactions with other BOSs. The definition of IA depends on the organizational roles that the BOS undertakes. IA usually includes the User Aid Agent (UAA), which manages the interactions between the BOS and its user, the Sensor Data Process Agent (SDPA), which is responsible for updating sense information from environment, and so on.

4.   Problem Solving Agent (PSA)

PSA is mainly used to realize problem solving and to create cooperative tasks by using the cooperative strategies, expertise, and domain knowledge. Besides the commitment knowledge such as the organizational structures and rules the BOS has, PSA also has cooperative knowledge such as heuristic model, cooperative strategies that the related acquaintances have, and its own knowledge base. The definition of PSA shows the special skills of the BOS.

5.   Common Facility Agent (CFA)

CFA is used to manage the public data, knowledge, and information within the BOS. It is often on the servers and linked with bases. It provides other agents with access operations to the public information. The CFA between BOSs can cooperate and provide the users with the transparent global information services. The CFAs of a BOS must include the Meta-Knowledge management Agent (MKA) and Global Workspace Agent (GWA), etc. The CFA used generally also includes the Database Management Agent (DMA) and the Model-base Management Agent (MMA), etc.

For example, in our prototype of DTIMS, a BOS, called Information Process Section, has 10 agents as follows.

1.   HA: Head Agent, which is called Information Process Section Chief
2.   MA: Visualizing Agent (VA), and distributed Assumption-based Truth Maintenance Agent (ATMA)
3.   IA: Sensor Data Process Agent (SDPA), User's Information inputting Agent (UIA), and User Aid Agent (UAA)
4.   PSA: Information Fusing Agent (IFA), and Situation Assessment Agent (SAA)
5.   CFA: the Meta-Knowledge management Agent (MKA) and Sharing Information Management Agent (SIMA)

There are two kinds of organizational relationships in the BOS model. One of them is formal organizational relationship, which includes superior, subordinate, colleague and so on. The other is informal organizational relationship, which may exist between any two agents in an organization. The informal organizational relationship is also a kind of cooperation relationship, which can be represented in an agent's acquaintance model.

The Computing Model of BOS

In this section, the principal ideas of the BOS computing model are introduced briefly. In the BOS, the communications between agents use the Knowledge Query and Manipulation Language (KQML). Three sorts of important message transmissions are required to satisfy the computing continuity of the BOS. They are as follows.

1. Controlling messages that HA sends to various agents in BOS, such as task decomposition, allocation message, schedule message, cooperation message and monitor message, and so on.
2. The control feedback information from the various agents in BOS to HA, which can be used to activate and coordinate the run of the agents.
3. The cooperative messages sent by all the agents (including within or among BOS).

Tasks and Events

"Tasks" means that problem-solving orders are input by users or issued by higher-level BOS, and cooperative tasks are from other cooperators. When a system runs, each task is concretized into a problem-solving goal in BOS. Complicated problem-solving goal can be decomposed into smaller ones, and the undecomposed basic problem-solving goal can be handled by several intelligent agents cooperatively.

In BOS, we define the concept of a "BOS event" (called "event" briefly). The computations are solicited by events. An event results in a new computation or makes an unfinished computation keep on.

An event is defined as one of the following cases:
1. Sending an outer message (i.e., KQML message from or to other BOS)
2. Accepting an outer message
3. Inputting a user command
4. Inputting a real time data information
5. Displaying a console
6. Outputting an effector information

For example, in our prototype of DTIMS, a BOS has following events:
1. HA sends a cooperative message to the other BOS

2. HA accepts a cooperative message from the other BOS
3. UAA inputs a user command
4. SDPA inputs the data information from the sensors, or UIA inputs the data information from the user
5. UAA displays a result to the user

Task Decomposition and Allocation

User commands are input into BOS by UAA. UAA interprets the commands and takes charge of completing the problem-solving goals (or problem-solving tasks) corresponding to the user command event. UAA has heuristic knowledge about the goals, intentions, and abilities of various agents in BOS. The planner of UAA decomposes and allocates the simple tasks according to the knowledge. The task implementation procedures are scheduled and monitored by its scheduler and monitor. Complicated tasks are handed over to HA.

KQML messages from outside of a BOS are processed by the special IA, in accordance with the cooperative knowledge. The problem-solving tasks committed by other BOS are handed over to HA for solutions.

A real time data input is processed by SDPA. According to different types of data, SDPA stores the newly inputting data in the corresponding CFA and generates corresponding problem-solving tasks in accordance with the rude data for processing and then hands them over to HA.

According to the scheduling strategy, HA first sequences all the problem-solving tasks or goals. Then, it works out a problem-solving plan for each task. The plan can either match one in the original plan case base or be worked out according to the meta-knowledge provided by MKA. After the plan has been worked out, HA stores the structure information about the related task plans in GWA so that the cooperative problem-solving agents can share this cooperative information. HA sends control messages about task allocation to all cooperative BOSs or problem-solving agents and supervises the implementation of the problem-solving procedure.

After HA receives the feedback information from other agents or BOS, HA synthesizes these results if they are result information. If they are failure information or other cases, HA will modify the original problem-solving plans.

The basic control algorithm of HA is as follows (in approximate Common Lisp language):

```
( loop
( setq L L+1 )  /* to a new control circle
( setq EL [ event-area value in HA ] )
```

/* read all events to be processed from event area
(When [EL no empty] do
  [scheduler generates the processing sequence SPQ of EL]
  /* SPQ is event scheduling sequence
  (dolist TR in SPQ
  /* TR is an event to be processed in SPQ. TR may be a new problem-solving goal g,
    /*cooperative problem-solving result r and the factor q resulting in plan
    /*modifications
    (case TR
  g : [planner generates the scheduling sequence of the target g;
    task-distri distributes task for g and adds them to TPQ];
      /* TPQ is the task planning sequence
  r : [r is added to the corresponding task result information, the results
  are synthesized];
  q : [modify TPQ according to q])) /* case and dolist ended
  (dolist H_L (T_i) in TPQ /* each task in the task planning sequence
    (case H_L (T_i)
  PSA_L (T_i) : [sends KQML messages, makes PSA_L (T_i) finish the
  corresponding subtasks;
    the monitor monitors the running results;]
  IA_L (T_i): [sends KQML messages and makes IA_L (T_i) finish the corre
  sponding interactive tasks;
    the monitor monitors the running results;]
  BOS_L (T_i): [results in outer message sending event, and the monitor
      monitors the running results;]
  MA_L (T_i): [sends cooperative information to other agents]
    /* calls for knowledge, data or function services))
    /* case and dolist ended
(if [the ending conditions are satisfied] then
  (GO TO END))) /* loop is ended

Cooperative Computing

    After PSA receives KQML messages, it completes the corresponding problem-solving goals and returns the solving results.

    All the tasks accepted by PSA are sequenced according to the scheduling rules and then carried out by PSA one by one. The completion of each task must cooperate with other agents in accordance with the cooperative knowledge. And the cooperative knowledge comes from its own intention base, belief base and task information or from BOS's sharing information such as MKA, GWA and DMA. During the cooperation, PSA can communicate with agents in the BOS. It can also communicate directly with agents in other BOS (i.e., the simple cooperative information) or with other BOS by means of IA (i.e., the complicated heterogeneous information transfer).

We can set some special IA that is in charge of the meta-knowledge communications, the complicated information exchanges, and the task-level interactions between BOSs. According to the knowledge in MKA and the current status in GWA, IA interprets and processes the received outer messages and then sends the related information or tasks to HA or the corresponding agents.

MKA, GWA and DMA manage the sharing cooperative knowledge in BOS, the global task structure information, and the data information respectively. The common information management agent between BOSs can cooperate and provide the users with the transparent global information services.

Synthesis and Output of the Results

If the results are synthesized by UAA, they are output to users in the corresponding forms. If the results are synthesized by HA, they are returned to the committed agents or other BOS in the committed forms.

Now we use the DTIMS prototype as an example to explain a cooperative computing.

When SDPA inputs the real time data information from the sensors, it checks the form of new information, records the new information, assesses the new information according to expertise, and sends the new information to the Information Fusing Agent (IFA). In the process of assessment, if SDPA found the new information useful to the other BOS, it sends the new information to HA; if SDPA found the new information important, it sends the new information to Situation Assessment Agent (SAA) to analyze the information thoroughly.

When HA accepts the new information from SDPA, it inquires of MKA about the cooperative knowledge. According to the knowledge from MKA, HA sends the new information to the related BOS. When IFA accepts the new information from SDPA, it fuses the new information with historical information and environment information. IFA sends the new fusion results to the UAA, SAA and SIMA.

When SAA accepts the new information from SDPA and the new fusion results from IFA, it assesses the new situation according to the expertise, and sends the new situation assessment results to the UAA and SIMA.

When UAA accepts the new fusion results from IFA or the new situation assessment results from SAA, it displays the results to the user on a travel map.

When SIMA accepts the new fusion results from IFA or the new situation assessment results from SAA, it records the results to the relevant databases.

Main Advantages of the BOS Model

The main advantages are as follows:

1. The complexities of designing the agents are decreased.

   In a multi-agent system, one agent usually cooperates with several other agents. And these cooperative actions are uncertain and interwound. Therefore, to get cooperation, each agent must have a large knowledge representation framework so as to illustrate various intentions, skills, knowledge, resources, goals of the agent concerned, and so on. In the BOS model, the problem solving actions of the intelligent agent are decomposed further in detail, which not only makes each agent in the BOS decrease its cooperative relations, but also makes the knowledge representations shorter and clearer, and the problem solving actions more specified as well. Meanwhile, the knowledge about the skills, goals, intentions, resources of the related agents are represented and managed by the BOS in a unified way. Therefore, the cooperation within a BOS help to make simple agent structures realize complicated cooperative actions.

2. The complicated cooperative relations are sequenced.

   By adding a managing layer to a BOS, the decomposition, allocation, supervision and cooperation mechanisms can be unified and carried out with the HA. So, the cooperation can be done on two layers, i.e. among agents and among BOSs, which simplifies the cooperative relations and strengthens the cooperative efficiency.

3. The hierarchy structure combines organically with the parallel structure.

   The organizational structures in a cooperative problem-solving system usually are classified in three types: hierarchy structure, parallel structure, and combined structure. If a certain agent in a BOS is another BOS or an abstract representative of the next layer, then by means of global commitment, BOS can model the organizational relations in an information system with any complexities.

4. Openness.

   When new agents or new functions are added in a BOS, they can be registered to the HA and are broadcast to other BOS by the HA so as to increase new cooperative functions. When a certain agent wants to solve problems but faces unfamiliar tasks, the tasks can also be handed over to the corresponding HA in order to seek new cooperative partners. In fact, the HA is playing the role of an intelligent facilitator here. This performance makes a multi-agent system be developed gradually and incrementally.

APPLYING BOS MODEL TO REALIZE ASSUMPTION-BASED COOPERATIVE PROBLEM SOLVING

Introduction to Assumption-Based Cooperative Problem Solving (ACPS) Model

Multi-Agent Systems function in a cooperative way in which various agents with different views and beliefs can reason cooperatively and in parallel so as to complete the large, complicated and difficult problems that a single agent cannot solve. An ACPS is put forward for processing effectively a great deal of complicated, incomplete, and inaccurate rude data. By accumulating the evidences and eliminating the contradictions in the cooperation dynamically, ACPS can support the continuous cooperative problem solving among multiple agents in the undetermined environments.

The ACPS model is different from the foregoing coordinated models such as FA/C (Carver, Cvetanovic & Lesser, 1991) and DATMS (Mason & Johnson, 1989), in which various agents mainly exchange the experimental intermediate results or share the results to assemble the global solutions identically among the agents. But in ACPS, various groups of agents (i.e., BOS) keep their own reasoning spaces. Their purposes to cooperate are: (1) to achieve their respective local problem solving (i.e., local decision making); (2) to support the higher level and abstract problem solving (i.e., the higher-level decision making). The differences appeared in the problem solving results are permitted. However, the reasoning spaces within various groups of agents (i.e., BOS) are unanimous and effective, and the cooperative problem solving results meet the related consistence.

Realizing ACPS by BOS

The design of the ACPS model is based on the assumption that the domain knowledge for each BOS (i.e., smaller group of agents) in the cooperative system to implement problem solving is all correct and consistent.

Set that the newly established formalized system is Γ, the languages provided by Γ can represent the knowledge of a given BOS_i and the assumption-based reasoning carried out in the BOS_i (de Kleer, 1986a; de Kleer, 1986b; de Kleer, 1986c).

The language Γ is composed of first-order language L and unary meta language relations for the members of L. Any axiom in L is still an axiom here, and the reasoning rules concerning the axiom supposes to be Modus Ponens and Generalization.

The set of the clauses in L, Sent(L), is also the set of the closed formulas in L. In accordance with the necessary and the accidental information, Sent(L) is divided into two subsets: basic closed formula and non-basic closed formula. They can be represented respectively by $Sent_N(L)$ and $Sent_C(L)$. That is, $Sent(L) = Sent_N(L) \cup Sent_C(L)$.

The significance to divide Sent(L) is that the clause in $Sent_N(L)$ is a closed formula including variable, which represents the common features one kind of individual has in the real world, and that the clause in $Sent_C(L)$ represents the information of individual constants depending on the language. Compared to the realities these constants represent, they are accidental. Therefore, $Sent_N(L) \cap Sent_C(L) = \varnothing$.

To describe all the knowledge and information of BOS_i in Γ, a class of special closed formula is introduced, i.e., the clause without any variables and constraint variables, which is called assumption. The assumption means the accidental knowledge that is assumed to be correct. For example, if fact a is correct, it is written as A(a). Suppose that set A is in contract with the clause set in L. Then, when the contradiction appears, certain assumed closed formulas are considered to be failure. So, they are deleted from the belief base (i.e., the BOS's assumption set).

Therefore, the knowledge of BOS_i are divided into two parts, which, if represented by the language Γ, are a binary group (K_i, A_i), where, K_i is a subset of Sent(L) while A_i is the set of the accidental knowledge which are supposed to be correct. (K_i, A_i) is called an assumption-based defeasible logic structure. K_i represents the basic belief set of BOS_i, which is constantly correct, i.e., $K_i \vdash \bot$ is never correct. A_i is the set of all the accidental knowledge which supposed to be correct, indicating the part of might-be-true heuristic information of BOS_i.

Set that the Multi-Agent System (MAS) is composed of n BOSs and MAS$=\{BOS_1, BOS_2, \ldots, BOS_n\}$. Each has a currently defeasible logic structure (K_i, A_i) (i=1, 2, ..., n). In the ACPS model, the cooperative problem-solving procedure is divided into three main parts, which are Selecting Mechanism, Reasoning Mechanism, and Distributed Truth Maintaining Mechanisms realized by agents in a BOS.

The tasks of the selecting mechanism of a BOS are to analyze the rude data and the experimental intermediate results of other BOSs, and on the basis of the argument structures of these results, to select more "reasonable" conclusions as special assumed data to add to the BOS's problem solving procedure in order to form the current defeasible logic structure (K_i, A_i), (i=1, 2, ..., n).

The selected results may be incorrect, but as the evidences are accumulated, the true facts can be found eventually. Thus, the uncertainties are decreasing. The experienced rules and strategies to implement the selecting mechanism of a BOS are extremely important for improving the efficiencies.

The main tasks of the reasoning mechanism are to realize the cooperative problem solving, and according to the current defeasible logic structure (K_i, A_i), to carry out the assumption-based reasoning. That a heuristic conclusion P is derived from BOS_i means the conjunction of K_i and A_i can derive P, and when contradiction is induced, A_i is ignored. Meanwhile, the reasoning mechanism calculates the "argument structure" and "environment" information for each derivative result and records them as a node, thus making a reasoning structural net. Furthermore, on the basis of the cooperative strategies, the reasoning mechanism should communicate the conclusions and the cooperative demands concerning the cooperation to the agents in other BOSs.

The major tasks of the distributed truth maintaining mechanism are to identify the contradictions in the reasoning structural net founded according to the reasoning mechanism and to remove the conflicts by means of cooperation among multiple agents to maintain the effectiveness of the reasoning. To identify contradictions is to check whether or not all kinds of constraint conditions comply with the rules. When contradictions are found and should be eliminated, not only all the nodes in their own BOS concerning the contradiction nodes must be updated, but also all the nodes concerning the changing nodes in other BOSs must be updated. This process is called the "related consistency for maintaining the cooperative reasoning structural net."

Therefore, in ACPS, the cooperative problem-solving procedure in MAS means that the agents in various BOSs select continually their own current defeasible logic structures, carry out cooperative reasoning according to these structures, maintain the distributed truth when any contradiction is derived, ignore the inconsistent assumption set, and select new defeasible logic structures to keep on reasoning. This process keeps on running repeatedly until the goals are attained. In this model, the key problems in cooperation are how to use effectively the experimental results of other BOSs to establish assumption, the maintenance and management of the assumptions, and how to eliminate rapidly the ill effects brought by the wrong conclusion propagations when contradictions appear.

It should be noted that: (1) the data structure of each BOS can maintain several incompatible assumption sets, but all the assumptions in (K_i, A_i) constituting the currently defeasible logic structures should be compatible. Only on these defeasible logic structures will the reasoning mechanism function, and just when contradictions appear in the solution, the inconsistent assumption sets are withdrawn and all their related conclusions are eliminated; (2) the inconsistency may exist among the current assumption sets of various BOSs in the system, but they do not influence the effectiveness of the cooperative problem solving; and that is because the cooperative process is a mutual selecting process of each other and the cooperation are implemented when no contradictions are found in the current assumption sets of both sides.

DESIGNS AND IMPLEMENTATIONS OF ACPS WITH BOS MODEL IN THE DTIMS

DTIMS is implemented on a PC computer for distributed traveling situation assessment tasks. Its organization chart is seen in Figure 1. The DTIMS is composed of three BOSs. Each BOS represents an independent information processing subsystem composed of groups of agents, which is distributed on different physical locations and is linked with the other BOSs mutually in network. Thus, these BOSs can form hierarchy cooperative organizations, compute in parallel, and process information cooperatively. This section briefly introduces the basic structures of this system and then discusses the cooperative problem solving among the same level BOSs by means of ACPS.

Fundamental Definitions

In the traveling situation assessment problem solving, there may exist uncertainties or mistakes in the primary input information. Therefore, the problem-solving system must have a mechanism to maintain several possible situation models and to make the compatible models share the information so as to form the current situation-analyzing report. In the DTIMS, the ACPS method is used to realize the cooperative problem solving and implement the mechanism mentioned above.

In the DTIMS, all the information concerning the external environments and all the conclusions generated in interpreting and analyzing this information are represented as proposition. They are classified in four types of propositions: precondition, assumption, derivation, and communication.

The precondition proposition represents the pre-defined domain knowledge or generally correct propositions. Its truth remains constant during the problem solving. For example, the topographic knowledge and the features of the recognizable objects in the observing field are unchanged.

The assumption proposition indicates that there is no logic basis and it is supposed to be correct by the selecting mechanism in the system according to certain rules. The states of its truth may change during the successful procedure of problem solving. For example, the platform assumptions, expansion assumptions, and external assumptions defined in the DTIMS may change in the process of problem solving.

The derivation proposition means that all the conclusions are derived from other propositions according to the problem solving rules such as Expanding Rules, Fission Rules, Recognizing Rules, and so on. One important class of this kind is the inconsistent proposition. The appearance of this proposition in the situation model shows mistakes in the situation analysis. For example, that a space group is not recognized indicates there exists a mistake in the object assumption, and that a space group movement is incomplete indicates there are mistakes in the expansion assumption, and so on.

The communication proposition is one that determines to be communicated to the agent of other BOS in accordance with the cooperative problem-solving rules. The definition of this class of propositions is mainly used to realize the cooperative problem solving and the distributed truth maintaining.

Data Structure

The design of the data structures is extremely important to the assumption-based reasoning and has a direct influence to the problem solving efficiencies. In the DTIMS, each BOS has a Global Workspace Agent (GWA) who is a CFA and is in charge of managing shared data structures within the BOS. Their major structure, called the reasoning-workspace-area, is a complicated two-dimensional area showing the topographic information. According to the topographical positions, all the observing object information can be found. Whenever a proposition is derived in the system, a new node is founded in the reasoning structural net. Its contents are as follows:

[node : node name;
node-type : proposition type;
node-content : proposition content;
as-label : proposition label
owner : BOS's name who derives this node;
inference-description : inference rule descriptions;
ante-list : antecedent node lists that derive this node;
conse-node-list : consequent node list whose deriving depend on this node;
a-struc : argument structure of this node]

The argument structure of a node includes the following contents:

(node-time: founding time of this node;
time: having observing time of this conclusion;
S: distance between the observing position and the center position of the
BOS's sensor;
agent-list: cooperative problem solving agent list;
CF: times which this proposition has been proved)

All the derivative nodes are linked by pointers according to the deriving relations so as to form several inference tree structures, i.e., an inference structural net. On the bottom layer of this net is the two-dimensional array, reasoning-workspace-area, and the nodes located at the highest abstract level constitute the current derived situation model.

In the DTIMS, the intermediate results are classified. So, when they are referred to by topographic positions and result types, the system can ensure that the same propositions are related on the same nodes in the inference structural net, thus giving a full play to the assumption-based inference priorities.

Furthermore, by checking the constraint conditions, the system can find the contradictory states and then analyze the inconsistent assumption sets according to the contradiction types, the inconsistent context can be recognized and eliminated, and the assumption-based inference effectiveness is improved.

Basic Cooperative Problem Solving Algorithms

Algorithm implementations can be described from three aspects of selecting, reasoning, and truth maintaining.

The Selecting Mechanism

The object assumptions and the expansion assumptions are founded respectively by IFA and SAA in the problem solving process. The assumption-based problem solving tasks are generated simultaneously. The external assumptions are completed by HA. The main procedure for a assumption being founded is as follows:

- To check if there are same conclusions in the BOS's inference structural net.
- If there is a same conclusion in the GWA of this BOS, to increase the creditability of this conclusion. Then, this procedure ends.
- To calculate respectively their argument structures. If the local conclusion is in contradiction with an external one, then according to a given rule, conclusions with greater argument structural creditability are selected. If the local argument structural creditability is greater, the external conclusion is

discarded, and the procedure ends. If the external message has greater creditability, a type of truth-maintaining task is generated first, which withdraws the exiting conclusion, and then changes the external conclusion into an external assumption, to insert into the inference structural net, thus generating a problem-solving task based on this new assumption, and this procedure ends.

- If there is no same conclusion in the local BOS, the external conclusion is turned into an external assumption, which is then inserted in the inference structural net so that an assumption-based, problem-solving task is generated and then the procedure ends.

The Assumption — Based Inference Mechanism

The assumption-based inference mechanism is mainly completed by the IFA and SAA. The rules to calculate the assumption are explained as follows:

Set the assumption set of the conclusion P is $AS(P)$, and according to the definition:

If $\forall a \in AS(P)$, a supposes to be true and $AS(P)$ is consistent, and so P is creditable;

If $\forall a \in AS(P)$, a is not creditable or $AS(P)$ is inconsistent, then P is not creditable.

1. if P is the precondition proposition, then, $AS(P) = \{\}$.
2. if P is the assumption proposition, then, when P is an object assumption or an expansion assumption, $AS(P) = \{P\}$;

   when P is an external assumption, $AS(P) = \{BOS : P\} \cup \overline{AS}(P)$, where

   $\overline{AS}(P)$ is the assumption set of P in the original agent, and $BOS : P$ denotes this external assumption from BOS.

3. If P is a derivation proposition, and $a_1 \wedge a_2 \wedge \ldots \wedge a_n \longrightarrow P$, then

$$AS(P) = \bigcup_{j=1}^{n} AS(a_j).$$

4. If P is a communication proposition, the information of $AS(P)$ will be used as the environmental information to be communicated to the corresponding cooperative agents together with P.

The problem solving of IFA and SAA includes the following abstract algorithm descriptive processes:

1.   to carry out derivations according to different tasks and the inference rules;
2.   to set up nodes for the derived new proposition, to calculate their assumption sets, and to record the inference rules;
3.   to compute the argument structure for new node;
4.   to judge whether the new node is contradictory one by the constraint conditions. If contradictory occurs, then turn to truth maintenance;
5.   to refer to whether there is this node in the inference structural net. If there is, the original node is updated. Otherwise it should be inserted into the net; and
6.   to determine whether this node needs to be communicated to other agents in accordance with the cooperative rules. If so, it is labeled communication proposition and the corresponding communication tasks are generated.

The Distributed Truth Maintaining Mechanism

By the constraint conditions the DTIMS system can discover the contradictory states. The contradictory-identifying activities appear mainly in the problem-solving procedures of IFA, SAA, SDPA and UIA. When any contradiction appears, the control function is transferred to the distributed Assumption-based Truth Maintenance Agent (ATMA). And the major tasks of ATMA are to eliminate contradictory and to make the problem solver always reason in a defeasible logical structure (K_i, A_i) that results from a conformable assumption set A_i. The main process is as follows:

1.   to determine the minimum assumption set T that can cause contradictions according to the contradiction types;
2.   to eliminate all the nodes whose labels are the superset of T as contradictory nodes;
3.   to carry out four to six circularly in regard to all the contradictory nodes to be eliminated;
4.   to withdraw these nodes from the inference structural net and to check whether these nodes are communication propositions;
5.   to generate communication tasks if they are communication propositions, and to make the cooperative agents carry out the distributed truth maintaining;
6.   to check whether there are succeeding nodes to these nodes. If there are succeeding nodes, they are all labeled as contradiction nodes; and
7.   after all the contradiction nodes are eliminated, the truth maintaining process ends.

CONCLUSIONS

It is of great significance to study the organizational structure of the multi-agent system for the distributed cooperative information processing, which can greatly quicken the development in many application systems. The examples are distributed sensor network, distributed network diagnosis, distributed information retrieving and collecting, distributed electronic bookstore management, coordinated robotics or no man driving vehicles, distributed perception processing, and distributed cooperative situation assessing tasks, etc.

The problem solving in BOS is neither centralized nor all localized, but distributed dynamically according to the solving tasks. So this method is suitable for the cooperative problem solving which is real-time, dynamical, and distributed. The theory behind BOS was tested and evaluated in a series of experiments in the context of the DTIMS. The main result of the experiments was that the distributed cooperative information is processed efficiently and the hierarchical system management is in perfect order, too.

Now we are applying the BOS model to the DTIMS. In the future, we are going to develop a software platform based the BOS model, called MBOS (Yao et al., 2001), which means multiply Basic Organization Structure for creating and deploying organizationally intelligent agents that can cooperate with other agents. We prepare to use MBOS to build an Organizational Decision Support System (ODSS).

ACKNOWLEDGMENTS

This research was partly supported by a project from NSFC, which Grant No. is 79800007.

REFERENCES

Bradshaw, J. M. (1997). *Software Agents*. Menlo Park, CA: AAAI Press.

Carver, Z., Cvetanovic, Z. & Lesser, V. (1991). Sophisticated cooperation in FA/C distributed problem solving systems. *Proceedings of the 9th National Conference on Artificial Intelligence* (pp. 191-197). Anaheim, CA.

Ciancarini, P. & Wooldridge, M. (2001). *Agent-Oriented Software Engineering*. Springer-Verlag Lecture Notes in AI Volume 1957.

de Kleer, J. (1986a). An assumption-based TMS. *Artificial Intelligence, 28,* 127-162.

de Kleer, J. (1986b). Extending the ATMS. *Artificial Intelligence, 28,* 163-196.

de Kleer, J. (1986c). Problem solving with the ATMS. *Artificial Intelligence, 28,* 197-224.

Decker, K. et al. (1995). *MACRON: An Architecture for Multi-agent Cooperative Information Gathering.* University of Massachusetts: CS Technical Report 95-11.

Ferber, J. & Gutknecht, O. (1998). A meta-model for the analysis and design of organizations in multi-agent systems. *ICMAS-98,* Paris, France, 128-135.

Fox, M. S. (1981). An organizational view of distributed systems. IEEE Transaction on Systems, *Man and Cybernetics, 11*(1), 70-70.

Jennings, N.R. (2000). On agent-based software engineering. *Artificial Intelligence,* 117, 277-296.

Jennings, N.R. (2001). An Agent-based Approach for Building Complex Software Systems. *Communications of the ACM,* 44(4).

Kirn, S. (1996). Organization Intelligence and Distributed Artificial Intelligence. In G.M.P. O'Hare and N.R. Jennings (Eds.), *Foundation of Distribution Artificial Intelligence* (pp. 505-526). New York: John Wiley & Sons, Inc.

Mason, C. L. & Johnson, R. R. (1989). DATMS: A framework for distributed assumption-based reasoning. In L. Gasser and M.N. Huhns (Eds.), *Distributed Artificial Intelligence 2* (pp. 293-318). London: Pitman/ Morgan.

Matsuda, T. (1992). Organizational intelligence: its significance as a process and as a product. *Proceedings of the International Conference on Economics/Management and Information Technology* (pp. 19-222). Tokyo, Japan.

Mike, P.P. et al. (1991). *Intelligent & Cooperative Information Systems.* Proceedings IJCAI-91, Workshop.

Wesson, R., Hayes-Roth, E., Burge, J. W., Statz, C., & Sunshine, C. A. (1981). Network structure for distributed situation assessment. *IEEE Transactions on Systems, Man and Cybemetics, 11*(1), 5-23.

Wooldridge, M. (1999). Intelligence Agent. In G. Weiss (Ed.), *Multiagent System: A Modern Approach to Distributed Artificial Intelligence* (pp. 27-78). London: MIT Press.

Wooldridge, M. & Ciancarini, P. (2001). Agent-Oriented Software Engineering: The State of the Art. In P. Ciancarini & M. Wooldridge (Eds.), *Agent-Oriented Software Engineering.* Springer-Verlag Lecture Notes in AI Vol. 1957.

Wooldridge, M., Jennings, N.R. & Kinny, D. (2000). The Gaia Methodology for Agent-oriented Analysis and Design. *Journal of Autonomous Agents and Multi-Agent Systems, 3*(3), 285-312.

Yao, L. (1995). *Distribute Cooperative Knowledge Model and Its Application in Situation Assessment*. National University of Defense Technology. Doctoral dissertation. 66-91.

Yao, L. (1997a). Assumption-based Distributed Cooperative Problem Solving. *Journal of Software (in Chinese), 8*(12), 914-919.

Yao, L. (1997b). Building the Organizational Model of DAI System. *Computer Engineering (in Chinese), 23*(3), 15-19.

Yao, L. et al. (2001). Multiply Intelligent Agent Developing Environment MBOS. *Compute World (in Chinese)*, 23(28), 11-12.

Yao, L. et al. (2002). Basic Organization Structure Model for Cooperative Information Processing. In M. Khosrow-Pour (Ed.), *Issues and Trends of IT Management in Contemporary Organizations* (pp. 836-839). Hershey, PA: Idea Group Publishing.

Yao, L. & Zhang, W. (2000). Basic Organization Structure Model for Cooperative Information Processing. *Mini-Micro Systems (in Chinese), 21*(6), 628-630.

Yao, L., Zhang, W., Chen, W., & Wang, H. (1999, July). Research on the Building Technology of Multi-Agent Systems. *Journal of Computer Research & Development (in Chinese)*, 36 (Suppl.), 50-53.

Zambonelli, F., Jennings, N.R., & Wooldridge, M. (2001). Organizational rules as an abstraction for the analysis and design of multi-agent systems. *International Journal of Software Engineer and Knowledge Engineering, 11*(3), 303-328.

Chapter II

Knowledge-Based Personalization

Tamara Babaian
Bentley College, USA

ABSTRACT

We present a novel method for software personalization. Personalization is understood broadly as a set of mechanisms by which an application is tailored to a particular end user and his or her task. The presented method outlined here is motivated by and remedies a few widely recognized problems in the way customization is carried out. The proposed method has been used in a collaborative system called Writer's Aid. It relies on a declarative specification of preconditions and effects of system's actions and applies artificial intelligence, automated reasoning, and planning framework and techniques to dynamically recognize the lack or availability of the personal information at the precise time when it affects a system action and initiates an interaction with the user aimed at eliciting this information in case it has not yet been specified.

INTRODUCTION AND MOTIVATION

Personalization has been identified as a key task to the success of many modern systems. As Riecken writes in the editorial of the special issue of Communication of the ACM devoted to this subject (Riecken, 2000, p. 28) "personalization means something different to everyone." There are various forms personalization can take; however, it can be broadly described as the set of mechanisms by which an application is tailored to a particular end user and his or her goal. Modern systems are increasingly more sophisticated, designed to carry out a multitude of tasks or operate using the enormous wealth of information available on the Internet. The effectiveness of a system helping a user achieve his goal, and the user's satisfaction from interacting with the system depends critically on the user's ability to identify and use relevant customizable options, configuring the system for optimal performance with his individual preferences and task-related information. However, the user's ability to provide this kind of *personal information* is often greatly impaired by the following drawbacks in the way personalization is implemented.

- Customization is carried out as a separate process that is taken out of context of the task in which such personal information is used, thus obscuring from the user the purpose and advantages of supplying such information.
- The amount of potentially useful personal information is sometimes over-whelming, thus the systems are installed with a set of settings that are considered typical. Further customization has to be initiated by the user. However, inexperienced users rarely take advantage of customization even if they are aware of potential benefits due to the lack of information on the available options. As a result, experience demonstrates (Manber, Patel & Robison, 2000) that the many users shy away from the customization while they can benefit from it a great deal.

The items above characterize the shortcomings in the user interaction model. On the other hand, there are problems developers of software face in designing for personalization. As Pednault (2000) points out, the underlying representation of "the human-side and the technology-side" is the key; however, representations currently in use at times lack flexibility to be easily adjustable and reusable. This is largely a consequence of the absence of a rigorous model of what constitutes personalization. The lack of such a model results in ad hoc representations used by most systems.

The approach to personalization that we present here is inspired by the view of interfaces as means for collaboration between humans and computers in solving the problem, rather than means of humans controlling the computers as articulated in Shieber (1996). As a theoretical framework, collaboration theory and its existing philosophical and formal mathematical accounts (Bratman, 1992; Grosz & Kraus, 1996; Cohen & Levesque, 1991) can inform both design and usability analysis of systems as well as give rise to new representations, highlight problems that need to be addressed to make interfaces better collaborative partners. Examples of interfaces that have been created following this view have already been built and are described in Rich Sidner and Lesh (2001), Babaian, Grosz and Shieber (2002), Ryall, Marks and Shieber (1997), and Ortiz and Grosz (2002).

Theories of collaboration postulate as the key features of a collaborative activity the commitment of the parties to a shared goal, shared knowledge and communication in the effort to establish agreement and mutual knowledge of the recipe for completing the task. Stemming directly from this view, in our approach the collaborator system has the ability to elicit personal information from the user at the time it is processing the task for which such information is critical. The novelty of our approach and its implementation also lies in defining the personalization task declaratively via informational goals and preconditions on the actions that the system would take in response to a user's request. This is enabled by the use of a knowledge base that stores the gathered preference information, and an automated reasoning and planning system that can reason autonomously about knowledge, lack of knowledge, and actions that the system may take to acquire necessary missing information. The system performs information gathering autonomously, by inspecting available personal information, such as, for example, a person's Internet bookmarks as well as by direct user querying. This approach to personalization ensures gradual adaptation of the system to the user's preferences. At the same time, the declarative nature of defining personalization information and system actions makes the system easily adjustable and extendable.

BACKGROUND

The problem of end user tailoring, also known as customization of software, is not new (see for example Morch, 1997). Recent explosion of the Internet and its ubiquity in our everyday life have created new challenges and opportunities for advancement of research on this subject, in particular, in the area of customizing information access interfaces. Numerous works have addressed the issue of information overload and the resulting need for effective information retrieval and presentation of the results tailored to the needs of each individual visitor. (A thorough review of these works is beyond the scope of this chapter.) Availability of logs of Web site usage has provided an excellent opportunity and an exciting domain for technologies such as Machine Learning and Data Mining (see Anderson, 2002 for a review). Two approaches to automated personalization on the Web have been explored and used most successfully: adaptive Web sites and collaborative filtering. Adaptive Web sites and Web site agents (e.g., Perkowitz & Etzioni, 2000; Pazzani & Billsus, 1999) attempt to dynamically tailor the layout and/or the contents of a Web site or suggest a navigation path for each individual user by observing the user's initial interaction with the Web site and matching it to the previously observed behaviors of others. Likewise, collaborative filtering (Amazon.com is probably the most familiar example) is a technique that makes a recommendation to a user based on the previous choices of users with similar interests or requests.

Applications of Machine Learning and Data Mining technologies to Web-based computing have been enabled by the availability of logs recording various details of interaction of millions of users with the Web sites. At the same time, non-Web-based systems (e.g., common desktop editors, spreadsheets, etc.) have benefited from the emerging culture of personalization and now commonly incorporate a few personalizable features, but the advancement of research in personalization of common desktop applications is not nearly as fast, partly due to the absence of detailed data on their actual usage. In this chapter we attempt to bridge the gap by presenting a method of software customization that is applicable to a broad set of software tools and not limited to just Web-based systems.

GOAL-DIRECTED PERSONALIZATION IN WRITER'S AID

Writer's Aid (Babaian et al., 2002) is a system that works in parallel with an author writing a document, helping him with identifying and inserting citation keys, autonomously finding and caching papers and associated bibliographic information from various online sources.

At the core of Writer's Aid is a knowledge base that contains system's knowledge about the state of the world, and an automated planner system. The planner has a description of the list of actions that Writer's Aid can execute and it can automatically combine the actions into a plan that will achieve a posted goal. Each action is described via preconditions that must be true prior to executing the action and the effects that the action brings about. Plan-generation is accomplished by representing both goals and actions using a logic-based language and using a reasoning engine that can infer what is true after performing a sequence of actions. For an example, consider the following action of searching user's personal directories for bibliographic collections:

Action 1: FindLocalBibliographies
  Preconditions: none
  Effects: Knowing locations of all bibliographic collections of a user.

Personalization in the Writer's Aid consists of the initial tune-up of the system to the user's parameters and the dynamic personalization that occurs while Writer's Aid works on accomplishing a user-posted goal and identifies a need for information.

Initial tune-up occurs at the time of installation. The goal of the initial tune-up is to establish and enter into the system certain user-specific parameters, such as the user's own locally stored bibliographic collections, his preferred on-line bibliographies, etc.

To direct the system to collect the data about location of local bibliographies it is sufficient to post the following goal on the list of goals to be accomplished during the tune-up:

Personalization-goal-1 = Knowing the locations of all of user's bibliographic collections

and in response, Writer's Aid will generate a plan (in this case consisting of a single Action 1) described above, which accomplishes Personalization-goal-1, and thus provides Writer's Aid with access to the user's personal bibliographies.

This declarative approach to the initial customization separates personalization from the rest of the code, making personalization design very flexible and more easily adjustable.

DYNAMIC PERSONALIZATION

Imagine the following scenario: Writer's Aid is working to locate a viewable version of a paper that the user requested. The plan for locating the paper includes an action of querying a known paper collection, namely ACM digital library. In order to avoid wasting time on searching collections of papers on subjects unrelated to the user's research field, this action contains a precondition that the paper collection be one of the user's preferred collections:

Action 2: QuerySourceForPaper (source, paper)
    Precondition: source must be User's Preferred Source
    Effects: Knowing whether source contains viewable version of paper.

Writer's Aid does not know if ACM digital library is the user's preferred bibliography, so it cannot establish the precondition unless it executes an action (namely Action 3 described below) of asking the user himself to obtain necessary information.

Action 3: AskUserAboutSource (source)
    Precondition: User permits system to post questions
    Effects: Knowing whether source is user-preferred source.

The user's response determines whether ACM digital library will be queried; it is also recorded in Writer's Aid knowledge base for future use.

Dynamic personalization occurs gradually, always within a context of a particular task, thus eliciting the user's input at the time it is used and providing the user with knowledge of how the personal information is being used by the system.

DISCUSSION AND FUTURE WORK

We have presented a novel approach to personalization that involves mixed-initiative interaction between the user and the computer system. We are working on the implementation of semi-automatic preference gathering in Writer's Aid and will perform laboratory user studies to investigate whether use of the proposed mechanism results in improved user satisfaction and system performance, compared to typical offline preference gathering.

Personalization via knowledge preconditions remedies commonly occurring problems with customization outlined in the introduction by adopting a mixed-initiative approach to customization. However, special attention should be given to those aspects of mixed-initiative interface that ensure the system acts in a manner that does not greatly disrupt the user's ongoing computing activity.

For example, an important requirement to the underlying knowledge representation and planning system is non-redundancy of information gathering, as it would be annoying if the system could not infer a fact that follows from the user's replies and it would be disastrous for the system if it ever repeated a question to the user. The planning system used in Writer's Aid, PSIPLAN, (Babaian, 2000) can infer all the facts that are implied by its knowledge base, and it never discards any valid information, thus ensuring non-redundancy of information gathering.

On the other hand, the user must have access to the same customization data as the system and be able (and aware of the way) to modify those settings at any time.

Deployment and experimental evaluation will doubtlessly identify ways of further improvement of dynamic personalization. A set of principles of mixed-initiative user interfaces introduced by Horvitz (1999) and the recent study of instant messaging interruption on the user's performance in the ongoing computing activity (Cutrell, Czerwinski & Horvitz, 2001) can provide a starting point for further investigations.

CONCLUSIONS

Representing a personalization task via a set of information goals addresses the problems with the way personalization is approached in most modern systems that are outlined in the beginning of this paper in the following ways:

- It leads to preference elicitation that occurs within the context of the particular task that requires personal information, thus informing the user of his choices, motivating the response and ensuring its accuracy.
- Personalization occurs gradually at the times when the personal information is critical to the satisfaction of a user's goal and is initiated by the computer system, thus relieving the user from potentially time-consuming task of specifying all preferences at once.
- Personalization defined declaratively via information goals separates customization of the interface from the overall system architecture making the interface more easily adjustable and extendable.

REFERENCES

Anderson, C. R. (2002). *A Machine Learning Approach to Web Personalization*. PhD thesis, University of Washington, USA.

Babaian, T. (2000). *Knowledge Representation and Open World Planning Using ψ-forms*. PhD thesis, Tufts University.

Babaian, T., Grosz, B. J., & Shieber, S. M. (2002). A writer's collaborative assistant. *Proceedings of Intelligent User Interfaces '02*, (pp. 7-14).

Bratman, M. E. (1992). Shared cooperative activity. *The Philosophical Review*, 101(2), 327-341.

Cohen, P. & Levesque, H. (1991). Teamwork. *Nôus*, 25, 487-512.

Cutrell, E., Czerwinski, M., & Horvitz, E. (2001). Notification, Disruption, and Memory: Effects of Messaging Interruptions on Memory and Performance. *Proceedings of Human-Computer Interaction - INTERACT '01*, (pp. 263-269).

Grosz, B. J. & Kraus, S. (1996). Collaborative Plans for Complex Group Action. *Artificial Intelligence*, 86(2), 269-357.

Horvitz, E. (1999). Principles of mixed-initiative user interfaces. *Proceedings of CHI'99*, (pp. 159-166).

Manber, U., Patel, A., & Robison, J. (2000). The business of personalization: Experience with personalization of Yahoo! *Communications of the ACM*, 43(8), 35-39.

Morch, A. (1997). Three levels of end-user tailoring: Customization, integration, and extension. In M. Kyng & L. Mathiassen (Eds.), *Computers and Design in Context* (pp. 51-76), Cambridge: The MIT Press.

Ortiz, C. & Grosz, B. (2002, forthcoming). Interpreting information requests in context: a collaborative web interface for distance learning. *Autonomous Agents and Multi-Agent Systems Journal.*

Pazzani, M. J. & Billsus, D. (1999). Adaptive Web site agents. In O. Etzioni, J. P. Müller, & J. M. Bradshaw (Eds.), *Proceedings of the Third International Conference on Autonomous Agents (Agents '99)* (pp. 394-395) Seattle, WA: ACM Press.

Pednault, E. P. D. (2000). Representation is everything. *Communications of the ACM*, 43(8), 80-83.

Perkowitz, M. & Etzioni, O. (2000). Adaptive Web sites. *Communications of the ACM*, 43(8), 152-158.

Rich, C., Sidner, C., & Lesh, N. (2001). Collagen: Applying collaborative discourse theory to human-computer interaction. *AI Magazine, Special Issue on Intelligent User Interfaces*, 22(4), 15-25.

Riecken, D. (2000). Personalized views of personalization. *Communications of the ACM*, 43(8), 26-28.

Ryall, K., Marks, J., & Shieber, S. (1997). An interactive constraint-based system for drawing graphs. In *Proceedings of UIST*, (pp. 97-104).

Shieber, S. (1996). A call for collaborative interfaces. *ACM Computing Surveys*, 8(4es) (electronic).

Chapter III

Customizing Digital Storefronts Using the Knowledge-Based Approach

Fiona Y. Chan
Hong Kong Baptist University, Hong Kong

William K. Cheung
Hong Kong Baptist University, Hong Kong

ABSTRACT

The concept of personalization has long been advocated to be one of the edges to improve the stickiness of on-line stores. By enabling an on-line store with adequate knowledge about the preference characteristics of different customers, it is possible to provide customized services to further raise the customer satisfaction level. In this paper, we describe in detail how to implement a knowledge-based recommender system for supporting such an adaptive store. Our proposed conceptual framework is characterized by a user profiling and product characterization module, a matching engine, an intelligent gift finder, and a backend subsystem for content management. A prototype of an on-line furnishing company has been built for idea illustration. Limitations and future extensions of the proposed system are also discussed.

INTRODUCTION

The development of Web technologies has brought a lot of advantages to merchants for moving their business on line. Within the past few years, a large variety of on-line stores have been started in the cyberspace. However, the survival rate is just around 50%, where some recognized dom.coms like Boo.com, Kozmo.com, and MVP.com are included (Helft, 2001). We believe that one important factor determining the success of on-line stores is whether the on-line shopping experience can be enhanced to such an extent that some customers choose to and continue to shop on-line. Along this direction, the concept of personalization has long been advocated as one of the edges to improve the stickiness of on-line stores. A survey, recently conducted by Cyber Dialogue, reveals that customers are more likely to purchase from a site that allows personalization, and register at a site that allows personalization or content customization (Rosenbaum, 2001). To achieve that, an on-line store needs to be enabled with adequate knowledge about customers' preference characteristics and use it effectively to provide personalized services with high precision. A typical example of personalized services is the use of recommender systems.

Recommender systems have been adopted by many big Web retailers, such as Amazon.com and CDNow.com for enhancing the on-line shopping experience of their on-line customers. Typically, they use an intelligent engine to collect and mine the customer's rating records and then create predictive user models for product recommendation. Software products of recommender systems are now available from various companies like NetPerception, Andromedia, and Manna, etc. Based on the underlying technology, recommender systems can be broadly categorized as:

- **Knowledge-based** (Towle & Quinn, 2000) where user models are created explicitly via a knowledge acquisition process (e.g., expert knowledge tells you that young customers consider product appearance more than durability).
- **Content-based** (Mooney & Roy, 1999) where user models are created implicitly by applying machine learning or information retrieval techniques to analyze user preference ratings and corresponding product features (e.g., the products that a customer rated high so far have the common attributes of being less colorful, easy to clean, and safe).
- **Collaborative** (Resnick et al., 1994) where user models are created solely by utilizing overlap of user preference ratings (e.g., customers with their "tastes" (ratings patterns) similar to yours like this set of products).

In the literature, there exist a lot of works on content-based and collaborative recommender systems. One of their common characteristics is that a substantial amount of good user preference ratings is required before precise recommendations can be provided. However, if a company is lacking such ratings information or it has new items arrived constantly, these two approaches will fail.

Here we argue that before such ratings information can be collected, the knowledge-based approach should provide a good complementary solution. With a similar rationale, Ardissono et al. (1999) proposed a knowledge-based system using for tailoring the interaction users using a shell called SETA for adaptive Web stores, where stereographical information is also used for user modeling. Sen, Dutta, and Mukherjee (2000) proposed an intelligent buyer agent which aims to educate the user to be a more informed customer by understanding the user query and providing alternatives using a pre-built domain-specific knowledge base, which is based on propositional logic representation. For automatic rule generation, Kim et al. (2001) have built a prototype system where the decision tree induction algorithm is applied to personalize advertisements.

As there is always a trade-off between personalization and privacy, what kind of knowledge needed to be acquired for exchanging personalized services is definitely an important concern of on-line customers. So, the question becomes, "how can the user information requirement be minimized while an acceptable level of recommendation service can still be provided?" In this paper, we restrict the user information needed to only demographic information and describe in details how a related knowledge-based system can be built to support an adaptive on-line store in providing customized recommendation services. Our proposed conceptual framework is characterized by a user profiling and product characterization module, a matching engine, an intelligent gift finder, and a backend management system. A prototype of an on-line furnishing company has been built and is used throughout the paper for idea illustration. The limitations and future extensions of the proposed framework will also be discussed.

SYSTEM OVERVIEW

Knowledge-based systems are characterized by the fact that its two important components, namely the knowledge base and the inference engine (sometimes also called the shell in expert systems) are separated. A typical example is the rule-based system where the knowledge base is represented in the form of a set of if-then rules and forward-chaining reasoning is used in the inference engine. The knowledge engineer can keep on expanding the knowledge base by acquiring more domain knowledge with the inference engine being unchanged at all.

In this project, instead of using the rule-based syntax, a feature vector-based representation is adopted. Also, we assume a conventional two-tier architecture, where domain knowledge is stored in a relational database and all the functional modules of the inference engine are run on the Web server. The knowledge required to be acquired and stored in the database for driving this customized on-line store include:

- **Generic products information**, e.g., product name, price, manufacturing country, etc.
- **Product characteristics**, e.g., degrees of reliability, design style, etc.
- **User demographic information**, e.g., sex, age, occupation
- **User preference profiles**, e.g., preferences on reliability, dressing style, etc.

The inference engine contains the following functional modules (see also Figure 1):

- **User profiling module,** which acquires the user demographic information via a simple questionnaire during membership registration and transforms the information to create a preference profile for supporting the subsequent matching.
- **Matching engine,** which computes the similarity score between user preference profiles and product characteristics to support personalized product ranking shown in the catalog or as special product recommendations.
- **Intelligent gift finder,** which can assist the customer via a wizard interface to identify possible gifts for a particular recipient.
- **Back-end management system,** for managing the contents for supporting the above modules, which is important as adding adaptability to an on-line store greatly increases its complexity and the store can easily become unmanageable.

To provide personalized product recommendations to customers based on their preferences, one needs to first create the representations for user preferences and product characteristics, and then define a measure for computing the similarity between them (see section titled "Matching Engine").

PRODUCT CHARACTERIZATION AND USER PROFILING

Generic Representation

A set of discriminative features $\Phi := \{\phi_1, \phi_2, ..., \phi_N\}$ has first to be identified based on domain knowledge. Then, the user preference can be represented as a vector of preference values on those feature representation $\mathbf{u} = \{u_1, u_2, u_3, ..., u_N\}$

Figure 1. An Overview of the Recommender System

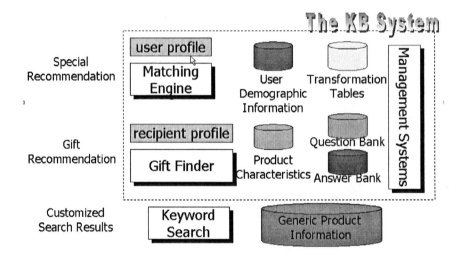

$\forall u_i \in [U_{\min}, U_{\max}]$ and the product can be characterized as a vector of values revealing the extent to which it possesses those features, denoted as $\mathbf{p} = \{p_1, p_2, \ldots, p_N\}$ $\forall p_i \in [P_{\min}, P_{\max}]$.

Product Characterization

Based on a chosen set of features, product characteristic vectors $\mathbf{p}$ have to be created for all the products. Unless for the cases where each product comes with a detailed product description so that some information extraction techniques can be applied, human effort for the creation of $\mathbf{p}$ is inevitable.

User Profiling

For acquiring user preference profiles $\mathbf{u}$, it can be achieved by filling in a questionnaire during the registration process. However, in practice, requiring the users to provide preference values for a long list of features is infeasible as the required effort may simply scare them from continuing to shop in your store. So, the questionnaire for a newly registered user has to be reasonably short and the questions should be easy enough for the user to provide answers. Typical examples are the demographic data like gender, age and occupation, here denoted as $\mathbf{d} = \{d_1, d_2, \ldots, d_M\}$ $\forall d_i \in \Delta_i$, where Δ_i is a set of possible stereotypical categories for d_i.[1] However, such a simple representation contradicts the requirement for a discriminative set of features. One solution is using domain knowledge to transform the demographic information $\mathbf{d}$ user into a preference profile representation $\mathbf{u}$ containing a rich set of features via a transformation $f_u(\mathbf{d}): \Delta \rightarrow [U_{min}, U_{max}]^N$, where $\Delta :=$

$\Delta_1 \times \Delta_2 \times \ldots \times \Delta_M$. The precision of the preference profile thus highly relies on that of the transformation.

Another issue related to user profile representation is about the importance of each individual feature. Under the aforementioned feature vector representation, user preferences on the features are assumed to be equally important. However, this is not the case in practice. Some users may consider "color" to be a more important feature than "durability" while some may find it the other way round. The situation can be even worse as this kind of information is usually unconscious for users and hard to be provided precisely. In our system, we model the relative importance of the feature with a weighting vector $\mathbf{w} = \{w_1, w_2, \ldots, w_N\}$ $\forall w_i \in [0,1]$ and $\sum_i w_i = 1$. Also, we introduce one more transformation $f_w(\mathbf{d}) : \Delta \rightarrow [0,1]^N$. This transformation can be interpreted as the relative importance of the features for different combinations of demographic categories. It is hoped that this can free up the user from providing subjective weighting values. Again, the precision of the transformation is crucial to the success of weighting application.

Obtaining the transformations that can effectively reflect the interests of the different demographic categories is by no means straightforward. Some possible objective means include conducting marketing surveys or analyzing past transaction records. Regarding their implementations, the input dimensions of the two transformations are equal to $\prod_{i=1}^{M} card(\Delta_i)$. Creating them directly may result in large storage requirements as well as tedious work in creating and managing them. By assuming the effect of each element in $\mathbf{d}$ on the overall transformation to be independent, the transformation for preference can be decomposed into a set of transformations $\{ f_{u_j}(d_j) : \Delta_j \rightarrow [U_{min}, U_{max}]^N \ \forall j = 1..M \}$, each corresponding to a particular element in $\mathbf{d}$. The storage requirement can then be reduced from $\prod_{i=1}^{M} card(\Delta_i)$ to $\sum_{i=1}^{M} card(\Delta_i)$. With the decomposition, the preference profile is then computed as:

$$\mathbf{u} = \{u_i = \frac{1}{M} \sum_{j=1}^{M} f_{u_j}^i(d_j)\} \quad \forall i = 1 \ldots N$$

where f^i denotes the ith element of f's output. The range of value for each element in $\mathbf{u}$ remains to be $[U_{min}, U_{max}]$. Similarly, the transformation for weighting can be decomposed as $\{ f_{w_j}(d_j) : \Delta_j \rightarrow [0,1]^N \}$. More details about the use of the weighting vector are described in the section titled "Matching Engine."

An On-Line Furnishing Company Prototype

To provide a concrete example for explaining the representation issue, we have built an on-line furnishing company prototype for idea illustration.[2] The furniture items include tables, sofas, beds, quilts, etc. For user profiling and product characterization, the set of features Φ we have used is shown in 2 and the range of value for each element in both representations is set to be $U_{min} = P_{min} = -1$ and $U_{max} = P_{max} = +1$. Products with softness = "-1" means that they are extremely hard, whereas those with softness = "1" means that the product is very soft. For demographic information $\mathbf{d}$, three attributes—gender, year of birth, and occupation—are adopted (i.e., $M = 3$). For the creation of the transformation functions $f_u(d_j)$ and $f_w(d_j)$ (see Figure 3 and Figure 4) as well as the product feature vectors $\mathbf{p}$, it is done manually based on domain knowledge.

After a user registers with our system, his or her basic personal demographic information will automatically be stored. If he or she logs onto the system again, a personal preference profile will be created based on the methodology previously described. Recommendation services can thus be provided.

MATCHING ENGINE

Given the user preference profile $\mathbf{u}$, the product characteristics $\mathbf{p}$ and the range of preference values, a similarity measure can then be defined. In our prototype, as the preference value range is $[-1,1]$, one obvious measure is the dot product between $\mathbf{u}$ and $\mathbf{p}$ weighted by $\mathbf{w}$, given as:

$$\text{sim}(\mathbf{u},\mathbf{p},\mathbf{w}) = \sum_{i=1}^{N} u_i p_i w_i$$

Figure 2. Examples of Product Feature Vectors, $\mathbf{p}$

Product ID	...	Colorful	Essential	Exotic	Easy to clean	Durable	Safe	Soft	Modern
10002	...	-0.4	0.8	0.4	-0.1	0.5	0.6	0.4	0.7
10023	...	0.6	-0.4	0.3	-0.2	0.4	0.3	0.1	0.6
10045	...	0.3	0.4	0.8	-0.2	-0.1	0.4	0.8	0.1

Figure 3. Examples of Preference Transformation, $f_u(d)$

Category	Colorful	Essential	Exotic	Easy to clean	Durable	Safe	Soft	Modern
35-45 yr old	-0.3	0.7	0.1	0.8	0.8	0.3	0.1	-0.4
Female	0.1	-0.2	0.2	0.5	-0.2	0.5	0.2	-0.1
Housewife	-0.5	0.8	-0.3	0.9	-0.4	0.1	-0.2	-0.1

with the output equal [-1,1].[3] Based on the similarity scores computed, personalized product ranking can be achieved. It can also be used to customize the catalog for browsing with the hope that the user can identify their intended products with fewer mouse clicks. The keyword search engine can also benefit by ranking the search results based on the scores so as to improve the chance that the intended items are put on the first few pages of the search results. Besides, when there is a list of new products, personalized recommendation services can be provided to further improve the quality of customer services.

INTELLIGENT GIFT FINDER

Profiling Gift Recipients

For on-line shopping customization, we used to focus on how to acquire the interest of the individual customers so as to provide just-in-time customized services. However, other than buying things for themselves, customers often buy product items to be presented to their friends as gifts. Most of the on-line stores try

Figure 4. Examples of Weighting Transformation, $f_w(d)$

Category	Colorful	Essential	Exotic	Easy to clean	Durable	Safe	Soft	Modern
35-45 yr old	0.03	0.18	0.06	0.33	0.24	0.08	0.04	0.04
Female	0.2	0.08	0.11	0.15	0.08	0.09	0.09	0.2
Housewife	0.04	0.17	0.08	0.31	0.22	0.1	0.04	0.04

Figure 5. A Snapshot of the Web-Based System

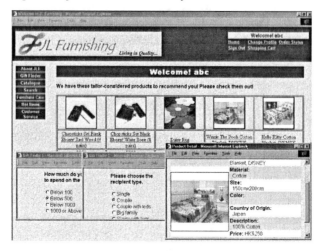

to fulfill the need by providing some advanced search functions, with the hope that the customers can manage to specify the preference of the gift recipients in the form of some complicated searching criteria. However, this does not conform to our usual shopping habit. Instead, we used to have dialogs with the salesperson in the store, describing some basic characteristics of the gift recipient with the hope that the salesperson could effectively provide some relevant recommendations to us for reference. With that idea in mind, our proposed system contains a module called *intelligent gift finder*. It operates like a typical wizard that asks users a sequence of dynamically generated questions for profiling the gift recipient. In our system, the questions are extracted from a pre-defined question bank[4] with a tree structure where the edges of the tree determine the next question to ask based on the answers of the previous question. Within the question bank, there are two sets of questions. One set of questions, denoted as Θ_H, is to help capture hard constraints to prune down the product search space (e.g., "what is your budget?"). The other set of questions, denoted as Θ_S, is to help capture the *preference profile* of the gift recipient (as described in the section titled "Product Characterization and User Profiling") for ranking the products in the reduced search space in a customized manner (e.g., "what is the gender of the gift recipient?").

Suppose a user has clicked on the wizard and answered K questions. Denote θ_i as the ith question, α_i as his or her corresponding answer. Also, denote $\Gamma(\theta, \alpha)$ as the set of feasible solutions corresponding to the question-answer pair (θ, α). The current set of feasible solutions should then be given as:

$$\Gamma_K = \bigcap_{i=1:K;\theta_i \in \Theta_H} \Gamma(\theta_i = \alpha_i).$$

For ranking products in Γ_K, we need to associate (θ_i, α_i) with some similarity measure. For questions capturing the recipient's demographic information, the associated preference and weighting transformations can be used, and the similarity score can be computed as:

$$\sum_{i=1:K;\theta_i \in \Theta_S} sim(f_{u_{\theta_i}}(\alpha_i), \mathbf{p}, f_{w_{\theta_i}}(\alpha_i)) .$$

See Figure 6 for a pictorial illustration. A concept similar to that of our gift finder has been used in the Decision Guide, which is developed by Personallogic and currently used in AOL.com.

Implementation and Related Management Tools

It is obvious that embedding the questions and answers into the program code greatly reduces the system's maintainability and extensibility. So, putting them into the database as part of the knowledge is a natural solution. As the question bank adopts a tree-like structure, the linking relationship between the questions has to be stored as well. To ease the effort for maintaining the question bank with a tree-like structure, an associated management tool has been developed accordingly. With the help of the tool, internal staff of the store can easily create, update and delete questions and answers. Also, they can easily specify how each question-answer pair is associated with the corresponding conditions to be used in searching the database, though prior knowledge on the database schema is still inevitable for the staff.

FUTURE EXTENSIONS

Personal Adaptation

One major limitation of the proposed framework is that it assumes that user preferences can solely be determined based on their demographic information. In fact, two customers with identical demographic information can only be considered to have the same preferences up to a certain extent on the average. If more precise personalized recommendation service is to be provided, a deeper level of personalized adaptation will be needed. For example, one can further adapt the preference transformations and weighting transformations acquired after the first registration to suit the specific characteristics of the customer. One possible direction is to use relevance feedback, i.e., to modify the transformations based on the characteristics of the customers' highly rated products in a weighted sum manner (Rocchio, 1971).

Figure 6. A Conceptual Illustration of How the Intelligent Gift Finder Works

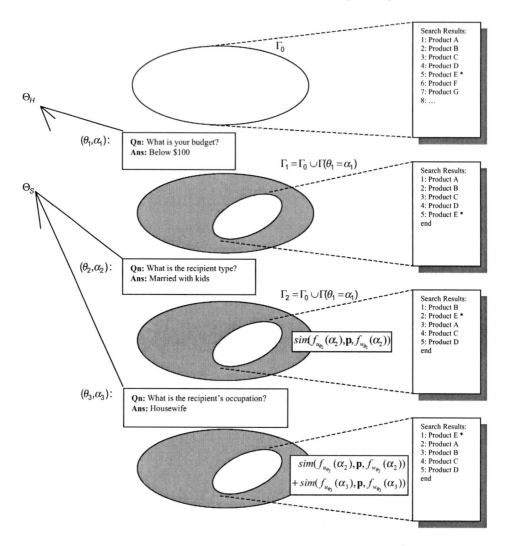

There is also another possibility, where one can rewrite the adopted vector representations in rule-based syntax and apply some uncertainty reasoning framework, like uncertainty theory (Hopgood, 1993). For example, if the feature vector [A, B, C] of stereotypical category X is [0.2, -0.8, 0.7], then it can be converted into:

> **IF X THEN** A is preferred; with certainty of 0.2
> **IF X THEN** B is preferred; with certainty of -0.8
> **IF X THEN** C is preferred; with certainty of 0.7

Consequently, highly rated products can then be used as additional pieces of evidence to refine the customers' individual preferences under the uncertainty theory in a disciplined manner. Currently, we are studying how to cast the problem under a Bayesian framework. Related open issues include:

- what kind of information should be acquired from the customer to support the personalized adaptation (e.g., customers' ratings, click-streams, etc.)
- in what manner they should be acquired (explicitly or implicitly)
- how the acquired information should be analyzed to represent the customer preference and combined with the existing transformation tables in an incremental and disciplined manner

Integration with Collaborative Methods

The collaborative filtering technique is known to be an effective method for identifying like-minded customers solely based on customer ratings and has been used by a number of recommender systems. It will be interesting to see how the knowledge-based approach can take the advantage of collaborative filtering to shorten its time in providing highly precise recommendations. One possibility that has been proposed in the literature is to compute *ratings for features* by aggregating *ratings for products* (Pazzani, 1999). Then, the predicted preferences on different features, which will be changed as more ratings are provided, can be used as relevance feedback or additional evidence with the hope to further increase the precision of the recommender system. Other works along this direction have been reported in the literature (Burke, 1999; Tran & Cohen, 2000).

CONCLUSION

In this paper, we have demonstrated how customers' stereotypical information can be used to provide customized product recommendations using a knowledge-based approach. In particular, we have illustrated how an intelligent gift finder, acting as an on-line salesman can be built for profiling a gift recipient and providing gift suggestions. Besides this, we have discussed several ways to further enhance the precision of the recommender system described.

ENDNOTES

[1]   Whether a user is willing to provide his or her demographic information is related to the privacy issue, which is out of the scope of this paper. In general, the user has to sacrifice a certain degree of privacy in order to gain customized services.

[2]   There are many related on-line companies, e.g., IKEA.com, Maxwellfurniture.com, etc.

[3]   If the range of preference value is changed, the Pearson correlation or the cosine value between the vector **p** and the vector **u** weighted by **w** can be used.

[4]   For the creation of the question bank, we believe there exist different cognitive or psychological theories governing how the questions should be set to achieve objective user profile acquisition. However, related considerations are out of the scope of this paper.

REFERENCES

Ardissono, L., Goy, A., Petrone, G., Segnan, M., & Torasso, P. (1999). Tailoring the interaction with users in electronic shops. In *Proceedings of the 7ᵗʰ International Conference on User Modeling,* (pp. 35-44) Banff, MA.

Burke, R. (1999). Integrating knowledge-based and collaborative-filtering recommender systems. *Artificial Intelligence for Electronic Commerce: Paper from AAAI,* Technical Report WS-99-01, 69-72.

Helft, M. (2001). The E-commerce survivors. *The Industry Standard Magazine.* Found on July 16, 2001 at http://www.thestandard.com/article/0,1902,27593,00.html.

Hopgood, A.A. (1993). *Knowledge-based Systems for Engineers and Scientists.* Boca Raton, FL: CRC Press.

Kim, J.W., Lee, B.H., Shaw, M.J., Chang, H.L., & Nelson, M. (2001). Application of decision-tree induction techniques to personalized advertisement on internet storefronts. *International Journal of Electronic Commerce,* 5(3), 45-62.

Mooney, R.J., & Roy, L. (1999). Content-based book recommending using learning for text categorization. In *Proceedings of SIGIR '99 Workshop on Recommender Systems: Algorithms and Evaluation,* (pp. 195-204) Berkeley, CA.

Pazzani, M.J. (1999). A framework for collaborative, content-based and demographic filtering. *Artificial Intelligence Review,* 13(5/6), 393-408.

Resnick, P., Iacovou, N., Suchak, M., Bergstorm, P., & Riedl, J. (1994). GroupLens: An open architecture for collaborative filtering of netnews. In *Proceedings of ACM 1994 Conference on Computer Supported Cooperative Work1* (pp. 75-186). Chapel Hill, NC.

Rocchio, J.J. (1971). Relevance feedback in information retrieval. In G. Salton (Ed.), The *SMART Retrieval System* (pp. 313-323) Englewood Cliffs, NJ: Prentice-Hall.

Rosenbaum, A. (2001). *Personalization Consortium News*. Found at http://www.personalization.org/pr050901.html.

Sen, S., Dutta, P.S., & Mukherjee, R. (2000). Agents that represent buyer's interests in E-commerce. *Knowledge-based Electronic Markets: Paper from AAAI*, Technical Report WS-00-04, 63-69.

Towle, B., & Quinn, C. (2000). Knowledge-based recommender systems using explicit user models. *Knowledge-based Electronic Markets: Paper from AAAI*, Technical Report WS-00-04, 74-77.

Tran, T., & Cohen, R. (2000). Hybrid recommender systems for electronic commerce. *Knowledge-based Electronic Markets: Paper from AAAI*, Technical Report WS-00-04, 78-84.

Chapter IV

Managing Process Compliance

Larry Y.C. Cheung
Loughborough University, UK

Paul W.H. Chung
Loughborough University, UK

Ray J. Dawson
Loughborough University, UK

ABSTRACT

The current best practice of providing reliable systems is to embody the development process in recent industry standards and guidelines, such as IEC61508 for safety and ISO9001 for quality assurance. These standards are generic, but every application is different because of the differences in project details. While current workflow systems have been used successfully in managing "administrative" process for some time, current products lack the ability to ensure that a process is planned and performed such that it complies with an industry standard that is necessary to support particular engineering processes. This chapter presents a Compliance Flow Workflow System for managing processes. Model-based reasoning is used to identify the compliance errors of a process by matching it against the model of standards used. Some examples drawing on a draft version of IEC61508 are used to illustrate the mechanism of modeling and compliance checks.

INTRODUCTION

In order to provide reliable systems or services, the current best practice of a development process is typically embodied in recent safety standards and guidelines, such as IEC61508. Once a standard has been adopted, it is important to manage compliance with the standard. By compliance we mean that there is a clear description of the design stages and, at each stage, the inputs (requirements) to that stage are fully and unambiguously defined, and finally the objectives and requirements of each practice of the standard are met. The standards are generic, but every application is different due to the differences in the project details. It is neither practical nor desirable to compel compliance at all points in the development process. Thus determining the degree of compliance with specified practices as the development progresses is a challenging task.

Most of the current research, such as by Emmerich et al. (1998), adopts a document-centred approach in which the development process is implicitly represented in the product. The compliance has been treated as a problem that is closely related to inconsistency management in specification, which is discussed in the literature (Easterbrook, Finkelstein, Kramer & Nuseibeh, 1994; Finkelstein et al., 1994). Such approach uses a document schema specification to elaborate and formalise the definitions of document structure suggested in the standard so that properties can be checked against them. Appropriate checks will be triggered only when events occur on documentation during the development process. This approach can ascertain that the expected qualified document is obtained, which matches current quality control practices where the compliance checks are performed at the end of development stages by individual assessors. However, it lacks the ability to manage the development process to proactively prevent unqualified products resulting from a wrongly planned process, which is an essential requirement for the conformance of rigorous standards like IEC61508.

IEC61508 is an international standard that focus on the *process* in which a safety product is designed and manufactured, not just the product itself. Therefore, the company can only legitimately develop an IEC61508-compliant product when its development process is compliant with the standard.

Some companies in our industry claim to have IEC61508 compliant products. In fact, they have only had an assessment done on a single product, not on their company's processes to design and produce

that product. This is a severe shortcut, and certainly not in keeping
with the intention of the standard (Moore, 2002).

A Workflow Management System (WfMS) is a system that aims to provide computer-based support for the task of workflow management, in which the execution of every process instantly conforms to its process plan. Most workflow products can only support simple, well-defined, consistent, and predictable administrative processes, but not the dynamic changing, complex, collaborative processes occurring in engineering projects (Alonso, Agrawal, El Abbadi & Mohan, 1997; Sheth, 1997; Moore et al., 1999). Recently, some attempts were made to use artificial intelligence (AI) to improve the adaptability of WfMSs, enabling them to deal with more complex processes (Dellen, Maurer & Pews, 1997; Myers & Berry, 1999; Jarvis et al., 1999; Stader et al., 2000).

Current workflow reference models, such as WfMC (1995) and Weske (1999), provide no support for maintaining process consistency against particular standards. In order to facilitate the extension to the current WfMSs to support process compliance management, the use of a software agent in isolation with a workflow engine, we believe, is the easiest way to bridge this gap as no amendment to the reference model is necessary.

Our approach to the compliance problem is to model the standards into a "Model of Standards," which will provide the required information about the standards in terms of the process management to enable compliance checks to be performed by a compliance agent called the "Inspector." Compliance checks will be performed between the Model of Standards and user-defined process plan during both process build and run time to identify the compliance errors. A set of ontologies is used to enable the compliance check. The Model of Standards comes with the system, but additions, amendments, and removals to and from a standard within the model are possible. It is also possible to have a user-defined development cycle as a standard with compliance checks still being performed without any problem.

Significant resources are devoted to managing standards, particularly in safety engineering projects. In such projects, much of the time of developers, managers and quality assurance teams is occupied with identifying breaches in compliance and with tracking and managing the compliance of a project. A workflow system with compliance management ability can not only shorten the development time and reduce the cost, but improve the quality of the product as well. Thus, our treatment of this problem is strongly industrially motivated. It is to be noted that we are not advocates of using an automatic checking process to substitute the regular assessment in an engineering project, as this would be too dangerous. Instead, we suggest taking advantage of workflow systems with compliance management ability to assist in the management of an engineering project. As the non-compliant, development processes are identified and handled earlier, the required product development time and cost will drop.

This paper mainly describes the work around compliance management where the international safety standard IEC61508 is used to perform the evaluation. The next section portrays the standard modeling. We then introduce the compliance agent and how it performs compliance assurance. The next section provides a discussion on the degree of coupling between the compliance agent and the Model of Standards. Finally, the chapter concludes with a summary of our principal contributions.

STANDARD MODELING

A standard is modeled into a Model of Standards, which later will be used in the compliance checking process. Compliance Flow has the capability of modeling a wide range of standards. It captures three important aspects of a standard in terms of workflow management:

1. The development lifecycle, which is used as the key framework to deal in a systematic manner with all the activities necessary to achieve the required quality of products or services.
2. The techniques, measures, tools, or methods that are recommended by the standard to be used to achieve specific objectives or requirements.
3. The required capability of a task performer. Capability refers to qualifications, roles, experiences, or other attributes identified by a standard, which staff must possess to be qualified to perform a specific task.

This approach has successfully modeled IEC61508 with its two important concepts: the Safety Lifecycle and Safety Integrity Levels (SIL). The Safety Lifecycle is the proposed development process necessary to achieve a required SIL. The SIL, a number between one and four, is an indicator for specifying the safety integrity requirements, with four having the highest level of safety integrity. The meta-model of standard modeling presented using the unified modeling language (UML) class diagram is illustrated in Figure 1.

The Use of Ontology

As the information provided by the Model of Standards will be used in compliance checks by matching it with the user-defined processes, the terms used in describing a concept of interest must be consistent. We take the advantage of

Figure 1. Meta-Model of Standard Modeling

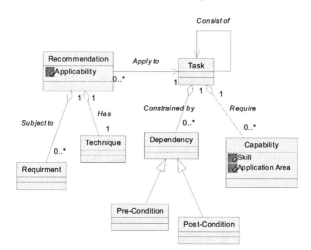

ontology to enable a matching process. An ontology is a data model that "consists of a representational vocabulary with precise definitions of the meanings of the terms of this vocabulary plus a set of formal axioms that constrain interpretation and well-formed use of these terms" (Campbell & Shapiron, 1995). These models can be shared and re-used by others in the same domain with minimised interpretation and ambiguity because they are modeled formally. An ontology is therefore an explicit representation of a "…shared understanding of some domain of interest…" (Uschold & Gruninger, 1996).

In Compliance Flow, all terms used to describe the concepts in the context of process management such as task, pre- and post-conditions, recommendation, and capabilities have to be selected from the ontology. A number of ontologies come with the system, including Process Ontology, Artefact Ontology, Capability Ontology, and Application Ontology, etc. The terms of an ontology are organised into a hierarchical structure in which a term located in a higher level implies a higher level of abstraction, while a lower level term represents a more concrete concept of object. A term can be changed, removed, or extended by users to adapt to the particular environment where the system is running. Therefore, a concept can be detailed by decomposing it into a set of more granulated pieces if necessary, each of which is also represented using a unique term. An example of ontology hierarchy is given in .

The Modeling of Task Framework

The Safety Lifecycle proposed by IEC61508 is modeled into a hierarchical task network (HTN) in which the tasks correspond to the activities in the Safety

Figure 2. An Example Hierarchical Ontology Network

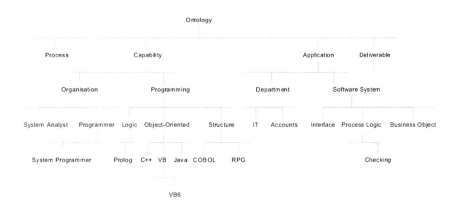

Lifecycle. A task is a basic unit of work, which can be hierarchically decomposed into subtasks until the required details are modeled, as long as the parent and child relationship between tasks is maintained.

Each task is associated with two sets of conditions: pre- and post-conditions. The post-conditions of a task are sometimes the pre-conditions of its subsequent tasks. Performing a task requires the fulfillment of its pre-condition, and to do so, the preceding tasks that can satisfy those conditions with their post-conditions must be completed successfully in advance. The post-conditions of a task will be achieved when the task is completed successfully. Therefore, the order of the execution of tasks is constrained by their dependencies.

IEC61508 views the requirements simply as the input to a distinct stage in the lifecycle, and the design specification as the output of that stage. The requirements and specifications are equivalent to pre- and post-conditions of tasks respectively as they have to be achieved under the recommended sequence in order to comply with IEC61508. A condition is presented in the form of checklists, and is stated as fulfilled when all items in the checklist are checked.

The Modeling of Task Requirement

The recommended techniques, measures, tools, or methods that have to be used for specific tasks to achieve the specified objectives are modeled with four parameters: (1) the task for which the technique is required, (2) the requirement for applying the technique, (3) the technique itself, and (4) the level of recommendation. The value of parameter two can be null, implying that no requirement is necessary to apply the technique.

IEC61508 introduces sets of techniques for specific development activities with different levels of applicability according to the SIL of the product to be developed. The SIL is normally achieved after the safety requirements are addressed. Therefore, the level of SIL (from one to four) becomes the requirement for applying the recommended techniques. These techniques are categorised into four levels of recommendation in IEC61508, namely Highly Recommended (HR), Recommended (R), No Recommendation (-), and Not Recommended (NR).

These recommendations can be modeled; for example, IEC61508 recommends that the technique "Structure Methodology" (parameter three) is HR (parameter four) during the achievement of the objective of Clause B.30 (parameter one) when the SIL of the product being developed is equal to one (parameter two).

The Modeling of Task Capability

The hierarchical ontology network provides a hierarchy of capabilities. For example, a programmer can do programming — more specifically, a system programmer has C++ programming capability. This hierarchical structure can ease the process of specifying capabilities since specifying a high-level capability implies that all its lower-levels are covered. A capability in our system is specified into two parts: the capability itself (skills, techniques, qualifications, role, etc.) and its application area. For example, a programmer can do C++ programming; he can apply this capability to the development of system interface. Each part uses its own hierarchy of terms, which are drawn from the hierarchical ontology network as shown in Figure 3.

COMPLIANCE AGENT AND COMPLIANCE CHECK

A compliance agent is a software agent responsible for ensuring that the processes in a workflow engine is planned and performed in accordance with a standard. In our system, the compliance agent is called the Inspector, who

Figure 3. Example Capabilities and their Application Area

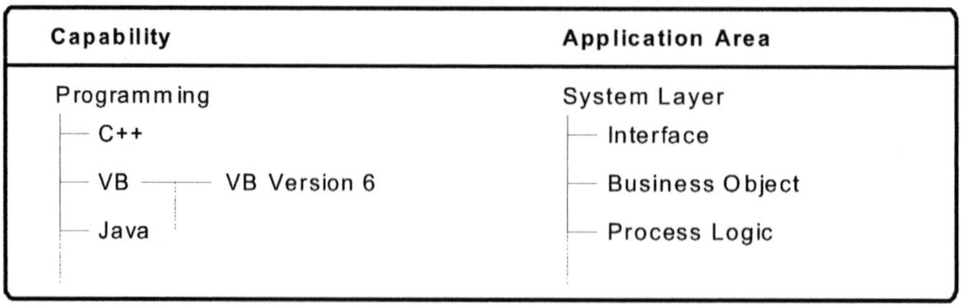

Capability	Application Area
Programming	System Layer
├─ C++	├─ Interface
├─ VB ─── VB Version 6	├─ Business Object
└─ Java	└─ Process Logic

continually monitors the planning and the execution of activities, ensuring that the compliance of a process conforms to a particular standard, in this case the IEC61508 safety standard. The Inspector performs the following duties:

- *During Process Build-Time:* The Inspector provides four kinds of consultative services (compliance checks) during task planning—namely correctness check (ordering), completeness check, capability check and cross-referencing to help users in devising a standard compliance plan.
- *During Process Run-Time:* The Inspector actively prevents the task from being executed incorrectly.
- *During Process Build-Time and Run-Time:* The Inspector ensures that the recommended techniques have been fully considered.
- *Correctness Check:* A correctness check will be performed when the Inspector services the requests from users for verifying that the placement of a particular specification in a design plan complies with IEC61508. To verify the correctness of a specification, two mapping mechanisms are required.

First is the existence check. It maps the specification of a user-defined process plan with the specifications identified in the Safety Lifecycle proposed by IEC61508.

Next is the ordering check. If the specification exists, the immediately previous specifications in the Safety Lifecycle are then mapped with the previous specifications in the user-defined process plan.

The success of both mapping mechanisms implies that the production of the specification is planned in the right sequence. An example is given in .

In Figures 4 and 6, rectangles with identifiers beginning with the letter T represent the tasks of a process, and circles represent pre- or post-conditions of tasks.

Figure 4. Example of a Correctness Check

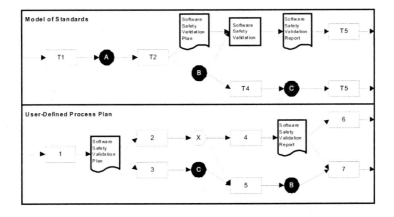

In Figure 4, to check the compliance of the specification titled "Overall Safety Validation Report" in the user-defined process plan, agent Inspector will first determine whether the specification has been defined in the Model of Standards by performing a search. If not found, it implies that the specification belongs to the type of user-defined specification that is beyond the scope of IEC61508 and will not affect the compliance of a process with the standard, and therefore no compliance check is required. Specification "X" in this example falls into this kind of situation. If found, agent Inspector will then map the immediately previous specifications defined in the Model of Standards, in this case the "Overall Safety Validation Plan," with the previous specifications in the user-defined process plan. If the mapping is successful, the ordering of the specification is correct, corresponding to its previous specifications. In this example, both mapping mechanisms are successful and therefore the specification is placed in a right position in the process plan.

Completeness Check

The second service, the completeness check, provided by the Inspector is used to ensure that required specifications defined in the Model of Standards have been included in a particular user-defined process plan. The Inspector will then map all the specifications in the Safety Lifecycle with the specifications in the user-defined process plan. If all specifications can be mapped, then the verification is successful. This implies that the objectives and requirements of every clause of the standard have been covered in the user-defined process plan. Otherwise, the Inspector will present the missing specifications visually on its interface. In this example, the user-defined process plan is incomplete as specification "A" is absent.

Capability Check

In a capability checking process, the capability possessed by a performer is matched against the capability required of a performer involved in executing a task. A performer may possess many capabilities. To enable capability matching, the two sets of capability, therefore, have to be captured and modeled in the same manner.

Figure 5. An Example of Capability Check

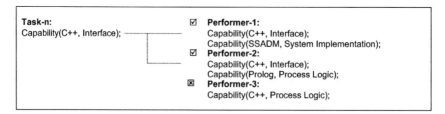

In Figure 5, Task-n requires its performer to possess C++ programming ability and experience in developing a system interface, denoted as Capability(C++, Interface). Performer-1 and Performer-2 have been identified as qualified staff by the compliance check as they possessed the required capability. However, finding a perfect matching (all the required capability fulfilled by a performer in exactly the same terms) can be difficult and sometimes impossible.

The reasons for the failure to find a perfect match in a capability check process are either due to the shortage of required capability or due to vague capability description. For example, if Performer-1 and Performer-2 are occupied by other projects, should we assign the task to Performer-3? How far is his capability from the requirement? For these cases, a fuzzy matching algorithm is developed to access the goodness of fit of a performer against the task, indicating the level of compliance of the performer's capability with a standard.

Cross-Referencing

Finally, through a cross-referencing function, the Inspector can identify the location of a particular specification in a user-defined process plan in the IEC61508 standard, presenting it in the Model of Standards. This service provides a user-friendly system interface, in which users can be aware of the progress of their ongoing works corresponding to the Safety Lifecycle in the standard.

The correctness check ensures that all the specifications in the user-defined process plan are devised in the right sequence. A completeness check ensures that all required specifications are included in the user-defined process plan. They are complementary to each other in ensuring that a user-defined process plan is fully planned and in the correct sequence in accordance with the standard.

With regard to task planning, the Inspector will not actively list down the non-compliance errors, forcing the user to respond. Instead, it will point out the errors to capture the user's attention, similar to the notion of the spelling check function in Microsoft Word where spelling errors are underlined to attract the user's attention. This is because planning normally starts from scratch and gradually evolves to a complete plan. It is assumed that non-compliance errors will always exist until the plan is completed. However, an enforced response is possible if the compliance check function is actively requested by users. Users can either fix the non-compliance error or let it go by providing an explanation, which will be logged for further reference.

Error Prevention

On the other hand, with task execution, the Inspector provides an active control to ensure that tasks are performed in accordance with IEC61508. A distinct feature of Compliance Flow is that it supports interleaving between task planning and task execution, which enables parts of the plans to be specified while the overall process is in progress. Thus, execution of some tasks may start while the overall process plan is still in progress and does not yet comply with the standard.

For example, the tasks towards the attainment of the Safety Integrity Level (SIL) of the product being developed are normally performed prior to the outlining of the system requirement details. If there is any further design process where the requirements according to IEC61508 should correspond to the SIL defined in the safety plan, then execution of the process will be prevented by the Inspector until the required SIL is achieved.

Recommendation Check

IEC61508 recommends sets of techniques or measures for safety related systems for the control of failures. These techniques are grouped and graded for each SIL, in which the rationale should be detailed for any HR techniques or measures not used. These recommendations are modeled into the Model of Standards and are used in the recommendation check process. In a user-defined process, a recommendation of a task is defined as a pre-condition of that task.

During process build-time, the Inspector will map the pre-condition of a task to the recommendations of the relevant task modelled in the Model of Standards to verify whether the required techniques have been selected in a process plan. The Inspector will list all the recommended techniques in the order of their suitability. If the user does not adopt the HR techniques or they choose alternatives with a lower level of recommendation, an explanation is required, which will be recorded in the system. When the user starts a task, the Inspector will check its recommendations again. If the required techniques are not adopted, a reason for the exception must be provided by the user or the execution of the task will be prohibited by the Inspector. An example of recommendation handling is given in .

In Figure 6, three techniques with different levels of suitability in the Model of Standards are defined, which will be used in preparing the Software Safety Validation Report when the SIL is equal to two. In the user-defined process plan where the SIL is equal to two, only two R techniques have been selected. These techniques are defined as pre-conditions of Task-4. After performing the recommendation check, the Inspector discovers that a technique titled "Functional and Black-box Testing" that is HR by IEC61508 is missing in the user-defined process plan. In this case, the execution of Task-4 is prohibited by the Inspector unless the reason for this exception is provided.

Figure 6. Example of Recommendation Handling

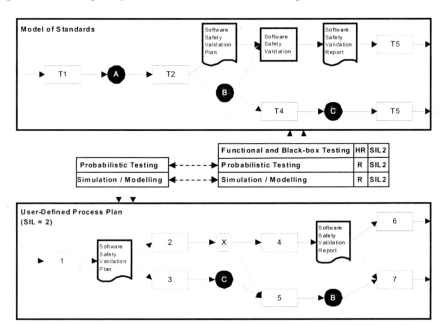

DISCUSSION

Development processes in engineering projects may vary due to uncertainties. Performing mapping between the user-defined process plan and the one proposed by the standard is the most flexible way to tackle the compliance problem. The degree of compliance relies greatly on the level of detail the information of the Model of Standards can provide and the mapping algorithm.

Occasionally, more than one industry standard may be involved in an engineering project. To deal with this situation, there are two approaches: (1) employ a number of compliance agents, each of which is responsible for handling one standard, or (2) employ only one compliance agent who is capable of handling more than one standard. The difference between these two approaches is the degree of coupling between the compliance agent and the Model of Standards.

The first approach has close coupling where every standard may be modeled in a different way and mapping algorithms for each standard would therefore vary. This approach may describe each standard more precisely since differences exist among standards; a different mapping algorithm will be developed to tackle some special features in a particular standard, so that a higher degree of compliance can be achieved. However, the system applicability is impaired as users cannot perform modeling themselves and programming work is required when the standard is updated or a new standard is required.

Our research is tended to the second approach where a generic standard modeling language is developed with the capability of modeling a wide range of standards together with a comprehensive mapping of algorithm to ensure a standard-complied process plan. Users are required to model a new standard only when necessary, and are allowed to amend an existing model to the one used in their organisation in order to achieve the necessary precision of compliance assurance, and consequently extend the applicability and flexibility of the system.

CONCLUSION

In this chapter we have introduced standard compliance as an issue of importance in engineering processes and have discussed our approach of standard modeling that is capable of capturing the main elements of standards for compliance checks. We have presented the Inspector, an intelligent compliance agent, and explained the compliance checking mechanism. We argue that an environment that allows users to be able to plan tasks without restriction is vital while compliance checks are taking place. This is possible as the process structure is not a concern in our approach.

Unlike other researchers, we believe that workflow systems provide the most suitable environment for supporting standard complied projects. We advocate taking advantage of software agent technology to bridge the gap where current workflow models provide no support for process consistency against any standards. Our approach is straight forward, in the sense that it requires relatively simple augmentation of workflow products. Currently the Inspector can only work with the workflow model in Compliance Flow that provides extra flexibility for supporting dynamic engineering processes. We expect that the compliance agent can eventually work with other workflow models through the use of standard interfaces (WfMC, 1995) proposed by the Workflow Management Coalition (WfMC).

REFERENCES

Alonso, G., Agrawal, D., El Abbadi, A., & Mohan, C. (1997). *Functionality and Limitations of Current Workflow Management Systems.* IEEE Expert, 12(5).

Campbell, A. E. & Shapiron, S. C. (1995). *Ontological Mediation: An Overview.* Proceedings of the IJCAI Workshop on Basic Ontological Issues in Knowledge Sharing. Menlo Park, CA: AAAI Press.

Cheung, Y.C., Chung, P.W.H., & Dawson, R.J. (2002). *Supporting Engineering Design Process with Compliance Flow — An Intelligent Workflow Management System.* Engineering Design Conference 2002. King's College, London.

Dellen, B., Maurer, F., & Pews, G. (1997). *Knowledge-Based Techniques to Increase the Flexibility of Workflow Management.* Data and Knowledge Engineering. North Holland.

Easterbrook, S., Finkelstein, A., Kramer, J. & Nuseibeh, B. (1994). Coordinating Distributed ViewPoints: The Anatomy of a Consistency Check. *International Journal on Concurrent Engineering: Research and Applications,* 2 (3), 209-222.

Emmerich, W., Finkelstein, A., Montangero, C., Antonelli, S., Armitage, S., & Stevens, R. (1999). Managing Standards Compliance. *IEEE Transanctions on Software Engineering,* 25 (6).

Finkelstein, A., Gabbay, D., Hunter, A., Kramer, J., & Nuseibeh, B. (1994). Inconsistency Handling In Multi-Perspective Specifications. *IEEE Transactions on Software Engineering,* 20 (8), 569-578.

IEC. (1997, December). *Draft Standard IEC61508 Functional safety of electrical/electronic/programmable electronic (E/E/PES) safety-related systems,* Parts 1 to 7. IEC 61508.

Jarvis, P., Moore, J., Stader, J., Macintosh, A., Casson-du Mont, A., & Chung, P.W.H. (1999). *Exploiting AI Technologies to Realise Adaptive Workflow Systems.* Proceedings of the Workshop on Agent Base Systems in the Business Context, held during AAAI-99.

Moore, J., Inder, R., Chung, P.W.H., Macintosh, A., & Stader, J. (2000). *Combining and Adapting Process Patterns for Flexible Workflow.* DEXA 2000 DomE: International Workshop on Enterprise and Domain Engineering, to be held in conjuction with DEXA 2000: 11th International Conference on Database and Expert Systems Applications. London, Greenwich.

Moore, J., Stader, J., Chung, P.W.H., Jarvis, P., & Macintosh, A. (1999). *Ontologys to Support The Management of New Product Development in the Chemical Process Industries.* International conference on engineering design ICED99. Munich, Germany.

Moore, L. (2002, Spring). *Epigram Profit from Safe Systems.* S. Nunns (Ed.). Moore Industries International, Inc.

Myers, K. & Berry, P. (1999). *Workflow Management Systems: An AI Perspective.* Technical Report, AIC. SRI International, USA.

Sheth A. (1997, September). *From Contemporary Workflow Process Automation to Adaptive and Dynamic Work Activity Coordination and Collaboration*. Workshop on Workflows in Scientific and Engineering Applications. Toulouse, France.

Stader, J., Moore, J., Chung, P.W.H., McBriar, I., Ravinranathan, M., & Macintosh, A. (2000, October). Applying Intelligent Workflow Management in the Chemicals Industries. In L. Fisher (Ed.), *The Workflow Handbook 2001* (pp. 161-181). Published in association with the Workflow Management Coalition (WfMC). FL: Lighthouse Point.

Uschold, M. & Gruninger, M. (1996). Ontologies: Principles, Methods and Applications. *The Knowledge Engineering Review*, 11 (2), 93-136.

Weske, M., Goesmann, T., Holten, R., & Striemer, R. (1999, March). *A Reference Model for Workflow Application Development Processes*, ACM SIGSOFT Software Engineering Notes. Proceedings of the international joint conference on Work activities coordination and collaboration, 24 (2), 1-10.

Workflow Management Coalition (WfMC). (1995). *Workflow Reference Model Version 1.1*. Retrieved in October 2000, available from http://www.wfmc.org/standards/docs/tc003v11.pdf.

Chapter V

Integrating the End User into Infrastructure Systems: A Customer Centric Approach to the Design and Function of Intelligent Transportation Systems

Thomas A. Horan
Claremont Graduate University, USA

ABSTRACT

This chapter analyzes the role of users in enacting Intelligent Transportation Systems (ITS) functions and services. Preliminary evidence from recent demonstrations and market research studies is reviewed with a focus on the role of travelers in producing and using information about traffic conditions and traveler options. The potential for systems development is then considered with specific regard to alternative mode travel, flexible travel, emergency, and commercial services. Based on these findings, several directions and recommendations are made for creating the next generation of ITS systems that enhance user-based elements. Several areas for research and development are recommended, including integrating a wider range of market segments into ITS systems planning, developing a better understanding of how users drive complex systems, and creating new institutional partnerships for delivering innovative services.

INTRODUCTION
The Electronic Generation of Infrastructure

Information technology is transforming the way civil infrastructures function (Zimmerman & Cusker, 2001). Whereas a century ago, transportation, water, and building infrastructures would have been built without regard to their electronic and communication properties, today information technology is increasingly integrated into the process of designing, building, and operating these infrastructures. Within this transformation, there is also an opportunity to integrate the end user more closely in the system. That is, rather than being treated as a "demand" on the system, the end user can be treated as an active integral part of the system. This article explores this development, and challenges thereof, within the context of the surface transportation system and with specific regard to the role of ITS in facilitating this user involvement.

ITS has emerged over the last decade as a major new vector in surface transportation investment. Spurred on by some $2 billion in federal support, states and localities throughout the United States have begun deploying a range of information systems that comprise the general ITS approach (U.S. Department of Transportation, 2001). As documented by the ITS National Systems Architecture (Iteris, 2000), these information systems serve a variety of surface transportation centers (e.g., traffic management, commercial vehicle administration, transit management) through active wireline and wireless communication to the infrastructure and vehicles traveling on the infrastructure (see Figure 1). However, these systems do not exist in a vacuum, but rather have the ultimate goal of improving travel for users of the transportation system. Within the wide array of technology-based services that constitute the ITS program, the principle focus of this article is how travelers obtain and use Advanced Traveler Information Systems (ATIS), such as real-time information about travel and traffic conditions. The implications, however, are broader, as these user-related ITS research and demonstrations suggest a next generation of information system design and use.

Figure 1. National ITS Architecture Overview

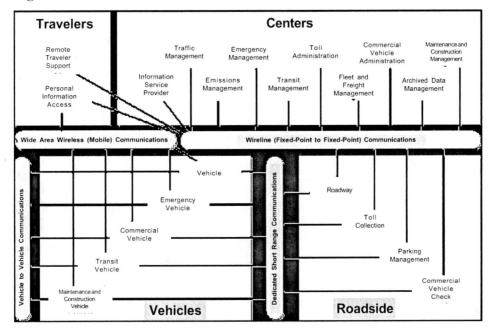

Source: U.S. Department of Transportation

THE INFRASTRUCTURE-CUSTOMER CONNECTION

Early ITS Demonstrations and Deployments

In the early stages of ITS (e.g., the late 1980s), the vision of ITS foresaw a strong public sector role in creating a consumer information platform. For example, the landmark plan for the federal program, *Mobility 2000* (1990), articulated the vision for a publicly supplied information system that would feed "value added" private sector traveler information services. Over the last decade, this vision has been tested throughout the United States via a range of ATIS demonstration projects. A common feature of these systems has been the publicly supported procurement of traffic and travel information and then its distribution usually through free means (e.g., radio, television, etc.). Such demonstrations were undertaken in scores of cities, including but not limited to Boston, Washington, D.C., Minneapolis, Seattle, and San Francisco (Lappin, 2000).

While the demonstrations were undertaken to test the proposition that high-quality information on transportation conditions could be obtained and disseminated, a major lesson from these demonstrations and deployments has been that *the relationship of the consumer to the infrastructure is more complex than at first envisioned.* This is true in terms of both the direction of the information flow between the infrastructure and the customer, and the perceived value and use of this information across consumer groups.

Starting with the direction of the information flow, several early field demonstrations have provided important hands-on experiences with getting accurate and reliable information about transportation system conditions (U.S. DOT, 2001). During the mid-1990s, perhaps the most visible demonstration was the TravInfo project in San Francisco. TravInfo sought to create a state-of-the-art, public sector-led platform for providing multi-modal information to travelers. In this highly visible case, the public sector information system became hampered by institutional and technical limitations in being able to deploy a publicly financed and managed traffic sensing system in a timely matter (Yim & Deakin, 2000).

These limitations in traffic system deployment have led to an interesting change in the flow of information. As a result of the TravInfo demonstration experience, the Bay Area Metropolitan Transportation Commission is now evaluating new *public-private partnerships in the production of traveler information*, including data emitting from wireless probes. That is, the consumer is moving to be a part of the information production, not just consumption. A similar, though perhaps less stark, pattern is occurring throughout U.S. metropolitan areas. Through cell-phones, call-ins and probes, the travelers and their cars are emerging as an active part of the surface transportation information system. This trend is being further tested in a new research program (Autonet) by the Cal-IT2 program at the University of California and represents a significant shift in the potential source of information (i.e., away from public sources and toward more private sources) (Smarr, 2002).

In terms of the value of the information, these demonstrations have occurred against the backdrop of market studies that have consistently revealed a modest "willingness to pay" for general travel information (Shuman & Sherer, 2001). However, these "stated" preferences understate the diversity of interest and use across different market segments. For example, in the model deployment initiative in Seattle, several different users were identified and different travel information sources were highly valued and used by these groups (Jenson et al., 2000). There is a strong interest, for example, in television-based video feed information services for those who use infrequently computer technology, while, not surprisingly, there is high interest and use of web-based information among the facile Internet users, who in this case tended to be younger.

Findings from Seattle and other sites point the way to a more detailed understanding of market niches for traveler information. For example, a recent summary on lessons learned from national ATIS field tests identified three market segments: "control freaks," "web-heads," and "information seekers" (Lappin, 2000). The former two, for example, are often market leaders in new ATIS services, and e-services generally; but it is the less technologically agile information seeker that represents a critically large segment, and within that domain this would include market niches such as the alternative-mode traveler, as well as what I would dub the "flexible traveler."

New Niches: Alternative Mode and Flexible Traveler

The alternative-mode traveler (e.g., bus rider) has been a vital constituent in the transportation system, yet it has been difficult to provide reliable and timely information to this user. As bus and light rail information systems become more integrated into regional ITS programs, this should provide a useful data source for travelers interested in bus and rail information. However, the alternative mode traveler information need not stop there. There are a variety of niches and circumstances where alternative transportation modes excel as a means of travel. These would include special transit systems in recreational and national park areas, car-sharing programs in university towns, and jitney systems to airports (Salon, Sperling, Shaheen & Sturges, 2000). As bandwidth becomes more available to primary residential and mobile users, there is a new opportunity to bring information about innovative systems to the attention of existing and potentially new alternative mode travelers.

In this regard, the SmartTrek project in Seattle is telling. Under the leadership of the Washington State Department of Transportation, the project has developed a rich array of information on various modes, including highway, rail, car-sharing, and ferries. Moreover, it is customizable to consumer needs, both in terms of types of information available (e.g., video, graphics) and platforms to which the information can be delivered (e.g., Internet, cell phone). While travel condition information is available through a variety of sources, the Puget Sound web site is by far the most extensive information source. Not surprisingly, the SmartTrek evaluation found a high degree of user satisfaction with this web-based travel information; over 90% of respondents thought that the regional online information was useful and that it affected their commute trip, either in terms of time of travel or means of travel (Jenson et al., 2000).

Flexible Travel

Another ATIS target market is the flexible traveler—the flexible traveler is perhaps the unsung hero of the transportation system. The flexible traveler has not been studied closely, but might provide an important ingredient to bringing "yield management" (perfected in the airline industry) to surface transportation systems. The flexible traveler is one who, as the name implies, could, and indeed would, change his travel time if he could have a more reliable trip time. The Washington, D.C., demonstration uncovered that ATIS systems were as useful for improving the reliability of service as they were for improving the timeliness of service (Wunderlich, Hardy, Larkin & Shah, 2001). That is, it is as important to know *with certainty* that one can make a 9:00 a.m. meeting as it is perhaps to save a few minutes on that commute and arrive, say, at 8:40 a.m. While the transportation-telecommunications literature has examined closely the impact of telecommuting programs, the impact of flexible commute arrangements is arguably as important, if not more important, to smoothing out spikes in travel demand.

While there has been a tapering off in the number of formal telecommuting programs, a more diverse and flexible array of work patterns seems to be emerging (Mokhtarian, 2000; Niles, 2001). Even in the slowing economy, flexible work arrangements remain critical. For example, based on a survey of over 1,000 employers, Hewitt Associates (2001) found that 73% of businesses offer flexible work options. The most common arrangements offered are flextime (58%) and part-time employment (48%). Other popular programs include work-at-home options (29%), job sharing (28%), compressed work weeks (21%), and summer hours (12%). Flexible travelers can adjust their work hours depending on any number of factors, one of which is perceived commute time. This form of partial telecommuting-flextime can be enhanced by accurate ATIS information on estimated travel times.

Flexibility can also be a part of the commercial traffic solution. This shift away from the peak has already occurred to some extent in the commercial industry and through proper use of transportation information could be encouraged even further. Commercial delivery services will often wait until the perceived peak period travel is over to deliver products and goods to congested urban areas. However, a recent national workshop on e-freight revealed that additional traffic and parking information could make the commercial delivery availability more efficient (Casgar, 2001). With the growth of small package delivery services, there has been a related growth in customer interest in on-time delivery, often around the peak travel time (e.g., business morning delivery). New systems that provide additional certainty for both consumer and operators can enhance individual productivity, as well as overall system performance.

Of course, economists have long argued that pricing provides the simplest, and hence, the preferred mode to convey information about demand relative to supply (Winston & Shirley, 1998). When demand increases relative to fixed supply (e.g., peak-hour capacity), the price rises, and when demand falls relative to supply, the price falls correspondingly. Travelers accept that when they assess their air travel choices—price sales occur off peak, and price premiums occur during business days. Yet, for most parts of the United States, "congestion pricing" or "value pricing" remains an untried option. Where Electronic Toll Collection (ETC) has been introduced, however, it is providing demonstrable time savings to users. For example, the evaluation of New York's E-Z Pass program found widespread technology acceptance among users (though there have been some problems with regard to customer support) (Vollmer, 2000). It is not surprising, therefore, that this E-Z Pass system is becoming a de facto standard for the middle Atlantic states as some seven states now use the E-Z pass system. These and related systems around the country are setting the stage by providing transactional platforms for a more dynamic and information-based transportation system.

Need for Mobile Emergency and Security Systems

The transportation system must function safely as well as efficiently and these twin objectives have an information analog: information systems are needed to facilitate rapid response to emergency situations throughout the transportation network. It is instructive to note that the advent of private sector telecommunications and cellular service has played a pivotal role in bringing the safety information network online. Between 1990 and 2000, the percent of 911 calls from mobile devices exploded from 20,000 to 120,000 *per day* (ComCare Alliance, 2001). The role of mobile telematics in detecting travel hazards and providing safety services has become substantial and a consortium has arisen to promote innovative services through a transportation-health care partnership.

Indeed, the advent of the new federal e-911 mandate (for being able to determine location based on a cell-phone call) will usher in a new era of mobile-related emergency service. The recent operational test in Minnesota of Mayday Plus demonstrated "next generation" possibilities for enhancing access to emergency services. This demonstration, conducted over the last two years, integrated cellular communications, Global Positioning Systems (GPS) satellite technology, and a special emergency response communications system installed at Mayo Clinic and Minnesota State Patrol emergency dispatch centers. The Mayday Plus system successfully provided authorities with automatic collision notification and related information on location and crash severity (Castle Rock Consultants, 2000).

Beyond this demonstration, operations such as the ComCare Alliance have created new institutional alliances to help ensure critical services are delivered within the narrow "golden hour" that exists for delivering medical treatment after an accident. With a large percent of fatal accidents occurring in rural areas, the new e-911 requirements provide an important tool for delivery of these critical safety services. Moreover, they highlight the innovative types of partnerships needed to deliver ITS across a broad range of users. In this case, it involves a new form of interorganizational system (IOS) partnership with healthcare providers, emergency service providers, and the state police. In this author's recent review of wireless systems, many factors have emerged as affecting the extent to which these IOS systems perform well. These include technical constraints on cell-phone coverage in remote areas, organizational constraints, such as seamless integrates across agencies, and policy-level dimensions constraints, such as reluctance to adequately fund statewide efforts (Horan & Schooley, 2002). These findings point toward the need to take an integrated view of information and communication systems in transportation. This approach integrates technological advancement with supporting socio-technical policy and organizational actions. These dimensions are considered further in the conclusions and recommendations.

CONCLUSIONS AND RECOMMENDATIONS

A common thread woven through these trends, market research studies, and demonstration projects is the emergent transformation of the transportation system from something that is industrial in its organization—a concrete, asphalt, and steel system that uninformed consumers travel in predictably inefficient ways—to something that is understood and used in a manner that is highly dynamic, user specific, demand-responsive, and information intensive. That is, it is a dynamic socio-technical system.

Changes in this dynamic socio-technical system need to be considered within the context of federal legislation. The federal ITS program was originally authorized in the 1991 federal transportation legislation (i.e., Intermodal Surface Transportation Efficiency Act of 1991). The program has enjoyed decade-long support from the federal government, along with substantial support from local government and the private sector. With the transportation legislation scheduled for reauthorization again in 2003, there has been some discussion with the ITS industry about the overarching policy concerns that would drive ITS usage over the next decade (Johnson, 2001). In this discussion, ITS is often seen as becoming part of "mainstream" transportation planning and operations. However, given the weakness of traditional transportation planning methods in terms of addressing specific user needs through technology, there are a variety of new directions that could be taken to enhance ITS as a user-responsive, socio-technical system. These are outlined below.

Adopt a User-Centric Perspective

Pursuant to the transportation legislation reauthorization scheduled for 2003, a new 10-year ITS Program Plan is being developed by the U.S. Department of Transportation. In the current version of this plan, the importance of the end user is recognized explicitly. The relevant section states the ITS program should focus on "providing effective, end-to-end, seamless, multi-modal transportation services for people wherever they live, work, and play regardless of age or disability…and helping make travel time more productive, by flexibly enabling more travel choices for more people" (ITSA, 2001). The challenge is to deliver a system that will indeed produce this seamless experience.

In catalyzing this vision, it is useful to consider the changes that have occurred in the air travel reservation system. Even the prescient Robert Crandall (former CEO of American Airlines) could not have foreseen the extent to which consumers would take control over their travel choice. The Sabre system was originally designed for the travel agent, but, of course, the World Wide Web changed all that, making the travel agent one of the many functions to be "disintermediated." In the spirit of these times, the Sabre system gave birth to Travelocity, which has since become a shining star in the otherwise darker e-commerce sky. Indeed, the travel industry has been revolutionized by these information system changes, as a new era of information intensive user-friendly systems continues to drive personal air travel. Looking more broadly at the e-commerce industry, among those enterprises that continue to shine, a fundamental principle is the dedication to a consumer focus, alternatively termed mass customization (e.g., Dell), personalization (e.g., Amazon), or, more generally, customer relationship management (CRM).

For the transportation professionals generally and the ITS program specifically, the corresponding challenge is to devise and execute an information system that can satisfy the individual traveler and affect overall system choice and performance. The lesson from CRM approaches (and the longer history of customer-centric management models) is that information systems can allow for both: generating overall system efficiencies and devising highly tailored relationships with customers (Vandenbosch & Dawar, 2002).

These findings beg the development of a more flexible transportation management network that can respond to personalized information and choice. While ITS has increasingly allowed information to be available to consumers, it has not achieved the level of user acceptance and use as the air travel reservation system enjoys. This is despite a recent nationwide effort to institute a national 511 traffic information system (ITSA, 2002). However, there is abundant reason to believe that information about choice enhances system efficiency. In surface transportation, choice has been constrained due to a number of policy, market, and technological circumstances. However, there are an increasing number of modal options being pursued in metropolitan areas — transit, light rail, car sharing, and e-commuting. The role of the ITS system should be to facilitate access to these modal options and a user-centric ITS system should be charged with providing this information intensive experience for these and other markets.

Create New Institutional Allegiances.

Underlying the tension in moving toward a customer-centric approach in surface transportation is the industry's institutional history with regard to capital projects. Traditionally, surface transportation policy has concerned itself with major project (i.e., highway) planning and construction concerns, rather than day-to-day customer satisfaction (Lockwood, 1999). The customer-driven focus suggested in this article highlights the need to link information systems directly to the customers. Transportation managers have little to fear of being disintermediated; in fact, they have much to gain from an informed traveler who will use the information to alter travel time or mode to enhance their personal mobility, and by consequence, enhance system mobility. While this objective may be laudable at a very general level, actually finding the precise style of institutional partnership can be quite challenging. The next generation of systems will do well by executing partnerships in travel-service, navigation, electronic tolling, safety, and mayday services in a manner that was hoped for but not executed in the first generation of ITS deployment.

For some, the recent retrenchment in the technology sector has given rise to concern about reliance on the private sector in providing information systems and services to the public. What happens when private sector partners cannot receive adequate return of investment to justify participation in ITS programs? For over a decade, the ATIS industry has struggled to establish itself as a profitable sector, and it now appears to function as a segment of larger database, mapping, and radio-advertising market segments. Similarly, in terms of transportation sensing and control systems, the major private sector participants often are rooted strongly in public sector contracting, which can lead to an orientation around obtaining and maintaining public contracts, rather than fulfilling the needs of the end user.

Perhaps the best way the public sector can reduce these uncertainties is to articulate its strategic commitment to being a steady consumer and purchaser of information systems that enhance user-based transportation services. The venue to articulating this strategic focus is the transportation planning process. The regional ITS architecture conformity requirements could be viewed as a starting point for this strategic vision, as these architectures lay out a general scheme for deploying ITS in the region. The next generation of information systems for surface transportation should build on this planning framework to articulate a strategic vision of customer-oriented transportation information services and systems that are fully integrated with the physical and institutional aspects of the transport system.

Research on Users in the System

Returning to the air travel analogy, the explosion of the information dimension of the airline travel business has an important message for infrastructure system designers — the consuming public is ready to take charge of its transportation choices. However, just as the Sabre information system needed to be in place before the benefits of yield management could be realized, the challenge for surface transportation professionals is to research and develop timely, useful, reliable, and interpretable information systems that the consumer can use to guide their choice of mode, time, and route of travel. Further, a corresponding challenge is to devise and execute an information system that can satisfy the individual traveler in this manner while having a positive effect on overall system choice and performance. In this vein, research is needed on how various ITS systems can become an integrated means by which travelers can develop customized traveler plans — plans that can benefit ostensibly from archival and predicative information on system performance.

This begs the research and development of an ITS management network that can respond to personalized information and choice. Research is needed on the specific user-information needs, delivery modes, and interface requirements for several major traveler groups, including, but not limited to, flexible travelers, e-commuters (e.g., teleworkers), and interregional and intermodal travelers. These services could utilize a variety of travel and traffic data. With regard to the latter, a major opportunity would be to develop new wireless based systems — including using vehicles as probes. As noted earlier, the AutoNet program at Cal-IT2 represents one approach to this research. As a complement to this engineering-based analysis of wireless network potentials, additional business and organizational analyses are needed to assess the public-private business models for delivering and maintaining such systems.

Research on Complex Systems Development

It is clear that managing complex systems like the surface transportation system necessitates a set of principles and knowledge at the interface of several fields: transportation, engineering, economics, social science, and information systems (Sussman, 2000). Yet, only now are we beginning to understand how these systems perform. The PeMS system under development by the University of California at Berkeley is an example of the next generation of an archival-predictive model that holds promise for using traffic data combined with management control means (Variaya, 2001). It suggests a new level of operations management that needs to be integrated with policy, financing, and engineering approaches to transportation management

In looking for research directions, an interesting parallel can be found from the energy sector. Recognizing the dynamic nature of energy systems, the Electric Power Research Institute (EPRI) has initiated a cooperative $30 million, five-year program with the Department of Defense to develop a fundamental understanding of how energy management can learn from complex system dynamics and, as a consequence, devise more reliable and adaptive energy systems (Amin, 2000). A similar effort may be needed in surface transportation. This would be a research program that draws upon advances in complexity theory, user-driven systems, and ITS lessons and developments to enhance the body of research on information intensive surface transportation infrastructure. Such an effort would be consistent with a recent National Science Foundation view that better theories and principles on IT and infrastructure performance are needed to ensure the competitive performance of the nation's civil systems (Bordogna, 2001).

CONCLUSION

In conclusion, the time is right to reconfigure the surface transportation industry to better plan, manage, and disseminate information relative to users of that system. During the first decade of ITS testing, the dominant paradigm was one of government-provided, industry-assisted forms of information to customers, with the hope that some customers would respond and that this response would affect transportation system performance. The "next generation" challenge for ITS is to devise a self-organizing information system, where the benefits of information are realized through a dynamic market system that provides incentives for just-in-time travel, travel substitution, and full-cost travel. The goal of such an enterprise should be to create a close connection between the traveler, the system, and the information guiding the system. Such a change has already occurred in air travel. Perhaps in twenty years, we will remember a time when it changed in surface travel.

ACKNOWLEDGMENTS

An earlier version of this paper was presented at the 2002 International IRMA Conference, Seattle, Washington, May 19-22, 2002. A practitioner-oriented version appeared in a special edition of TR News, *Intelligent Transportation Systems: Determining Directions,* pages 31-37. Findings reported in this paper are drawn from a study completed by Horan and Reany, titled *Network Management Approaches: Cross-Industry Comparisons and Implications for ITS Development,* Report Prepared for California PATH Program, August, 2001.

REFERENCES

Amin, M. (2000). National Infrastructures as Complex Interactive Networks. In T. Samad & J. Weyrauch (Eds), *Automation, Control and Complexity, New Developments and Directions* (pp. 263-286). New York: J.W. Wiley.

Bordogna, G. (2001, May 26). *Infrastructure for the Future: Assembling the Pieces.* Presentation at NSF/ICIS Workshop, Bringing Information Technology to Infrastructure. Washington, D.C.

Casgar, T. (2001). *E-Freight: Metropolitan Implications.* Conference Report Prepared for Federal Highway Administration and Environmental Protection Agency. Washington, D.C.: Foundation for Intermodal Research and Education.

Castle Rock Consultants. (2000). *Mayday Plus Operational Test Evaluation.* Prepared for Minnesota Department of Transportation. Minneapolis, MN.

ComCare Alliance. (2001, November). *Wireless fact sheet, 2001.* Retrieved on January 29, 2003 from http://www.comcare.org/research/topics/wireless.html.

Hewitt Associates. (2001). *Findings from 2001 Worklife Survey.* Lincolnshire, IL.

Horan, T. & Reany, W. (2001). *Network Management Approaches: Cross-Industry Comparisons and Implications for ITS Development.* Report Prepared for California PATH Program. Berkeley, CA: University of California, Berkeley.

Horan, T. & Schooley, B. (2002). *Managing Complex Networks: The Case of Interorganizational Systems in Emergency Medical Services* (report draft). Claremont, CA: Claremont Information and Technology Institute.

Intelligent Transportation Society of America (ITSA). (2001). *Intelligent Transportation Systems Ten Year Program Plan* (draft). Washington, D.C.: Intelligent Transportation Society of America.

Intelligent Transportation Society of America (ITSA). (2002). *511 Proceedings of the Deployment Conference: Answering America's Call for Travel Information.* Washington, D.C.: Intelligent Transportation Society of America.

Iteris. (2000). *ITS National Systems Architecture: Overview.* Prepared for U.S. Department of Transportation. Washington, D.C.: U.S. Department of Transportation.

Jenson, M., Cluett, C., Wunderlich, K., DeBlasio, A., & Sanchez, R. (2000). *Metropolitan Model Deployment Initiative: Seattle Evaluation Report, Final Draft.* Washington, D.C.: U.S. Department of Transportation.

Johnson, C. (2001, May 6). *ITS and TEA-21.* Presentation to the ITS America Annual Meeting. Miami Beach, FL.

Lappin, J. (2000). What Have We Learned from Advanced Traveler Information Systems and Customer Satisfaction. In *What Have We Learned About Intelligent Transportation Systems,* (pp. 65-86) Washington, D.C.: U.S. Department of Transportation.

Lockwood, S. (1999, December). Realizing ITS: The Vision vs. The Challenge. *ITE Journal,* 24-27.

Mobility 2000. (1990). *Mobility 2000 Presents Intelligent Vehicles and Highway Systems.* Dallas, TX: Texas Transportation Institute.

Mokhtarian, P. (2000). *Telecommunications and Travel.* Paper Prepared for Millennium Series. Washington D.C.: Transportation Research Board, 2000.

Niles, J. (2001). *Transportation and Technology: A Dynamic Relationship.* Seattle, WA: Discovery Institute.

Salon, D., Sperling, D., Shaheen, S., and Sturges, D. (2002). *New Mobility: Using Technology and Partnerships to Create a More Efficient, Equitable, and Environmentally Sound Transportation System.* Washington, D.C.: Transportation Research Board.

Shuman, R., & Sherer, E. (2001). *ATIS U.S. Business Model Review.* Report Prepared for U.S. Department of Transportation. Washington, D.C.

Smarr, L. (2002, February 18). *Extending the Internet with Sensornets: Supporting Science and Emergency Preparedness.* Keynote Address to American Association for the Advancement of Science, Boston, MA, February 16, 2002.

Sussman, J. (2000). *Introduction to Transportation Systems.* Boston, MA: Artech House.

U.S. Department of Transportation. (2001). *ITS Evaluation Summaries.* Retrieved on April 16, 2002 from http://www.its.dot.gov/EVAL/documents_RMTIS_ATIS.html.

Vandenbosch, M. & Dawar, D. (2002). Beyond Better Products: Capturing Value in Customer Interactions. *Sloan Management Review,* 43(4), 35-42.

Varaiya, P. (2001). *Freeway Performance Measurement System: Final Report*. Report Prepared for California PATH Program. Berkeley, CA: University of California, Berkeley.

Vollmer Associates. (2000). *E-ZPass Evaluation Report*. Prepared for New York State Freeway Authority. New York.

Winston, C. & Shirley, C. (Eds.)(1998). *Alternate Route: Toward Efficient Urban Transportation.* Washington, D.C.: Brookings Institution.

Wunderlich, K., Hardy, M., Larkin, J., & Shah, V. (2001). *On Time Reliability Impacts of Advanced Traveler Information Services: Washington, D.C. Case Study*. Washington, D.C.: Mitretek.

Yim, Y. & Deakin, E. (2000). *TravInfo Field Operational Test Institutional Evaluation Final Results*. Report Prepared for California PATH Program. Berkeley, CA: University of California, Berkeley.

Zimmerman, R. & Cusker, M. (2001, May 26). Bringing Technology to Infrastructure: A White Paper for a Research Agenda. Paper prepared for NSF/ICIS Workshop, Bringing Information Technology to Infrastructure, Arlington, VA, June 25, 2001.

Chapter VI

Implementing the Shared Event Paradigm: Architecture, Issues and Lessons Learned

Dirk Trossen
Nokia Research Center, Boston, USA

Erik Molenaar
University of Technology, Aachen, Germany

ABSTRACT

Shared collaboration between distributed users gains more importance due to the globalization of organizations and institutions. Besides exchanging audiovisual data, sharing spreadsheets or graphics is of utmost importance, especially in scenarios for tele-working or tele-education. Although the Internet has gained more ground in our daily work, most applications nowadays are not prepared for shared collaboration, and it is expected that this non-awareness of distribution will remain persistent for most of the applications. For that, application-sharing technologies have been developed to encounter the problem sharing these kinds of applications among a set of distributed users. Two different paradigms to realize application sharing can be distinguished, namely sharing the application's output or the application's evolving state. In this chapter, the realization of an application-sharing service is presented, based on the latter paradigm, which is mostly suited for closed development or teaching scenarios. The requirements for the service as well as its realization are outlined, together with the lessons we learned from this realization.

INTRODUCTION

For collaboration among a group of users, sharing audiovisual, textual, graphical, or even interface-related information is the essence of systems that realize *computer supported collaborative work* (CSCW). Several toolkits have been developed and studied in the past. Since most applications being used in private and work life nowadays are merely usable on the computer on which they are executed, collaboratively working with a single application is the most challenging part of CSCW. This is not only true because these applications are not aware that they are executed in a distributed environment, but also, in particular, because of the numerous possibilities of data to be shared among the distributed users when performing a local application.

Thus, the distribution of the application's functionality over the network has to be added transparently and, more importantly, subsequently without changing the application's semantic. The effect has to be created at each remote site that the application is running locally and, therefore, can also be controlled by any remote user with a more or less immediate effect to the application.

Two different paradigms can be distinguished to tackle the above-mentioned challenges, namely *Output Sharing* and *Event Sharing*. In Trossen (2001), a qualitative comparison of both paradigms is presented, outlining the different application scenarios for both paradigms. It was concluded that the latter is best suited for closed group environments with a limited set of input data to be shared. As a consequence, it seems to be a promising candidate for shared engineering (Trossen, Schueppen & Wallbaum, 2001), multimedia presentation, or tele-teaching scenarios.

This chapter presents a realization of the event-sharing paradigm, called *Multipoint Event Sharing Service* (MESS), outlining the architecture and the implementation issues to be addressed. For that, a component-based architecture is presented, which is mapped onto an object-oriented design to bring the system to life. The currently provided functionality and obtained performance is described, which is very encouraging, especially for the targeted application scenarios.

However, the realization encounters several difficulties, which will be presented as the lessons we learned from our work.

The remainder of the chapter is organized as follows. After giving some background information on different techniques for application sharing and their applicability, we will define the requirements for the presented architecture. Based on these requirements, we will outline the architecture and realization of the application sharing service. We will also discuss the lessons we learned from our implementation, and give pointers for further reading. The chapter concludes eventually with a discussion of our future work.

BACKGROUND

The realization of application sharing involves the synchronized transfer of application-specific data among users, and it faces several challenges to be solved (Trossen, 2001):

- *Amount of transferred data*: The amount of data per packet to be transferred is part of the indicator for the generated network load.
- *Number of interception points*: Each technique adds certain points to the local system to intercept the required information that needs to be distributed among the session members. First, the information has to be extracted for building the appropriate packet to be sent. Second, the packet has to be transferred through the protocol stack degrading the overall system performance. Additionally, together with the amount of transferred data (see above), the resulting number of bytes to be sent over the network can be used as an indicator of the generated network load.
- *Heterogeneity*: Sharing applications independent from each member's operating system is crucial for a wide applicability of the technique. This requires appropriate software at each site.
- *Latecomer's support*: Joining the session later should be supported without leading to inconsistencies of the shared application's state.
- *Shared data problem*: Using any kind of input data within the shared application should not lead to inconsistencies of the distributed copies of the application. For instance, no inconsistencies should occur when copying local input data into a shared spreadsheet.
- *Synchronization*: The shared instances of the application have to be synchronized to ensure consistency of the workspace among all users due to the different processing speed of the sites and the different delays of the transmission lines.

Two different paradigms can be distinguished to tackle the abovementioned challenges, namely *Output Sharing* and *Event Sharing*, presented in the following subsections, summarizing the findings in Trossen (2001).

Sharing GUI Technique

The first technique is to share the application's GUI output with the set of users. For feedback from the receivers, any input data like mouse or keyboard events is transferred back to the sender and fed into its local event loop for control. Figure 1 illustrates this technique. The server host runs the local application. *Rendering data* is transferred from the server to the receiver group using a specific protocol, e.g., a reliable multicast transport protocol. Obtaining the rendering data can be realized either on *windows engine level* or on *graphics engine level*, resulting in different numbers of interception points (Trossen, 2001).

As indicated in Figure 1, *event data* is sent back to the server to be fed into its local event loop for a remote control of the application. Usually, transferring event data to the server is controlled by means of *floor control* (Hao & Sventek, 1996), i.e., the appropriate host is selected based on a *social protocol* with an associated floor, representing the right to control the application.

Latecomer's support is provided by invoking a full refresh of the local GUI resulting in a transfer of the entire GUI content to the receiver group. Furthermore, the shared GUI approach allows a heterogeneous receiver group, assuming appropriate rendering engines on the client's side. As shown above, the input event data is the only data to be synchronized with the local application, which is realized by means of floor control. Any additional data, like files or local device data, is held locally with the server's host. Hence, there is no *shared data* problem to deal with. However, the different processing speeds of the client rendering engines have to be considered for synchronization of the workspace. For that, *synchronization points* can be used, which have to be acknowledged by each member.

Figure 1. Sharing GUI Approach

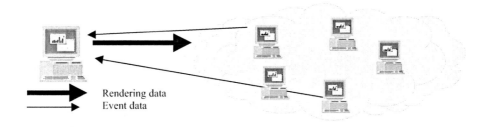

Rendering data
Event data

Sharing Event Technique

The second technique to solve the shared application problem is the *sharing event* approach. The assumption being made is that if a set of identical applications is executed with the same start state and evolves using the same sequence of events, its timeline evolution is identical on each site. Hence, the basic approach of this technique can be outlined as follows:

- define the start state to be distributed among all group members
- start local copies of the application to be shared on each host
- distribute input events of the current controlling group member to evolve the current application's state

This technique is demonstrated in Figure 2. In contrast to the shared GUI approach, there is no central server after starting the shared application. The initiator of the shared application session is merely used for defining the start state of the application. Any input data is transferred from the current floor holder to *all* group members. There is no central entity to which the input data is sent first to determine the new output.

Additionally, the *number of interception points* can be reduced drastically since only the main input event handling loop of the current floor holder has to be intercepted and the (relatively) small packets are to be distributed to the other participants (Trossen, 2001).

However, it can easily be seen that the *homogeneity* of the environment is crucial due to the requirement having a local application instance. Hence, hetero-geneous environments are not supported. *Latecomers* can be supported through maintaining a history of the event evolution that is distributed to the recently joined participant.

Figure 2. Shared Event Technique

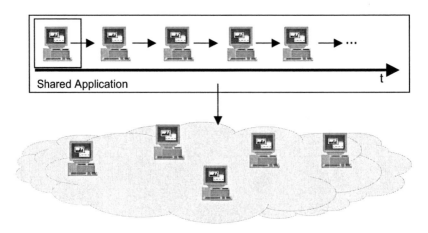

A special treatment is necessary handling the *shared data problem*. If there is any local data to be fed into the local instance, this case has to be handled to ensure consistency among the different copies.

Similar to the shared GUI technique, the different processor speeds have to be considered for synchronization. Inserting *synchronization events* is a common solution for this problem.

Applicability of the Techniques

Each approach for tackling the application-sharing problem has its specific advantages and weaknesses. The first technique, either sharing the GUI on higher or lower level, is well-suited for heterogeneous environments and when using input data that cannot be shared among the other participants.

However, the shared event approach has also specific advantages, which makes this technique attractive for specific scenarios. Due to the local copy of the application, the additional load on each host is expected to be much lower, which increases the responsiveness of the system and thus improves the user's perception of the system. However, the problem of ensuring the consistency of each user's view when using shared data restricts the applicability of the approach either to not using shared input data or to using the technique in local environments where data sharing is feasible to some extent. Furthermore, this technique is not applicable in heterogeneous scenarios.

The following table shows typical scenarios for shared applications and the applicability of both paradigms in these scenarios. It is worth mentioning that the list is only meant to outline sample scenarios. Thus, the list is neither exhaustive nor exclusive.

It can be seen that the shared event technique is not applicable to the last two scenarios due to the heterogeneous character of these situations, while the first three scenarios are fairly good examples where the shared event approach promises to provide a higher responsiveness of the system and therefore an improved user's perception. Especially the multimedia presentation is hardly conceivable using the shared GUI approach due to the large amount of data to be transferred, which is

Table 1. Scenario Examples and Paradigms Applicability

Scenario Description	Shared GUI	Shared Event
Multimedia presentation in a local environment	--	++
Programming environment in a lecture	-	++
Development environment in a closed user group	-	+
Spreadsheet in an heterogeneous Internet environment	++	-
Accompanying presentation in an Internet lecture	++	-

avoided by the local copy of the application when using the shared event technique. Furthermore, due to the local character of the scenarios, the shared data problem can be handled much easier.

It can be summarized that the shared event technique is better suited for local environments and high demands on the responsiveness of the shared application, while the shared GUI approach is to be preferred in heterogeneous environments and when having problems with data to be shared.

REQUIREMENTS AND ISSUES TO BE SOLVED

The main requirement for an application-sharing service is to enable a synchronous view of an application on several participating computers. In Trossen (2001), the idea was formulated to investigate the possibilities of applying the event-sharing paradigm and the gain it can offer. In this work, a realization of an event-sharing service is proposed. Its design will be a consequence of the requirements, presented in this section. Before outlining the requirements, some definitions and theoretical background are needed.

Definitions and Background

The *state* of an application describes the current snapshot of the application itself and all resources it addresses. *Resources* can be anything that is not the application itself, but is changed or used by the application to determine its behavior. Examples are files, registry entries, or the system time. Phenomena that change the application's state are called *events*.

A *stable state* of the shared application is given, if the execution behavior of all instances is equivalent. For example, if a menu entry is selected, the same action belonging to the corresponding menu entry should be performed on all machines. This stable state will sometimes be referred to as being in a *consistent* or *equivalent* state.

Deterministic behavior of an application means that if a set of this application is started in an equivalent state, and the same set of events is presented to those instances, then the same state transitions will happen for all instances. It is important to realize that this definition of deterministic behavior is more relaxed as other definitions, in the sense that resources that an application might need are considered as part of the environment. Where other definitions might assume that an application is no longer behaving deterministically if, for example, the system time of the local machine is used, this definition regards the system time as a part of the environment.

Given an application that behaves deterministically, the following statement is valid:

Theorem 1: A set of instances of an application that behaves deterministically can be held in a stable state if the starting state and all events can be captured.

The proof of this statement is a simple induction: Assume all instances in stable state at the beginning. Since every event can be captured, these events are fed into each instance to initiate a transformation of state. Because of the definitions of state and event, the successor states are stable again from a viewpoint of a neutral observer somewhere in the session.

Requirements

Apart from the major requirement that the application to be shared must behave deterministically, the following requirements for the application-sharing service can be defined to keep the shared instances in stable state over the timeline.

- All participating instances must start in an equivalent state.
- During runtime of the session, all events that change the application's state must be captured and broadcast to all participants.
- If some events access resources, these must be provided to all participants.
- Synchronization of instances must be offered.

In addition to these functional requirements, the following minor requirements have to be addressed by a realization.

- An interface with the participant has to be offered.
- Distributed messages have to be marshaled, i.e., being transferred in a common syntax.
- Latecomer's support has to be addressed.

Since a shared-application service is using resources from existing conferencing systems, such as Trossen (2000), the following requirements for this part of the system can be derived:

- Conference management, i.e., joining and leaving conferences, should be provided.
- Floor control is required to prevent multiple participants to control the application simultaneously.
- Reliable message transport shall be provided with global ordering of messages.
- If possible, multicast capabilities shall be utilized.

MULTIPOINT EVENT SHARING SERVICE (MESS)

The abovementioned requirements will be used as a foundation for the design of an application sharing service called *Multipoint Event Sharing Service* (MESS), which is based on the event-sharing paradigm. We will first outline the architecture of the service before we present realization issues that we encountered.

Architecture

The left part of Figure 3 shows the components of the MESS architecture, reflecting the practical proof of Theorem 1, i.e., the concept of starting in an equivalent state and evolving during runtime of the session.

This concept is reflected through the *Starter/Static Replicator* and the *Dynamic Replicator* components. For these components to function, they need some utility components. At the currently controlling application side, the *Interceptor* gathers required event information. The resources that are used by these events are recognized through the *Resource Grabber*. The actual sending of both the needed resources and the events are prepared by the *Sender/Synchronizer*. This component also takes care of the synchronization and offers latecomer support. The required conferencing and data transmission functionality is provided by the *Conferencing* component, and the interaction with the participant and coordination of components are performed through the *Controller*.

This component architecture can be transformed in a UML framework, as shown in the right part of Figure 3. It is a straightforward mapping of the components onto classes with dedicated methods. This framework acts as the foundation of the actual implementation of the MESS architecture.

The tasks of each component are described in more detail in the following sections.

Controller

The Controller has to start the service, implement the chosen policy for conference management, and provide a mechanism for a token management policy.

Interceptor

The Interceptor gathers required event information to be shared among the users and to be used for synchronization. Two kinds of events need to be handled. The first includes events originating from the user (*user events*). Examples are mouse movement, mouse buttons pressed, and keyboard keys pressed. The second type of events originates from the system. These *system events* have to be handled separately. As an example consider an application that renders and shows an animation. The animation speed will depend on the processing speed of each

Figure 3. MESS Architecture

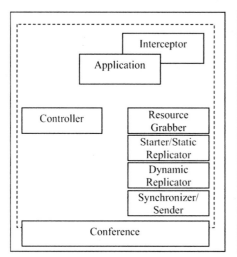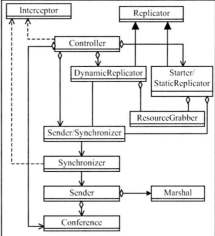

individual computer. If the event-sharing service merely shared the user events, the participating computers would get more out of sync during runtime, since their speed is not the same, although they were started synchronously. To cope with this effect, the progress in execution can be monitored and steered by system events. These events are not actually required to be shared since they are caused by the program execution as such, and therefore they should appear on all participating instances of the application. However, monitoring these events is required for synchronization.

Resource Grabber

The task of the Resource Grabber is to locate and identify all resources, including the application, on the controlling end-system and distribute this information among the group to ensure a consistent state of the application.

Starter/Static Replicator

This component takes care of all instances of the application to be in an equivalent state upon startup. It decides what resources will be distributed, and it takes care that the local settings for each participant are brought in a consistent state. For that, the input of the Resource Grabber is used.

Dynamic Replicator

The Dynamic Replicator is responsible for keeping all participating applications in an equivalent state after the session has started by appropriately sharing event information, determined by the Interceptor, among the group.

Synchronizer/Sender

The Synchronizer/Sender is responsible for synchronization and latecomer support. For synchronization of user events, these events are broadcast, while all application instances are halted locally. After successful delivery, the next user event is processed. For system events, the application is halted after *n* events have been counted. These events are not broadcast since they are generated by the system on each of the participating instances. Only after *n* system events have been processed on all instances, application progress is resumed. For latecomer support, a form of state dependent startup of the participating application is needed, which could be provided using a log file of previously occurred events.

Conference Control

This component deals as an interface to the underlying conferencing system, using functionality for conference management, floor control, and transport functionality.

Realization

The proposed MESS architecture was implemented as a prototype to demonstrate the feasibility of the event sharing approach. Although the current design allows for sharing all types of events and resources, the actual implementation has to make certain tradeoffs to keep the realization simple and feasible, but also to demonstrate the potential of the proposal. As a naive approach, one could try to watch and share every thinkable resource. This is neither necessary nor desired. Instead, one has to make a tradeoff between maximizing the limitation in bandwidth and system overhead on one hand, and to minimize the amount of applications that need services that are not implemented as a result of the first on the other hand.

As a consequence, no system events are shared at this time, and there is no synchronization among the participants. Moreover, resource distribution among the participants is not provided. The current demo application is merely meant to experiment with the distribution of user events and to test the resulting functionality of applications that are shared in such a primitive environment. This functionality reflects the most important part of the service, namely the evolution of the application's state and, therefore, demonstrates the ability of the concept to provide application sharing for certain scenarios. However, the missing functionality is easily integrated, since it mostly deals with capturing additional events, and synchronizing these appropriately at the controlling site.

As demonstration scenarios, simple text editing as well as rotation of complex 3D objects are performed. The latter in particular happens in shared engineering scenarios, as described in Trossen, Schueppen and Wallbaum (2001), and is well-suited to demonstrate the potential since it generates heavy graphical output that is difficult to capture appropriately with output sharing systems. However, due to the missing synchronization functionality, the computers usually run out of sync after a certain timeframe, which demonstrates the necessity of this functionality, i.e., to slow down the faster end-system(s) appropriately.

EVALUATION AND LESSONS LEARNED

The MESS architecture can be evaluated as regards to complexity, functionality as well as resulting performance.

The proposed components add certain *complexity* to each end-system. The variety of state information to be grabbed and distributed usually varies in modern operating systems, e.g., script files or registry settings. However, collecting this information can be realized at central points by intercepting appropriate system calls, e.g., for reading registry settings. Similar to state information, event interception can also be realized centrally by intercepting appropriate system calls. Thus, the added overhead to the operating system is usually fairly minimal and centralized.

Although the proposed MESS architecture provides application-sharing *functionality* for any kind of application with deterministic behavior, the actual functionality highly depends on the maturity of chosen implementation detail. For that, a tradeoff has to be made between the set of supported applications and the chosen complexity. For instance, the demonstration application shows that synchronization is necessary for many scenarios, though surprisingly many scenarios can be covered with limited or even no synchronization at all.

Performance of the proposed architecture can be evaluated in two dimensions. First, the added overhead to the system due to the interception to gather and distribute event information is a major performance measure. For that, the demonstration application shows that this additional overhead is fairly small. However, adding more system events and resources to the pool of information certainly decreases the overall performance, although the transmitted information remains small. As a second measure, the bandwidth consumption of the service is of importance. An estimation for the bandwidth consumption during runtime can be made based on the text-editing demonstration. Assume a reasonable amount of entered text, e.g., 250 characters per minute. Further, assume one sync event after each pressed key as a conservative approach. Thus, the bandwidth consumption would be less than 700 bits per second with an event size of 16 bytes and a synchronization message size of two bytes. In the example of rotating 3D objects, the overhead to the system and the consumed bandwidth is even smaller since user events are usually generated with a smaller frequency. However, the bandwidth consumed for distributing resource information heavily depends on the amount of gathered information and the application as such. The more resources are used, the more information has to be distributed, either during startup or runtime of the session.

As a summary, the most important lesson we learned was that the basic concept of event sharing works with an impressive speed by leveraging local processing speed for the application functionality. However, we also learned that the integration of some system events with an additional synchronization to cope with different processing speeds highly increases the spectrum of applications that can be used with the system.

FURTHER READING

Most available application-sharing systems implement the GUI sharing paradigm, of which many are based on the *X-Windows* system, comprised of a central server on which the application is executed. The application's output is redirected to *X Windows clients* for rendering. Extending this system to a multipoint scenario, as done in Altenhofen et al. (1993), Minenko and Schweitzer (1994), and Wolf, Froitzheim, and Schulthess (1995), enables a shared application system for cooperative working. However, floor control facilities have to be added for coordinated control, which was done in Altenhofen et al. (1993) and Minenko and Schweitzer (1994).

Despite the wide deployment of X Windows systems, their applicability is mainly restricted to Unix systems. Although X Windows client software is available for other platforms, the problem remains to share, for instance, MS Windows software on other platforms. Hence, the heterogeneity problem is only partially solved when using an X Windows system. To tackle this problem, the ITU proposed a protocol for multipoint application sharing (ITU, 1998), defining platform-independent rendering and interception functionality. The disadvantages of this approach are mainly its underlying shared GUI approach, and therefore the overhead on the server system and the usage of an ineffective transport system, which is defined in the ITU T.120 standard.

The work in Hao and Sventek (1996) realizes the event-sharing paradigm by replicating the entire data workspace before starting the application copies. Dynamically including shared data is not supported. Synchronization among the different copies is ensured for every incoming event, leading to a significant overhead instead of using specific synchronization events for overhead reduction. Moreover, the event mapping and distribution is realized on a central server. Hence, the proposal follows a distributed application, but a centralized control approach.

FUTURE WORK

The proposed MESS architecture allows for sharing start state and event evolution of applications among a set of local copies in a shared workspace scenario, i.e., it implements the event-sharing paradigm. However, the functionality of our demonstrator is currently restricted for the sake of simplicity.

In our future work, this functionality is to be increased, starting with the synchronization functionality to cope with out-of-sync effects. Moreover, finding some optima for the applications that can be served by the MESS while keeping the used bandwidth to a minimum is a field of future work.

In addition to enriching functionality, more systematic evaluation scenarios have to be defined to become a clear view of the overhead added to the system. Moreover, the demonstration system is used within a project, realizing a workspace for shared engineering (Trossen et al., 2001).

CONCLUSION

This chapter presented the issues and the lessons we learned when implementing the multipoint event sharing service (MESS). For that, we outlined the basic techniques of two different paradigms to tackle the problem of sharing applications via networks, namely sharing an application's output or sharing the application's state via the network. We showed that for specific scenarios that have an inherent locality of shared data and a homogeneity of end-systems, the event-sharing paradigm seems to be a promising candidate to increase the efficiency of application sharing. For the realization of this paradigm, we defined a set of requirements to be fulfilled, which were the foundation for our architecture of MESS. The components of this architecture were outlined together with the realized objects.

Our prototype showed promising results with respect to its simplicity on the one hand and the increased performance on the other hand, although the simplicity has to be re-evaluated when considered in a full-blown implementation. However, it was shown that with a fairly simple set of events, a fairly wide spectrum of applications is enabled that can be shared via networks. As for future work, the main task lays in the integration of more and more events, in particular system events, in our prototype. Furthermore, the appropriate grabbing of dynamically used resources remains the key issue for certain scenarios, which will be addressed in our future work.

REFERENCES

Altenhofen, M. et al. (1993). The BERKOM Multimedia Collaboration Service. *Proceedings ACM Multimedia.* Anaheim, USA.

Hao, M.C. & Sventek, J.S. (1996). Collaborative Design Using Your Favorite 3D Application. *Proceedings IEEE Conference on Concurrent Engineering.* Toronto, Canada.

ITU-T. (1998). *Multipoint Application Sharing.* ITU-T Recommendation T.128. Geneva, Switzerland.

Minenko, W. & Schweitzer, J. (1994). An Advanced Application Sharing System for Synchronous Collaboration in Heterogeneous Environment. *SIGOIS Bulletin*, 15 (2), 40-44.

Trossen, D. (2000). Scalable Conferencing Support for Tightly-Coupled Environments: Services, Mechanisms, and Implementation Design. *Proceedings IEEE International Conference on Communications.* New Orleans, LA, USA.

Trossen, D. (2001). Application Sharing Technology: Sharing the Application or its GUI? *Proceedings of IRMA Conference.* Anchorage, Alaska, USA.

Trossen, D., Schueppen, A. & Wallbaum, M. (2001). Shared Workspace for Collaborative Engineering. *Annals of Cases on Information Technology (Volume 4).* Hershey, PA: Idea Group Inc.

Wolf, K. H., Froitzheim, K. & Schulthess, P. (1995). Multimedia Application Sharing in a Heterogeneous Environment. *Proceedings ACM Multimedia.* San Francisco, CA, USA.

Chapter VII

The Effect of Training Set Distributions for Supervised Learning Artificial Neural Networks on Classification Accuracy

Steven Walczak
University of Colorado at Denver, USA

Irena Yegorova
City University of New York, USA

Bruce H. Andrews
University of Southern Maine, USA

ABSTRACT

Neural networks have been repeatedly shown to outperform traditional statistical modeling techniques for both discriminant analysis and forecasting. While questions regarding the effects of architecture, input variable selection, learning algorithm, and size of training sets on the neural network model's performance have been addressed, very little attention has been focused on distribution effects of training and out-of-sample populations on neural network performance. This article examines the effect of changing the population distribution within training sets for estimated distribution density functions, in particular for a credit risk assessment problem.

INTRODUCTION

As the availability of information continues to grow (e.g., through the World Wide Web or other electronic record keeping), the complexity of business decision making increases proportionally (Walczak, 2001b). Decision support systems, data mining tools, and artificial intelligence programs attempt to facilitate business decision making or solve business problems. Neural networks, a nonparametric modeling technique, have been shown to work well for many types of business problems (Li, 1994; Patuwo, Hu & Hung, 1993; Widrow, Rumelhart & Lehr, 1994; Zahedi, 1996). Additionally, many researchers have demonstrated empirically that neural network models outperform the more traditional statistical models including regression, logit, decision trees, and discriminant analysis (Bansal, Kauffman & Weitz, 1993; Patuwo et al., 1993; Piramuthu, Shaw & Gentry, 1994).

What factors enable the nonparametric neural network models to outperform the traditional parametric statistical methods? All parametric statistical methods, including regression and Bayesian classification, necessitate that the population distribution or variable distributions adhere to pre-defined characteristics such as a multivariate normal distribution (Klecka, 1980). When variable distributions are unknown, as frequently happens in business problem solving (e.g., bankruptcy prediction, credit assessment, and investment risk analysis), then the more traditional methods, including Bayesian classification, cannot be applied accurately (Patuwo et al., 1993). Nonparametric approaches, such as neural networks, are needed to determine group conditional distribution functions when *a priori* distributions are unknown (McLachlan, 1992).

An unanswered question, however, in the field of neural networks is the effect of unequal population distributions and their maintenance as a representative sample or alteration as a stratified sample in the training group used to build the neural network classification model. A heuristic that is normally followed by neural network researchers is to include the greatest amount of data possible in the training samples (Hung, Hu, Shanker & Patuwo, 1996; Hu, Zhang, Jiang & Patuwo, 1999; Patuwo et al., 1993; Smith, 1993; Zahedi, 1996), which promotes the usage of a representative training sample that maintains distribution differences.

Another potential problem with the use of stratified training sets is that the effect of unequal distributions is greatest when the overall population has very few elements (e.g., a 90/10 distribution between two categories over 100 samples leaves only 10 samples of the smaller category to be divided across the training and test sets) and in practice many interesting business problems have limited data sets (Smith, 1993). Berardi and Zhang (1999) specifically state that small group classification with neural networks is particularly sensitive to sampling variations. Although recent evidence suggests that neural network training may be optimized with very small data sets (Walczak, 2001a), most researchers still feel more confident if larger training sets can be instantiated. A common method for maximizing the size of the training set when small real-world data populations exist is to utilize either bootstrapping or jackknifing (Efron, 1982). The jackknife process, which is a specialization of the bootstrap method, would create N different training sets of size N-1, with each data sample being used as the hold-out test sample a single time. The aggregation of the N test results effectively approximates the results of an overall model (Efron, 1982). Unfortunately, the use of either the bootstrap or jackknife methodology necessarily creates a representative training sample that closely emulates the data distribution inequalities found in the population.

This chapter examines the effect of using stratified training samples when data samples have an unequal distribution for a two-group classification problem in the domain of credit scoring for bank loans. A modified bootstrap process is created to maintain predefined distributions within the training sets. The results empirically indicate that equal distributions of each category within the training set produces the optimal generalization capabilities of neural network classification models, while representative training samples (especially when the probabilities of group membership are widely disparate) will produce sub-optimal results.

BACKGROUND ON NEURAL NET BUSINESS CLASSIFICATION MODELS

As previously stated, neural networks are widely used for solving business classification problems. When building neural network models of business problems, several questions must be answered. Among these questions that are addressed in the next section are which variables to use as input values (Smith, 1993; Tahai, Walczak & Rigsby, 1998) and the quantity and arrangement of hidden nodes (Walczak & Cerpa, 1999). Both of these decisions will have an effect on the performance as well as the complexity of the problem that may ultimately be solved by the neural network models. Another design decision for the neural network developer is which learning algorithm to use to train the weights of the resulting neural network model. Because historic examples with known outcomes are available for training purposes, only supervised learning methods are considered in this chapter.

Previous research on classification models has demonstrated that the "learning vector quantization" learning method is well-suited for classification type problems (Walczak, 1998), and so the learning vector quantization method is evaluated in the research reported in this chapter. Additionally, the backpropagation learning method is commonly used (Fu, 1994; Widrow et al., 1994) and has been proven to be able to solve most complex association problems (Hornik, 1991; Hornik, Stinchcombe & White, 1989; White, 1990). Since other reported research is largely focused on the backpropagation learning method, this method will also be evaluated in the research reported in this chapter to enable comparison to other research.

Two of the more common applications of neural network classification models in business domains (Zahedi, 1996) are for bankruptcy prediction (Fletcher & Goss, 1993; Raghupathi, 1996; Sharda & Wilson, 1996; Wilson & Sharda, 1994) and credit/loan appraisal (Piramuthu et al., 1994; West, 2000). West (2000) indicates that a lender using a neural network credit scoring system was able to achieve a 10 percent improvement in accuracy over their previous system.

Some of the interesting aspects of previous research are that three of the five cited studies use a population of paired samples with representative training sets, so that the failed and non-failed groups or default and full repayment groups have equal probability of occurrence. Fletcher and Goss (1993) use a sample size of 36 firms and rely on an N-fold cross validation to handle the small amount of data, which in practice is the same as a bootstrap. Small data sets are a common problem in developing business classification models. Piramuthu et al. (1994) use two different data sets, each with equal probabilities of membership, that have 36 and 100 samples respectively for loan default classification (two groups) and credit risk classification (five groups) and a 10-fold cross validation (bootstrap) is used to overcome the small sample sizes.

Wilson and Sharda (1994) performed some early experiments in the domain of bankruptcy classification that examined the effect of different distributions between two groups on test sets that also had varying distributions. They used three combinations of training and test sets: 50/50, 80/20, and 90/10 distribution probabilities with the second number representing bankrupt firms. Their preliminary findings indicated that classification results for the nine different neural network models was best when the distribution of the training set matched the distribution of the test set. Hence, a representative training sample that preserves the distribution inequalities of the population produces the optimal performance. Hu,

Hung, Shanker and Chen (1996) follow the representative training sample philosophy to construct neural network models that classify Sino-foreign joint ventures as unsuccessful or successful, with the population having a 90/10 probability distribution. The initial results for the Sino-foreign performance classification problem were sub-optimal.

Later results on bankruptcy problem that utilizes three different group membership probabilities (Sharda & Wilson, 1996), indicated that the stratified 50/50 training group (representative for the 50/50 test set only) outperformed all other representative or stratified training set neural network models on all combinations of test set distributions (50/50, 80/20, and 90/10). Unfortunately, the other bankruptcy and credit scoring neural network research forces a 50/50 representative distribution and test set by limiting the population and, hence, the sensitivity of the smaller group in the real-world to the training set distribution cannot be effectively measured (Berardi & Zhang, 1999).

METHOD

Before presenting the methodology used to investigate the effect of representative versus stratified training sets for classification problems that have unequal population distributions, the impetus for considering a non-representative training set is examined.

Need for Stratification in the Training Set

Whenever a classification problem has equal probability of membership in each of its categories, then the issue of representative versus stratified training sets is eliminated. However, when unequal probabilities of group membership exist, a classification model maximizes its generalization performance by weighting predictions accordingly (Klecka, 1980; McLachlan, 1992). This means that if a two-group classification problem has a probability of membership in the first group of 80 percent, then it should be 80 percent likely that any unclassified sample belongs to the first group. Alternatively, an 80 percent classification accuracy may be achieved by placing all new observations into the first group, regardless of actual group membership. Although placing all out-of-sample or new objects into the group with the largest membership achieves a very-high classification accuracy, it is uninteresting since effectively the decision process has been eliminated and all objects are treated as equivalent in the world.

The presence of any significant inequality within group distributions may cause certain neural network and statistical models to maximize their performance by effectively eliminating membership in the smaller group. As an example, a logistic regression model was constructed for the previously mentioned Sino-foreign joint venture (Hu et al., 1996). This logistic regression model achieved a classification performance of almost 91 percent, which was over two percent above the closest neural network model, by classifying all of the joint ventures as not-so-successful (Group 2). The distribution between the not-so-successful group and the successful group was 90.84/9.16 for both the training and evaluation samples. The disparity of the exclusion effect just discussed increases as the probability of group membership in the smaller group approaches zero.

Problem and Data Description

The classification problem used to investigate the effect of stratified versus representative training samples is a loan default/repayment problem. The data set is the same as used by Yegorova et al. (2000; 2001) and is acquired from the files of a regional economic development lender whose role, among other things, is to provide financing to small companies that are expected to promote job growth and contribute to the local economy. A cross-sectional review of the industries involved reveals a variety of businesses including woodworking, paper, boating, and equipment manufacturing to support fishing and lobstering. The sample used in this paper is limited to loans extended to small, expanding manufacturing businesses, since this category has the largest percentage of loans and also includes a proportion of loan defaults, thus creating a two-group classification problem. The scope of this sample is also limited because homogeneity of data is critical to the predictive capacity of failure prediction models, as discussed in Scherr (1982).

The lender's terminated loan portfolio includes 102 loans made to expanding manufacturing companies. Terminated loans are defined here as loans that are either paid off by the borrower or are in default. Loans that were in non-accrual status as of the sample date, but not charged-off by the lender, were excluded from the sample. This elimination process and incomplete data resulted in only 61 loans with 15 defaults in the final sample. The sample covered loans that were made by the lender from 1983 to 1998. The sample data have a 75/25 distribution for the paid off and defaulted loans made by the lender.

Data from the lender and transformations include 138 variables representing various loan characteristics comprised of non-financial data as well as common balance sheet and income statement items. Data were collected for two consecutive time periods, when available, so that differences and growth rates could be calculated. Selection of the input variables may have a significant effect on the performance of neural network, as well as statistical, models (Smith, 1993; Tahai et al., 1998; Walczak & Cerpa, 1999).

The focus of the presented research is to evaluate the effect of stratified training sets and is not concerned with the construction of an optimal loan default evaluation model, and as such selects nine variables that are common elements in a number of financial ratios and their reciprocals. The nine variables selected for the presented research models are current assets, liability, current liability, inventory, working capital, equity, sales, cash, and long term debt. These variables should provide a breadth of information regarding the loan recipients and still minimizes the size of the neural network to limit extraneous effects from noise and over-fitting of the data set. Use of the actual ratio and reciprocal values may serve to further increase the classification performance of the reported neural networks (Yegorova et al., 2001).

Neural Network Architecture and Training Set Construction

Initially, two different learning algorithms are evaluated: backpropagation (BP) and learning vector quantization (LVQ). Each neural network has the nine independent input variables (listed in the previous section) and two dependent output variables. The two output variables serve as categorical variables for full repayment and default status on the loans. The use of two output variables representing the different classifications is required by the LVQ training method and consequently is also used for the BP training method to eliminate any unforeseen biasing effects from a different architecture. Additionally, the use of the two categorical output variables also eliminates any arbitrary decision regarding the optimum cutoff value for a single valued output to be mapped to the two classification groups, and a winner-take-all strategy is used to select the predicted category from the two output variables.

Effective comparison of classification performance across multiple neural network models requires that noise or variance sources be minimized. Therefore, a single neural network architecture must be selected for evaluating the effect of changing the distribution in the training sets used to build the corresponding neural network models, and other training variables such as the momentum term and learning coefficient are kept constant for all of the neural network models. Each neural network model will be trained/developed with its respective training set and tested a single time on the test set of out-of-sample data items. This means that the only variation between the neural network models performance should be derived solely from the differences in the training set composition, which is derived from the different distributions described below.

Several different architectures are evaluated to approximate an optimal neural network model for the specified independent variables. Since a single architecture, actually one for each neural network learning algorithm employed (BP and LVQ), the different architectures are all initially developed using the representative training sets and the architecture that has the best classification performance is then used with all of the other training sets for comparison. This approach will necessarily bias the results in favor of the representative training set neural network models, but avoids the problem of other bias effects introduced through variations in the neural network's physical architecture.

The size of the neural network architectures is minimized to avoid difficulties from over-fitting the data, and each architecture has its quantity of hidden nodes incremented by two until generalization performance starts to decline, indicating over-fitting of the data (Walczak & Cerpa, 1999). The best performing architecture, using the representative training sets, for the BP algorithm is a two-hidden layer architecture with eight perceptrons in the first hidden layer and four perceptrons in the second hidden layer, while the best performing architecture for the LVQ algorithm has a Kohonen layer of 18 elements.

The data set is then divided into training and test sets to build and evaluate the generalization performance of each of the two networks. The first collection of training and test sets is generated using the jackknife methodology (a specialization of the bootstrap method) (Efron, 1982), which holds out a single data sample and uses the remaining 60 data samples as the training group. This process is repeated 61 times so that every data sample may serve as the single test case and the neural network is completely re-trained with each of the 60 new training sets to generate an unbiased model. The jackknife method produces a collection of representative training sets that maintain the 75/25 distribution between the two classification groups.

A technique that is similar to N-fold cross validation or bootstrapping is developed to create and evaluate different stratified training sets. The "modified bootstrap" is a mixture of the jackknife methodology, which guarantees that every member of the population will be used in a hold-out sample, and the bootstrap, which enables multiple random samples to be held-out simultaneously, thus creating a smaller training set. The size of the training sets is governed by the quantity of samples from the smallest classification group. As an example, for the loan evaluation data set, a 50/50 stratified training set would only permit 14 or 15 (depending on the sample item to be held out) members of the larger 46-member group. Each member of the smaller group is held out a single time, similar to the jackknife, with training set elements from the larger group randomly selected to satisfy the distribution requirements. This process is repeated until all elements have served as an out-of-sample test item a single time. Due to the reduction in the quantity of the larger group members required for the training set, multiple item tests may be performed on a single neural network model (derived from a single training set), but care must be taken not to duplicate the test evaluation of any population member so as not to introduce any artifacts.

Using the "modified bootstrap" method just described, training sets that satisfy a stratified distribution of 60/40 and 50/50 are instantiated and used in determining the effects of stratification of the training sets. A possible side effect from using the modified bootstrap method is that the size of the training set is constrained by the quantity of samples in the smallest classification group, such as a maximum training set size of 28 to 30 samples for the 50/50 stratified distribution training set. Since fewer members of the known population are present in the training set, a negative generalization bias may ensue (Smith, 1993). Results for the three different training set distributions are presented in the next section and even if a training bias is introduced through the modified bootstrap method, the stratified training sets still far outperform the representative training set.

RESULTS AND DISCUSSION

The results of the LVQ neural network models for each of the three different training set distributions, one representative and two stratified, are presented in Table 1. It should be noted that because of the jackknife and "modified bootstrap" approaches, the classification accuracy for the both the LVQ and BP neural networks are for all 61 members of the population and generated from the aggregation of up to 61 different training sets (for the representative 75/25 training group using the jackknife with only 15 training sets needed for the "modified bootstrap" 50/50 training group).

Table 1. LVQ Neural Network Classification Performance for Three Different Training Set Distributions

Training Set Distribution	Repayment (Group 1) Classifications (N = 46)	Default (Group 2) Classifications (N = 15)	Overall Classification Accuracy
Representative 75/25	33 (71.74 %)	4 (26.67 %)	60.66 %
Stratified 60/40	36 (78.26 %)	6 (40.00 %)	68.85 %
Stratified 50/50	37 (80.43 %)	10 (66.67 %)	77.05 %

The smaller Group 2 classifications appear to mirror the probability of membership in the training set until the equally distributed 50/50 stratified training set is used, and then it jumps to well over 50 percent classification accuracy. As a further test of this statement, stratified training sets are constructed using the modified bootstrap approach with a group distribution of 65/35. The newly constructed training sets are then used to build neural network classification models that are subsequently used to evaluate only the loan default Group 2 test cases. This experiment yields a classification accuracy of the loan default, Group 2, members of 37.5 percent. Future research is needed to determine if there exists a minimum distribution threshold that must be surpassed in order for classification accuracy of an LVQ neural network model to exceed the simple group membership probability.

While the classification accuracy of the smaller loan default group members continues to rise as the probability of group membership approaches equality across the two groups, a corresponding decrease in the classification accuracy of the larger full repayment group members does not occur. This result is unexpected since the much heavier emphasis, in the representative and intermediate stratified training sets, for membership in the full repayment group, Group 1, should bias the classification results of the associated neural network model accordingly.

To demonstrate, the 61 members of the loan classification population are divided into two distinct groups: one that contains only the 46 members of Group 1, the full repayment group, and the other that contains only the 15 members of Group 2, the loan default group. This produces two populations that have membership probabilities of 100/0 and 0/100 respectively. A jackknife procedure is used to build LVQ-trained neural network models to predict the group membership of these two populations, using the same architecture previously described, with two output categorical variables. The resulting neural network models both produce 100 percent accuracy in classifying all test cases as belonging to the corresponding group. These two monotype populations demonstrate that very large biases (maximum in this case) can produce corresponding probabilistic (certainty) biases in the output of a neural network.

The LVQ neural networks are trying to accommodate the presence of two groups in the population. The difficulty arises in that the representative group does not provide enough information for the LVQ neural network to adequately distinguish between the two-group membership criteria. Even though the number of Group 2 (loan default) members in the training set stays the same (as in the representative set) in the stratified training sets, the relative importance of the Group 2 members increases to 40 and 50 percent of the population, as recognized by the training set. The more balanced representation prevents the larger group from dominating the training and enables the LVQ neural network to more adequately determine the membership criteria for all of the classification groups. This balanced knowledge from the 50/50 stratified training set is what enables the neural network to improve its classification accuracy for both groups in the classification problem. Since the classification accuracy for both groups (and overall) increases as stratification moves towards an even distribution, the evenly stratified training set clearly produces optimal results for the LVQ neural network learning algorithm.

How do the LVQ and BP neural networks evaluate with respect to standard statistical models? Because of the two categorical dependent variables, regression analysis may not be used. For any two-group classification problem, pure chance will average a 50 percent classification accuracy rate. Real-world problems also may not have well-defined *a priori* distributions, so the use of a Bayesian classifier is problematic. However as stated before, business classification problems frequently have a collection of historic examples with known outcomes, which is the reason that supervised learning neural network models can be developed. The *a priori* population distributions may be approximated by using the distributions found in the collection of historic training and test set samples, or for the loan risk classification problem a 75/25 distribution. This implies that care must be taken to collect representative data samples for model development and analysis.

A simple Bayesian classification algorithm that utilizes the *a priori* distribution knowledge produces a mean overall classification accuracy of 62.9 percent. While the representative training set develops a neural network model with classification accuracy below the Bayesian level, both neural network models trained with stratified training sets have superior performance.

Classification results for the backpropagation neural network models, trained with all the different training set distributions, are presented in Table 2. The neural networks trained using the BP training algorithm appear to have become trapped in a local minima and produced classification predictions for all members of the population, when trained using a representative training set, as belonging to the full repayment group. This is similar to the problem encountered by Hu et al.'s (1996) logistic regression model. The BP neural network "learned" to maximize its performance by classifying all new data samples as belonging to the group that has the highest probability of membership. While this did produce an overall prediction accuracy of 75.41 percent, the fact that no defaulting loan applicants are identified carries a large cost to the lending institution for the classification errors (Berardi & Zhang, 1999).

As expected, the classification accuracy for the larger group decreases as the distribution shifts towards being more even, while the classification accuracy for the smaller group increases. The overall classification accuracy improves by 4.2 percent. While the overall classification accuracy is best with the evenly distributed

Table 2. BP Neural Network Classification Performance for Three Different Training Set Distributors

Training Set Distribution	Repayment (Group 1) Classifications (N = 46)	Default (Group 2) Classifications (N = 15)	Overall Classification Accuracy
Representative 75/25	46 (100 %)	0 (0 %)	75.41 %
Stratified 60/40	40 (86.96 %)	6 (40 %)	75.41 %
Stratified 50/50	36 (78.26 %)	12 (80 %)	78.69 %

training set's neural network model since the increases to the smaller groups correct classifications exceeds the decreases to the larger groups correct classifications, the fact that the two individual group accuracies are moving in opposite directions implies that further evaluation is needed to determine the "best performing" neural network model.

Berardi and Zhang (1999) suggest that the cost of misclassification should be used for evaluating the performance of classification neural network models. The direct costs for the lending institution are lost interest on the loans for misclassifying the repayment group members and lost value of the loan for misclassifying the default group members. Other indirect or hidden costs, such as the unavailability of funds for a repayment class loan due to a default loan being made and the possibility of bankruptcy or other problems for a repayment group member that is unable to obtain the primary loan, are not considered. Values for loans made by the modeled lender are displayed in Table 3.

Misclassification costs for the representative model are then just the lost total loan to the default group since all loans are classified as repayable, which results in a total cost for using the representative model of $1,296,652. The misclassification costs for the other two neural network models have mixed components (from misclassifications of members in both groups) and will be approximated using the average values displayed in Table 3 and assume equal monthly payments for the duration of the loan. The respective costs, using the aforementioned calculation method, for the 60/40 and 50/50 neural network models are then $1,039,773 and $695,633.

The 60/40 stratified backpropagation neural network model is more cost effective than the representative model (although both have misclassifications costs of over one million dollars). This indicates that using the direct costs to the lender,

Table 3. Lender Values for Loan Amount, Interest Rate, and Duration of Loan

Class	Total Loan	Average Loan	Avg. Annual Interest Rate	Average Duration
Repay	$5,223,402.38	$113,552.23	0.108707	6.28 years
Default	$1,296,652.00	$86,443.45	0.109333	5.47 years

it is more costly to misclassify a default borrower than a repay borrower. The evenly distributed stratified BP neural network model reduces the misclassification costs of the lender from using a representative training sample by $601,019 or an almost 54 percent misclassification cost reduction. Bearing in mind that only direct identifiable costs are used in this empirical study, the evenly distributed training set produces the highest performing neural network model for both the LVQ and BP method neural networks.

SUMMARY

The research presented in this article demonstrates that neural network solutions to two-group classification problems with small data sets are optimized when the training sets used to build the neural network classification models are stratified to contain equal membership from each group. This is particularly important for those real-world problems that have unequal membership probabilities. These findings may help explain some of the less than optimal results from previous research (Hu et al., 1996) with neural networks that utilize representative training samples from unequally distributed populations. For the loan repayment classification problem presented in the article, moving from a 75/25 representative training set to a 50/50 stratified training set increased the classification accuracy of the LVQ neural network model by over 21 percent for generalization to real-world populations and also realized an estimated misclassification cost reduction of $601,019.

A modified bootstrap method is described to enable the maximum use of population members in training sets, while still maintaining a stratified balance between the group memberships in the training set. Additional research is needed to extend these results to N-group classification problems, where N is greater than two, with unequal probabilities of membership in the various groups.

The research results described in this chapter examine unequal population distribution effects on a real-world, two-group classification problem. Additional research is needed to examine if the proposed research methodology of utilizing evenly distributed group membership in training sets for supervised learning neural networks is extensible to multi-group (three or more groups) real-world problem sets.

REFERENCES

Bansal, A., Kauffman, R.J., & Weitz, R.R. (1993). Comparing the Modeling Performance of Regression and Neural Networks As Data Quality Varies: A Business Value Approach. *Journal of Management Information Systems*, 10(1), 11-32.

Berardi, V.L., & Zhang, G.P. (1999). The Effect of Misclassification Costs on Neural Network Classifiers. *Decision Sciences*, 30(3), 659-682.

Efron, B. (1982). *The Jackknife, the Bootstrap and Other Resampling Plans*. Philadelphia, PA: Siam.

Fletcher, D., & Goss, E. (1993). Forecasting with neural networks: An application using bankruptcy data. *Information & Management*, 24(3), 159-167.

Fu, L. (1994). *Neural Networks in Computer Intelligence*. New York: McGraw-Hill.

Hornik, K. (1991). Approximation Capabilities of Multilayer Feedforward Networks. *Neural Networks*, 4, 251-257.

Hornik, K., Stinchcombe, M., & White, H. (1989). Multilayer Feedforward Networks Are Universal Approximators. *Neural Networks*, 2(5), 359-366.

Hu, M.Y., Hung, M.S., Shanker, M.S., & Chen, H. (1996). Using Neural Networks to Predict Performance of Sino-Foreign Joint Ventures. *International Journal of Computational Intelligence and Organizations*, 1(3), 134-143.

Hu, M.Y., Zhang, G., Jiang, C.X., and Patuwo, B.E. (1999). A Cross-Validation Analysis of Neural Network Out-of-Sample Performance in Exchange Rate Forecasting. *Decision Sciences*, 30(1), 197-215

Hung, M.S., Hu, M.Y., Shanker, M.S., & Patuwo, B.E. (1996). Estimating Posterior Probabilities in Classification Problems With Neural Networks. *International Journal of Computational Intelligence and Organizations*, 1(1), 49-60.

Klecka, W.R. (1980). *Discriminant Analysis*. Newbury Park, CA: Sage Publications.

Li, E.Y. (1994). Artificial neural networks and their business applications. *Information & Management*, 27(5), 303-313.

McLachlan, G.J. (1992). *Discriminant Analysis and Statistical Pattern Recognition*. New York: Wiley.

Patuwo, E., Hu, M.Y., & Hung, M.S. (1993). Two-Group Classification Using Neural Networks. *Decision Sciences*, 24(4), 825-845.

Piramuthu, S., Shaw, M., & Gentry, J. (1994). A classification approach using multi-layered neural networks. *Decision Support Systems*, 11(5), 509-525.

Raghupathi, W. (1996). Comparing Neural Network Learning Algorithms in Bankruptcy Prediction. *International Journal of Computational Intelligence and Organizations*, 1(3), 179-187.

Scherr, F.C. (1982). Failure Forecasting Functions. *Baylor Business Studies*, Vol. 12.

Sharda, R., & Wilson, R.L. (1996). Neural Network Experiments in Business-Failure Forecasting: Predictive Performance Measurement Issues. *International Journal of Computational Intelligence and Organizations*, 1(2), 107-117.

Smith, M. (1993). *Neural Networks for Statistical Modeling*. New York: Van Nostrand Reinhold.

Tahai, A., Walczak, S., & Rigsby, J.T. (1998). Improving Artificial Neural Network Performance Through Input Variable Selection. In P. Siegel, K. Omer, A. deKorvin, & A. Zebda, (Eds.), *Applications of Fuzzy Sets and The Theory of Evidence to Accounting II* (pp. 277-292). Stamford, CT: JAI Press.

Walczak, S. (1998). Neural Network Models for A Resource Allocation Problem. *IEEE Transactions on Systems, Man and Cybernetics*, 28B(2), 276-284.

Walczak, S. (2001a). An Empirical Analysis of Data Requirements for Financial Forecasting with Neural Networks. *Journal of Management Information Systems*, 17(4), 203-222.

Walczak, S. (2001b). Neural Networks as a Tool for Developing and Validating Business Heuristics. *Expert Systems with Applications*, 21(1), 31-36.

Walczak, S., & Cerpa, N. (1999). Heuristic Principles for the Design of Artificial Neural Networks. *Information and Software Technology*, 41(2), 109-119.

West, D. (2000). Neural Network Credit Scoring Models. *Computers and Operations Research*, 27(11/12), 1131-1152.

White, H. (1990). Connectionist Nonparametric Regression: Multilayer Feedforward Networks Can Learn Arbitrary Mappings. *Neural Networks*, 3, 535-549.

Widrow, B., Rumelhart, D., & Lehr, M. (1994). Neural Networks: Applications in Industry, Business, and Science. *Communications of the ACM*, 37(3), 93-105.

Wilson, R.L., & Sharda, R. (1994). Bankruptcy prediction using neural networks. *Decision Support Systems*, 11(5), 545-557.

Yegorova, I., Andrews, B.H., Jensen, J.B., & Smoluk, B.J. (2000). A Successful Loan Default Prediction Model for Small Business. *The Credit and Financial Management Review*, 6, 53-61.

Yegorova, I., Andrews, B.H., Jensen, J.B., Smoluk, B.J., & Walczak, S. (2001). A Successful Neural Network-Based Methodology for Predicting Small Business Loan Default. *The Credit and Financial Management Review*, 7 (4), 31-42.

Zahedi, F. (1996). A Meta-Analysis of Financial Applications of Neural Networks. *International Journal of Computational Intelligence and Organizations*, 1(3), 164-178.

Chapter VIII

Executive Information Systems Use in Organisational Contexts: An Explanatory User Behaviour Testing

George Ditsa
University of Wollongong, Australia

ABSTRACT

Executive Information Systems (EIS) are designed to enhance the managerial roles of executives, including other senior managers, in organizations. Despite reported growth in the popularity of EIS, there are reports of low usage of these systems that, in part, contributes to their failures in organizations. The majority of prior EIS research has focused on documenting the features, benefits, development methodologies, and implementation of the systems. However, very few research studies address the problem of low EIS usage from behavioural point of the user. This chapter reports on a research on the use of EIS in organizational settings. The primary focus of the research is to investigate factors that explain users' behaviour towards using EIS. It is also aimed at identifying the relative importance of those factors that determine the use of EIS. The research model is based on Triandis' theoretical framework, a model from organizational behaviour. The research model is used to hypothesis that EIS use (behaviour) is determined by EIS experience and ability to use EIS (habits); subjective norms, roles, values and social situations (social factors); perceived usefulness of EIS (consequences); user satisfaction with EIS information, system, support, and plan (affect); and EIS development processes, management processes and organisational environment (facilitating conditions). Field data obtained by survey questionnaire from CEOs, CFOs and one other executive from 255 organisations using EIS in Australia were used to test and confirm the appropriateness of the behavioural model through correlation and regression analyses. The results of the study have some implications for research and practice.

INTRODUCTION AND RESEARCH PROBLEM

The success or failure of information systems (IS) has been the focus of studies by IS researchers in the past decades. Underutilisation of IS has generally been identified in the IS literature as one of the sources of IS failures, and system usage is even often used as a surrogate of IS success. As hardware and software capabilities continue to advance at an alarming rate, the problem of low system usage still remains (e.g., Weiner, 1993; Johansen & Swigart, 1996; Venkatesh & Morris, 2000).

Information is one of the crucial resources to an organisation in the following areas (Choo, 1998): sense-making of the external environment, knowledge creation, and decision-making. Executives' demand for suitable information systems to support their managerial activities has led to the development and implementation of executive information systems (EIS). These systems are tailored to meet the managerial demands of individual executives. Along with the success stories for these systems, however, there are many examples of EIS failures, some of which are due to the non-use of the systems (Glover, Watson, & Rainer, 1992; Schenk, 1992; McBride, 1997).

Whereas these systems have attracted a growing number of research studies in recent times, a review of the EIS literature reveals that few studies have been done on the real use (that is, the active engagement) of the systems. The majority of the prior EIS research studies have focused on documenting the features, benefits, development, methodologies, and implementation of these systems by using case studies and interviews (e.g., Rainer & Watson, 1995; Nandhakumar & Jones

1997; McBride, 1997; Watson, Houdeshel & Rainer, 1997; Bajwa, Rai & Brennan, 1998; Vandenbosch, 1999; Watson & Carte, 2000; Scholz, 2000). The research studies on this side are much more thorough and extensive than on the use side. Of the limited research studies on the use side, very few used appropriate reference theories that address system use as a behaviour (Trice & Treacy, 1988). These studies are also mixed, with only a very small number addressing the problem of low EIS usage. Put simply, the research approaches to resolve EIS failures are more technical and technological than social, cultural, political and organisational.

Although recent studies (Bergeron, Raymond, Rivard & Gara, 1995; Carte, 1999; Watson & Carte, 2000) indicate there is a growing popularity of EIS, and new concepts such as enterprise resource planning (ERP), data warehousing, data mining, OLAP, ROLAP, MOLAP, Internet, Intranet, Extranet and the Web are giving rise to a renewed need to provide executives with a meaningful view of corporate information, the of problem low EIS usage still remains.

The growth in popularity and the marked lack of empirical research studies to address the problem of low EIS usage necessitate this research study. The results of this study are aimed at helping suggest those social, cultural and organisational factors that need to be considered in the development and implementation of EISs to improve their usage in organisations.

In the following sections of this chapter, the research questions are presented, followed by the theoretical perspective for this study. Definitions of EIS and a brief overview of EIS are then presented, followed by some previous research studies on EIS usage. The chapter continues by presenting the nature of executives' work and how EIS fits into their work. The theoretical framework, the research model, the hypotheses, and the research methodology for the study are next presented. Finally, the chapter concludes by presenting results of the study with discussions and then some suggestions for future trends.

RESEARCH QUESTIONS AND CONTRIBUTIONS

Information systems are social systems. Studies (e.g., Sauer, 1993; Poulymenakou & Holmes, 1996; Nandhakumar, 1996) have suggested that the success or failure of an IS cannot be explained purely in technical terms, and that the roots of successful IS lie in the social and organisational context. Studies of the Stock Exchange Taurus system (Currie, 1995), the London Ambulance system (Beynon-Davies, 1995), the Confirm system (Oz, 1994) and some others (Sauer, 1993; Mitev, 1996; McBride, 1997) have also indicated that the complex interaction of the social, cultural, political and organisational elements with the technical elements results in the failure of ISs.

The success or failure of IS is therefore inextricably linked with the dynamics of the organisation within which they exist. McBride (1997), who studied the rise and fall of an EIS in a UK manufacturing company over nine years, concludes that, "no study that concerns itself with how to develop a successful IS and how to avoid failures can reach many reasonable conclusions unless it addresses issues of context and culture" (p. 277). Social, cultural, and organisational factors are equally linked with system use (Bergeron et al., 1995; Carlson & Davis, 1998; Venkatesh & Morris, 2000).

Bergeron et al. (1995), in their study of EIS usage using Triandis' framework, suggest, "future investigations should aim for a cumulative tradition by continuing to employ Triandis' framework as a theoretical foundation to further understand the phenomenon of EIS use" (p. 142). They also suggest "unobtrusive operationalisation of EIS use in addition to self-report measures" (p. 142).

Given the preceding considerations, the primary aim of this study is to identify, examine, and provide some understanding of the social, cultural, and organisational factors that explain the behaviour of executives towards using EIS. The study employed a model from organisational behaviour as a theoretical foundation. The main research questions for the study are:

1.   What are the major social, cultural, and organisational factors that explain the behaviour of executives towards using EIS in organisational settings?
2.   What is the relative importance of these factors in determining EIS use by executives in organisational settings?

Contributions envisaged to be made by this study include:
- Improvement in the development and implementation of EIS
- Better education and training for EIS use
- Improvement in EIS usage, leading to the success of EIS in organisations
- Better allocation of scarce resources for EIS
- Provision of further research into EIS usage factors
- Provision of further research into usage factors for other information systems

THEORETICAL PERSPECTIVE FOR THIS STUDY

A number of researchers have studied different aspects of the phenomenon of individual reactions to computing technology from a variety of theoretical perspectives, including the Technology Acceptance Model (TAM), which is an adaptation of the Theory of Reason Action (TRA) (e.g., Davis, 1989; Davis, Bagozzi & Warshaw, 1989; Adams, Nelson, & Todd, 1992; Venkatesh & Davis, 1996; Kim,

1996; Venkatesh, 1999; Venkatesh & Morris, 2000; Elkordy, 2000; Elkordy & Khalil, 2002); Diffusion of Innovations (e.g., Moore & Benbasat, 1991; Compeau & Meister, 1997), the Theory of Planned Behaviour (TPB) (e.g., Mathieson, 1991; Taylor & Todd, 1995), Social Cognitive Theory (SCT) (e.g., Compeau & Higgins, 1995a, 1995b; Hill, Smith & Mann, 1986, 1987) and Activity Theory (e.g., Engeström & Escalante, 1996; Nardi, 1996; Kuutti, 1996, 1999; Engeström, 1999; Blackler, Crump & McDonald, 1999). This body of research has produced some useful insights into the cognitive, affective, and behavioural reactions of individuals to technology, and into the factors which influence these reactions.

According to Compeau, Higgins and Huff (1999, p. 1), in each of the theories noted above, behaviour (e.g., the use of computers) is viewed as the result of a set of beliefs about technology and a set of affective responses to the behaviour. The beliefs are represented by the perceived characteristics of innovating in Innovation Diffusion research, by perceived usefulness and perceived ease of use in TAM, by behavioural beliefs and outcome evaluations in TPB, and by outcome expectations in SCT. Seddon (1997) refers to these as the net benefits (realised or expected) accruing from the use of a system. Affective responses are typically measured by attitudes towards use — an individual's evaluation of the behaviour as either positive or negative. These commonalities in the models reflect a belief in the cognitive basis of behaviour.

Compeau et al. (1999, p. 1), however, suggest that while TAM and the Diffusion of Innovations perspectives focus almost exclusively on beliefs about the technology and the outcomes of using it, SCT and the TPB include other beliefs that might influence behaviour, independent of perceived outcomes. The TPB model incorporates the notion of Perceived Behavioural Control (PBC) as an independent influence on behaviour, recognising that there are circumstances in which a behaviour might be expected to result in positive consequences (or net benefits), yet not be undertaken due to a perceived lack of ability to control the execution of the behaviour. PBC encompasses perceptions of resource and technology facilitating conditions, similar to those measured by Thompson, Higgins and Howell (1991), as well as perceptions of ability, or self-efficacy (Taylor & Todd, 1995).

However, none of the above theoretical frameworks addresses explicitly the social, cultural, political and organisational factors that may influence and/or explain the user's behaviour to use IS.

A model developed by Triandis (1971, 1980) from organisational behaviour addresses explicitly the net beliefs as well as the social, cultural, and organisational factors that influence or explain behaviour. The TAM, which is derived from Ajzen and Fishbein's Theory of Reason Action (TRA), is mostly used as a theoretical framework for IS use research studies. Triandis' model has some similarities with

TRA and forms the theoretical foundation for this study. The model is described later in this chapter.

DEFINITIONS OF EIS

There are various definitions for EIS by researchers, depending upon the perspective through which one sees the systems. What many EIS researchers think of an EIS can be summed up as,

Any information systems that can present critical information timely, clearly and accurately, and reveal the interrelationships and driving factors between key performance indicators (KPIs) to enable a faster and more accurate decision-making.

Typically, Kelly (1998) defines an EIS as "set of tools designed to help an organization carefully monitor its current status, its progress toward achieving its goals, and the relationship of its mental model of the world to the best available clues about what's really happening" (p. 3); whereas Thierauf (1991) defines an EIS as "a computer system that deals with all of the information that helps an executive make strategic and competitive decisions, keeps track of the overall business and its functional units, and cuts down on the time spent on routine tasks performed by an executive" (p. 10); while Watson Rainer and Koh (1992, p. 14), define it as "a computerised system that provides executives with easy access to internal and external information that is relevant to their critical success factors."

Bergeron et al. (1991) present an EIS as "an information system supported with a mainframe computer, or a personal computer, used for various business functions on a current basis by the CEO or a member of the senior management team" (p. 7). A similar definition of EIS was introduced by Elam and Leidner (1995) as "a computer-based information system designed to provide a senior manager access to information relevant to his or her management activities" (p. 89); whereas Turban (1993) defines it as "a structured, automated tracking system that operates continuously to keep management abreast of what is happening in all important areas both inside and outside the corporation [and] is designed to support the complex and multi-dimensional nature of top-level decision making" (p. 404).

Pervan and Phua (1997) think of EIS as "computer-based information systems designed to provide senior executives with easy access to integrated information from a variety of internal and external data sources, to support their analytical, communication and planning needs" (p. 64). whereas Bidgoli (1998, p. 93) defines it as "a computer-based information system that provides executives with easy access to internal and external information with drill-down capability related to the critical success factors for running current and future business operations."

Rightly or wrongly, a unique definition for these systems will seem to "box" them and limit the range of capabilities that the systems have as they evolve. Although EIS have spread and are spreading to other levels of organisations and may be engaged by other users in other functional areas, in the context of this study an EIS will be defined simply as:

A computer-based information system designed to aid executives in their managerial roles.

While definitions are useful, in a complex area such as EIS a better understanding is obtained by looking at their characteristics and how different they are from traditional IS.

AN OVERVIEW OF EIS

EISs are mostly concerned with data and ways of interacting with the data. They are designed as structured reporting systems that filter, extract, and compress a broad range of relevant current and historical information, which are either internal or external to the organisation. They are used, in part, to monitor and highlight the critical success factors of an organisation as defined by the user.

New technologies such as data warehousing and data mining, enterprise resource planning (ERP) and the Web have recently increased the popularity of EISs rather than replace them (Carte, 1999; Bashein & Markus, 2000). These technologies gave the impetus for the widening use of EIS by managers whose decisions must be timely in an increasingly competitive and uncertain environment (Bergeron et al., 1995). Data warehousing, for example, is generally regarded as the prerequisite for effective decision support or data mining systems, and ROLAP and MOLAP (relational and multidimensional operations for online analytical processing) have given rise to such concepts as "slicing" and "dicing" of data, which have added more flexibility and ease to the use of EIS (Bashein & Markus, 2000).

EISs differ from traditional information systems in the following ways:
- Specifically tailored to executive's information needs and decision-making style
- Able to access data about specific issues and problems as well as aggregate reports
- Provide on-line status access, trend analysis, exception reporting, and "drill-down" capabilities
- Access a broad range of internal and external data
- Particularly easy to use (typically mouse or touchscreen driven)
- Used directly by executives without assistance
- Able to extract, filter, compress, and track critical data

- Contain superb graphics capabilities such that information can be presented graphically in several ways
- Very user-friendly and require minimal or no training to use, so they can be used by the executive directly
- Provide instant access to supporting details of any summary displayed on an EIS screen.

Recent studies (Wheeler, Chang & Thomas, 1993; Frolick & Robichaux, 1995; Bergeron et al., 1995; Bashein & Markus, 2000) show EISs are spreading to other levels in some organisations. Subsequently, they are referred to in some organisations as "enterprise-wide information systems" or "everyone's information systems," which still befit the acronym EIS; whereas in other organisations they are known by vendor product names such Enterprise Business Intelligence Systems, Balanced Scorecard, or simply Scorecard.

THE NATURE OF EXECUTIVES' WORK AND HOW EIS FITS IN

According to Rockart (1979), "there is no position in the organisational hierarchy that is less understood than that of the executives" (p. 82). Furthermore, the functions and the way those functions are performed vary between organisations and between executives within organisations. Indeed, one of the reasons for EIS failures reported by many EIS researchers is the lack of understanding of the nature of executives' work by the system designers.

An executive's role in an organisation has, however, traditionally been related to identifying problems and opportunities and making the decision of what to do about those problems and opportunities. In addition, executives are expected by their subordinates to play other leadership roles. Much of the work of executives revolves around developing agendas, goals, priorities, strategies and plans (that may not be documented); establishing networks; and developing corporate relationships between people inside and outside the organisation who may play a role in developing and implementing future agendas (Hoven, 1996).

Weter (1988) indicates that each executive has a unique way of performing his or her job and breaks the work functions as follows:

- Reviewing reports from subordinates on the activities of many areas of the organisation
- Monitoring news of the outside world
- Meeting with managers in the organisation to discuss operations and strategy

- Identifying problems and opportunities and formulating plans to capitalise on them
- Leading the people who work with him or her to carry on their goals.

In relation to levels of management and decision-making activities, management activities in an organisation fall into the following three categories, based on Anthony's framework for planning and control (Anthony, 1965):

Strategic planning: The process of deciding on objectives of the organisation, changes in these objectives, the resources used to attain these objectives; and the policies that are to govern the acquisition, use, and disposition of these resources.

Tactical (Management) control: The process by which managers assure the resources are obtained and used effectively and efficiently in the accomplishment of the organisation's objectives.

Operational control: The process of assuring specific tasks are carried out effectively and efficiently.

Each activity has different information requirements. The operational control decision levels are based on highly detailed information generated by or available within the organisation. They require a high information frequency and the information must be recent as well as accurate. Strategic planning is at the other end of the continuum, relying on summary or aggregated information as well as data from external sources. Both the scope and variety of the information are quite large. The information requirements for management control fall between the other two levels.

The overall picture is that at the strategic level executives are concerned with planning and in the other levels they are concerned with the controlling of those plans. However, all executives do planning and controlling in proportion to the different levels of the organisation.

Perhaps Mintzberg's (1973) model is probably the best-known characterisation of the activities of executives. He categorises executives' activities into ten distinct roles, which are divided into three groups: *interpersonal roles, informational roles,* and *decisional roles.* These three groups each involve dealing with information or acting upon information, and an effective EIS can assist an executive in all these roles.

EISs are designed with the capabilities to assist the executive to quickly search and scan the organisation's environment for any threats and opportunities for prompt and appropriate decisions. They are designed as tools to support and improve the decision-making process of executives by providing the basic usable and relevant information from both the internal and external environments of the organisation. In addition, because executives devote a significant amount of time to acquire and analyse information through their interactions with people and processing of documents, EISs are also designed to save considerable amount of time by facilitating the collection, storage, retrieval, and analysis of information. The "what-if" analysis capabilities of an EIS combined with the decision maker's imagination and judgement is to help executives in arriving at decisions quickly and more accurately.

PREVIOUS RESEARCH STUDIES ON EIS USAGE

The focus of prior EIS research studies can be classified broadly into two groups. One group of studies focuses on EIS development and implementation, while the other group focuses on EIS usage (see Table 1). The research studies on the development and implementation side are more thorough and extensive than the studies on the usage side and form the bulk of the EIS literature.

The research studies on EIS usage are relatively few and mixed, with only a very small number addressing the actual use of the systems. Of this small number, too, only very few use appropriate reference theories to address system usage. The focus of these research studies seems to be in line with the four suggested frameworks by Carisson and Widmeyer (1990) for researching EIS usage based on executives management activities; that is, (1) EIS as a decision-making or problem-solving tool, (2) EIS as a scanning and searching tool, (3) EIS as an internal monitoring tool, and (4) EIS as a communication tool. This seems to be adhered to with almost a complete neglect of research studies into the real use of the systems. The managerial activities should rather filter into determining the real use of the systems by the target users.

The focus of the few research studies on EIS usage can be broken into six areas (see Table 1). Of the six areas, only the focus on factors that influence or explain EIS use deals with the actual engagement of the systems, without which the five others cannot be realised. The research studies on the actual engagement are quite few, and of the few only a small number used appropriate reference theories to address system use as a behaviour (e.g., Bergeron et al., 1995; Kim, 1996; Elkordy, 2000; Elkordy & Khalil, 2002).

As can be seen from Table 1, whereas some of the research studies on EIS usage are looking at the impact of using the systems on managerial activities in general and the decision-making process in particular, others are looking at the overall benefits, such as increase in profit, better communication, increased confidence in decision-making, access to unavailable information, and reduction in staff and clerical personnel from using the systems. While some other studies are looking at the use of the systems to respond to major business problems being intensified by global recessionary and competitive forces, such as adaptability to customer requirements, quality improvement and cost-containment, some others are looking at the mode of use of the systems, such as searching, scanning, and improving executives' mental model of the organisations. And while some of the studies are looking at the patterns of EIS use by executives, others are simply seeking answers to how frequently EISs are used by executives.

As mentioned above, it is only the sixth of the area of research studies on EIS usage in Table 1 — factors that influence or explain EIS use — that deals with the real use of the systems. System use being a behaviour (Trice & Treacy, 1988), appropriate reference theories are also necessary to study it. The following sections outline the theoretical framework that forms the basis of this study.

THEORETICAL FRAMEWORK, RESEARCH MODEL, AND HYPOTHESES

Trice and Treacy (1988) asserted that system use is a behaviour whose determinants are not well understood in IS research, and that system use can best be explained by referring to an appropriate reference theory. This assertion has

Table 1. Classification of EIS Research Studies by Research Focus

Focus of Research Study	Researchers (for example)
Development and implementation	Wetherbe, 1991; Glover et al., 1992; Watson, Rainer & Koh, 1992; Rainer & Watson, 1995; Frolick & Robichaux, 1995; McBride, 1997; Nandhakumar, 1996; Nandhakumar & Jones, 1997; Watson, Houdeshel & Rainer, 1997; Bajwa et al., 1998; Li & Jordan, 1998; Vandenbosch, 1999; Carte, 1999; Watson & Carte, 2000; Scholz, 2000; Kumar & Palvia, 2001; Poon & Wagner, 2001
Usage: i. Impact of use on - managerial activities - decision-making	Rockart & DeLong, 1992; Leidner & Elam, 1994a; Schenk, 1992; Leidner & Elam, 1994; Elam & Leidner, 1995; Hoven, 1996; Handzic, 1997; Singh et al., 2002
ii. Overall benefits from use	Wallis, 1992; Nord & Nord, 1995
iii. Use to respond to competitive advantage and other business problems	Volonino et al., 1995
iv. Mode of use (e.g., searching and scanning)	Frolick et al. 1997; Vandenbosch & Huff, 1997; Vandenbosch, 1999
v. Pattern of use (including frequency of use)	Seeley & Targett, 1999; Thodenius, 1995
vi. Factors that influence/explain use	Young & Watson, 1995; Bergeron et al., 1995; Kim, 1996; Elkordy, 2000; Elkordy & Khalil, 2002

guided some system use studies (e.g., Trice & Treacy, 1988; Davis et al. 1989; Young & Watson, 1995; Kim, 1996; Venkatesh, 1999; Venkatesh & Morris, 2000), with Fishbein and Ajzen's (1975) theory of reasoned action (TRA) as the conceptual framework of choice employed to link user beliefs and attitudes to behaviour. Some researchers (Thompson et al., 1991; Bergeron et al., 1995) have sought to explain personal computer usage and information systems use by grounding their research models on a similar, but richer, theoretical framework developed by Triandis (1971, 1980).

This research study employs Triandis' framework as theoretical foundation. The research model for this study is derived from this theoretical framework, which takes into consideration the social, cultural, and organisational factors that explain the behaviour of executives to use EIS. The research model is used to test empirically the hypothesised relationships among the factors. A further analysis is done to determine the relative importance of the independent variables in explaining EIS use by executives.

Triandis' Theoretical Framework

Some IS researchers (e.g., Trice & Treacy, 1988; Davis, 1989; Davis et al., 1989; Venkatesh & Davis, 1996; Kim, 1996; Elkordy, 2000; Venkatesh, 1999; Venkatesh & Morris, 2000; Elkordy & Khalil, 2002) relied on Fishbein and Ajzen's (1975) TRA, in their attempts to explain user behaviours. While TRA is very useful, it is somewhat incomplete in that it leaves aside factors that could also have influence on behaviour intentions and on behaviour itself. In an attempt to encompass a larger number of relevant variables, Triandis proposed a theoretical network of interrelated hypotheses around the constructs of attitude and behaviour, placing them in the broadest possible context.

With reference to his framework in Figure 1, Triandis (1980) states that *behaviour* has "*objective consequences,* (that occur 'out there' in the real world) which are *interpreted* (occur inside the person)" (p. 198). He argues that as a result of these interpretations, the person feels *reinforced.* Reinforcement, he states, "affects the *perceived consequences* of the behaviour in two ways: it changes the *perceived probabilities* that the behaviour will have particular consequences and it changes the *value of these consequences*" (p. 198). These probabilities and values, Triandis argues, in turn constitute one of the determinants of *behavioural intentions* to behave, which are one of the determinants of behaviour. Triandis further argues that *habits* and *relevant arousal* are also determinants of behaviour. But even when the intentions are high, the habits well-established, and the arousal optimal, there may be no behaviour if the geography of the situation makes the behaviour impossible; thus, *facilitating conditions* are seen as important determi-

Figure 1. Triandis' Theoretical Framework — Showing Relations Among the Major Variables

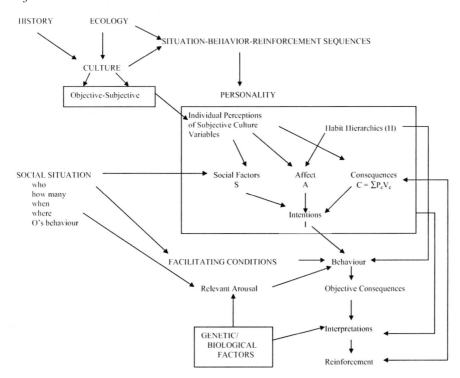

nants of behaviour. The interpretation of the objective consequences, Triandis argues, may differ because of genetic or biological influences or because of the previous situation-behaviour-reinforcement sequences that the individual has encountered in his or her history, that is, the individual's *personality*. Personality, Triandis states, internalises the *culture's* way of perceiving the social environment, called the *subjective culture* of a group.

According to Triandis, *subjective culture* consists of *norms* (self-instructions to do what is perceived to be correct and appropriate by members of a culture in certain situations), *roles* (which are also concerned with behaviours that are considered correct, but related to persons holding a particular position in a group, society, or social system), and *values* (the broad tendencies to prefer certain states of affairs over others — what make a group or a category of people to distinguish between, for example, good and evil, clean and dirty, beautiful and ugly, natural and unnatural, normal and abnormal, logical and paradoxical, and rational and irrational). These internalisations, according to Triandis, correspond with, but are not identical to, the group's subjective culture, and form the *social factors* that influence the intention to behave. In addition, Triandis argues, previous experiences of the individual with particular behaviours result in *affect* towards the behaviour, which in turn are among the determinants of intentions. Triandis adds that personality is an outcome of *situation-behaviour-reinforcement* sequences and the *subjective culture* to which the individual is exposed. This subjective culture, Triandis explains, reflects the human-made part of the environment, which is shaped by *historical* and *ecological* forces. In turn, personality has an impact on the way people will interpret the objective consequences of the behaviour.

Triandis argues that any behaviour occurs in a particular situation, which influences the facilitating conditions and the relevant arousal of the person while simultaneously activating specific levels of the social factors. For interpersonal behaviour the *social situation* includes particular individuals, in a behaviour setting, as well the other's previous behaviour.

Triandis notes that the arrows in the model show the directions of probable causality. Though he admits that there are several bidirectional relationships, which are not shown in order to keep the diagram simple.

Triandis defines *habits* as "situation-behaviour sequences that are or have become automatic, so that they occur without self-instruction" (p. 204). According to Triandis, habits are what people usually do and the individual is usually not conscious of the sequences—for example, driving a car. They are closely related to an individual's past experience and ability to perform a given act. His model suggests that the habitual nature of a behaviour, in addition to intentions, will have an influence on the individual's response to a given situation. Triandis argues that habits are more important than intentions for many behaviours. Thompson et al. (1991), who ignored habits in their studies, acknowledged that habits "are clearly an important determinant of behaviour" (p. 130).

Triandis on the other hand defines *behaviour* as "a broad class of reactions by an organism to any stimuli (internal or external to the organism) [which] includes *acts*" (p. 201). *Acts* he defines as a "socially defined pattern of muscle movements" (p. 201). He gave an example of specific acts of hitting someone. Such acts, he said, have no meaning in themselves, but acquire meaning from the social context, particularly the perceived causes of the acts. "For instance, 'to hit' is very different if it is done accidentally, as a joke, to 'correct' a naughty child, or with the intention to hurt" (p. 201). According to the framework, behaviour consists of the frequency, duration, and/or intensity of the reactions by an organism to stimuli. *Behavioural intentions,* which trigger behaviour, are defined as "instructions that people give to themselves to behave in certain ways" (p. 203). They involve ideas such as "I must do X," "I will do X," and "I am going to do X," and are influenced by social factors, affect, and the behaviour's consequences (p. 203).

The clear distinction that can be drawn between *habits* and *behaviours* from Triandis' framework is that whereas habits are automatic and occurring in the individual without self-instruction and with the individual usually not conscious of the reactions, behaviours are not. It can be deduced from the framework that *habits* are *behaviours* that have become automatic and acquired through the individual's past experience and ability to perform an act.

Relevant arousal is a physiological factor. Triandis states, "the physiological arousal of the organism that is relevant to the act facilitates the act, and increases its probability" (p. 205). The model suggests that relevant arousal directly influences behaviour and is influenced by genetic and biological factors, as well as by the social situation—that is, the behaviour setting.

According to Triandis, it may happen that an individual has the intention to do something, but is unable to do it because the environment prevents the act from being performed. Consequently, the level of *facilitating conditions* is an important factor in explaining an individual's behaviour and must be taken into account. In turn, facilitating conditions are dependent on the social situation.

Triandis (1971) argued that behaviour is influenced by social norms, which depend on messages received from others and reflect what individuals think they should do. In his later work, Triandis (1980) expanded this term and called it *social factors,* which he describes as "the individual's internalisation of the reference group's subjective culture, and specific interpersonal agreements that the individual has made with others, in specific social situations" (p. 210). Thus, in addition to influencing intentions, social factors are themselves dependent on the social situation, and on the individual's perception of subjective culture variables.

Affect relates to the individual's feelings of joy, elation, or pleasure, or depression, disgust, displeasure, or hate towards a given behaviour. Positive feelings will increase the intention toward a given behaviour, while negative feelings will decrease them. Affect is influenced by the individual's habits and by his or her perceptions of subjective culture variables.

The *Consequences* factor is considered as a function of the *perceived consequence* of the behaviour and the *value of each consequence.* Perceived consequences, what Davis (1989) called perceived usefulness in TAM, refers to the probability that a given consequence will follow from performing a behaviour. The value of the consequence is the "affect attached to the consequence" (Triandis, 1980, p. 203). The model hypothesised that the higher the expected value of the behaviour, the more likely the person will intend to perform it. Consequences are influenced by an individual's perception of subjective culture variables as they do to social factors and affect variables. According to the model, consequences, in addition to influencing behaviour through intentions, are influenced by behaviour. That is, the objective consequences of a behaviour are interpreted by the individual, and "as a result of these interpretations, the person feels reinforced" (p. 198).

The Research Model

Bergeron et al. (1995), who based their research model on Triandis' framework, suggested in their conclusion that "future investigations should aim for a cumulative tradition by continuing to employ Triandis' framework as a theoretical foundation to further understand the phenomenon of EIS use" (p. 142). In line with this suggestion, the research model for this study is based on Triandis' framework, as shown in Figure 2. The model is in line with that used by Bergeron et al. (1995) in a similar study. While, however Bergeron et al. ignored culture and social situation factors in their model, subjective-objective culture and social situation factors are taken into account in the operationalisation of the social factors construct in this study.

The affect construct consists of satisfaction with information similar to that of Bergeron et al. This model, however, takes into account satisfaction with the EIS system and support instead of satisfaction with access and assistance respectively, as in Bergeron et al.'s model. In addition, satisfaction with the EIS system plan is included in the constructs for this study. The facilitating conditions construct consists of EIS development processes, EIS management processes, and organisational environment. In line with Triandis' framework, the consequences construct consists of perceived usefulness (consequences) of EIS use. The behaviour construct consists of the frequency of EIS use and the internalisation of EIS use, similar to that of Bergeron et al. (1995).

Similar to Bergeron et al. (1995) and Thompson et al.'s (1991) studies, genetic or biological factors are not included in this research model. Similarly, behavioural intentions are not included in line with the suggestions of Bergeron et al., Thompson et al., Moore and Benbasat (1991), and Ajzen and Fishbein (1980). This study seeks to explain behaviour towards the use of EIS, but not to predict it, as done by Bergeron et al. (1995); therefore, a longitudinal study is not also necessary.

The measurement of the variables in this research model is based on Triandis' (1980) suggested operationalisations of constructs defined in his framework, in addition to other relevant studies (e.g., Bergeron et al., 1995; Thompson et al., 1991).

Habits are operationalised by assessing the number of years of an executive's experience in using EIS and his or her ability to use the systems. Consequences are operationalised by assessing executive's perceived consequences (usefulness) of using EIS in his or her work and assessing the impact of using EIS on his or her performance. Social factors are operationalised by measuring the subjective norms, roles, and values and the social situations on the executive in using EIS. Affect is operationalised by measuring the executive's satisfaction with the information provided by the EIS, with the EIS itself, with the support provided in using the

Figure 2. Research Model for EIS Use

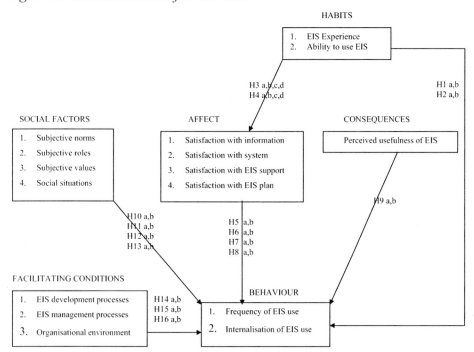

system, and with the system plan now and into the future. Facilitating conditions are operationalised by measuring what effect the EIS development processes, the EIS management processes, and the organisational environment have on the executive's behaviour in using the EIS. Finally, behaviour is operationalised by measuring the frequency and the internalisation of EIS use. (Detailed operationalisation of the constructs is provided in Appendix A.)

Research Hypotheses

The hypotheses to be tested based on the research model are as follows.

According to Triandis' framework, habits have a major contribution to the explanation of behaviour. This is supported by a previous study (Sugar, 1967, cited in Thompson et al. 1991), which shows that habits are a strong predictor of behaviour. Sugar (1967) measured the attitudes, norms, and habits of college students concerning cigarette smoking. On a separate occasion, the same students were offered a cigarette. The strongest single predictor of behaviour was found to be habit, followed by norms and attitudes being the least. According to Triandis, habits are closely related to an individual's past experience and ability to perform a given act, and in his earlier work in 1972 (in association with Vassiliou, Vassiliou, Tanaka, and Shanmugam, and with the assistance of Davis, Kilty, McGuire, Saral and Yang) he also acknowledged experiences as habits. Previous IS studies also identified computer experience as determinants of user attitude towards information systems.

According to the framework, habits lead to the derivation of some satisfaction or dissatisfaction (affect), which in turn explains behaviour, while habits themselves directly explain behaviour. The framework asserts that the frequency of doing or using something constitutes a behaviour and the internalisation of the probabilities and values of an act constitutes one of the determinants of behavioural intentions to behave, which are one of the determinants of behaviour. Accordingly, it is hypothesised that:

H1a: EIS experience positively correlates with the frequency of EIS use.
H1b: EIS experience positively correlates with the internalisation of EIS use.
H2a: Ability to use EIS positively correlates with the frequency of EIS use.
H2b: Ability to use EIS positively correlates with the internalisation of EIS use.

Previous research studies indicate that executives who had been using computer systems for a greater length of time were seen to have better attitudes in terms of user comprehension and participation (Raymond, 1988). Similarly, Sanders and Courtney (1985) found the length of DSS use to be positively related to user satisfaction.

Swanson (1974) defines user satisfaction as a set of user beliefs about the relative value of an information system in terms of providing timely, accurate, and easy-to-understand information to support his or her decision making. This definition, however, focuses on only one component of user satisfaction – information satisfaction. Previous studies have shown that users' satisfaction with the quality of information provided by a system, with the features of the system, and with the support provided by the support group or information centre are correlated with user satisfaction of information systems. Tafti (1992) synthesised the research in this area into information satisfaction, system satisfaction, and support group satisfaction, each of which consists of unique attributes, which correlate with user satisfaction of information systems. Previous studies (Amoako-Gyampah & White, 1993) also show that system plan correlates with user satisfaction of information systems. Accordingly, it is hypothesised that:

H3a: The longer the experience with EIS, the higher the satisfaction with EIS information attributes.
H3b: The longer the experience with EIS, the higher the satisfaction with EIS features.
H3c: The longer the experience with the EIS, the higher the satisfaction with EIS support group.

H3d: The longer the experience with the EIS, the higher the satisfaction with EIS plan.

H4a: The more the ability to use EIS, the higher the satisfaction with EIS information attributes.

H4b: The more the ability to use EIS, the higher the satisfaction with EIS features.

H4c: The more the ability to use EIS, the higher the satisfaction with EIS support group.

H4d: The more the ability to use EIS, the higher the satisfaction with EIS plan.

H5a: Satisfaction with EIS attributes positively correlates with the frequency of EIS use.

H5b: Satisfaction with EIS attributes positively correlates with the internalisation of EIS use.

H6a: Satisfaction with EIS features positively correlates with the frequency of EIS use.

H6b: Satisfaction with EIS features positively correlates with internalisation of EIS use.

H7a: Satisfaction with EIS support positively correlates with the frequency of EIS use.

H7b: Satisfaction with EIS support positively correlates with the internalisation of EIS use.

H8a: Satisfaction with EIS system plan positively correlates with the frequency of EIS use.

H8b: Satisfaction with EIS system plan positively correlates with the internalisation of EIS use.

The perceived consequences construct is consistent with the expectancy theory of motivation proposed by Vroom (1964). The basic premises of expectancy theory is that individuals evaluate the consequences of their behaviour in terms of potential rewards and base their choice of behaviour on the desirability of the rewards. Perceived consequences are also what Davis (1989) refers to as perceived usefulness in the technology acceptance model. Davis (1989) defines *perceived usefulness* as the extent to which a person believes that using a particular technology will enhance his or her job performance. Perceived usefulness, which reflects perceptions of the performance-use contingency, has been closely linked to outcome expectations, instrumentality, and extrinsic motivation (Davis, 1989; Davis et al., 1989, 1992). A significant body of TAM research has shown that perceived usefulness is a strong determinant of user acceptance, adoption, and usage behaviour (e.g., Davis, 1989; Davis et al., 1989; Mathieson, 1991; Taylor & Todd, 1995; Venkatesh & Davis, 1996; Venkatesh, 1999; Venkatesh &

Morris, 2000; Elkordy, 2000; Elkordy & Khalil, 2002). Accordingly, it is hypothesised that:

H9a: Perceived usefulness positively correlates with the frequency of EIS use.
H9b: Perceived usefulness positively correlates with the internalisation of EIS use.

As described earlier, subjective culture consists of norms, roles, and values. Subjective norms are defined by Fishbein and Ajzen (1975) as the degree to which an individual believes that people who are important to him or her think he or she should perform a behaviour in question. Superior, peer, and subordinate influences in the workplace have been shown to be strong determinants of subjective norms in the technology domain (Mathieson, 1991; Taylor & Todd, 1995; Venkatesh & Davis, 1996; Venkatesh, 1999; Venkatesh & Morris, 2000; Elkordy, 2000; Elkordy & Khalil, 2002). It follows that subjective roles and values, which are also social factors, will as well have superior, peers, and subordinate as determinants. Subjective culture constitutes the work group influences on the individual at the workplace. Bergeron et al.'s (1995) studies show that social factors determine EIS users behaviour. And according to Triandis (1980), subjective culture is the subjective aspect of the social environment.

According to Triandis' framework, any behaviour occurs in a particular social situation, which triggers specific levels of social factors. Adamopoulos's (1976, cited in Triandis 1980) study of the perception of social situations, using an adaptation of the role differential, reveals two dimensions: formality-informality (reflecting the public-private character of the situation) and constraining-unconstraining (reflecting the number of different behaviours that can appropriately occur in the situation). According to Triandis, social situations include behaviour settings. A behaviour setting has place-time coordinates, it consists of physical entities and process, and it evokes particular behaviours. Triandis cites a classroom as a behaviour setting that has a particular location and a particular time when a class meets; it also has physical entities such as chairs and tables, black/whiteboards, and in it people act in certain ways, e.g., talk, listen, take notes, and so on.

Following the information on the previous page, it is hypothesised that:

H10a: Subjective norms positively correlate with the frequency of EIS use.
H10b: Subjective norms positively correlate with the internalisation of EIS use.
H11a: Subjective roles positively correlate with the frequency of EIS use.
H11b: Subjective roles positively correlate with the internalisation of EIS use.
H12a: Subjective values positively correlate with the frequency of EIS use.
H12b: Subjective values positively correlate with the internalisation of EIS use.
H13a: Social situations positively correlate with the frequency of EIS use.
H13b: Social situations positively correlate with the internalisation of EIS use.

EIS development, as revealed by the literature review, attracts much of the EIS research effort. Much of the effort in this area is directed at creating or suggesting the right conditions for deriving the maximum benefits from the systems. Critical factors for successful EIS development have been linked to executive sponsorship, user involvement and participation, technical and other resources, plan for development and spread, management of data problems, and resistance. One of the main reasons for user involvement and participation, for example, is to facilitate implementation — that is, to ensure follow-up, overcome resistance, ensure acceptance, avoid conflicts, and ensure continuous resources or support (Nandhakumar & Jones, 1997). Nandhakumar's (1996) in-depth case study of EIS in an organisation suggests that, in addition to these development success factors, developers need to have some understanding of the social and organisational contexts in which the systems are used. He mentioned contextual elements such as assumptions, beliefs, shared norms, and perspectives.

Systems development processes are ongoing and, therefore, create facilitating conditions for the use of the systems. As well, management processes, such as company policies and rules, with regards to information systems use in organizations, will create facilitating conditions for their use. Policies regarding EIS can be, say, making the systems accessible to executives anywhere, anytime. This may require the provision of laptops and connectivity facilities, which will allow executives to dial into the systems at home, on business trips, or even overseas. McBride's (1997) nine-year case study of the rise and fall of an EIS in the UK manufacturing company also suggests the importance of the interactions between the business environment, the organisational environment, and the perceptions and interpretations of events and facts by stakeholders on the success or failure of an information system.

From the above analysis, it will therefore be appropriate to investigate how these facilitating conditions explain EIS users' behaviour to use the systems. Accordingly, it is hypothesised that:

H14a: EIS development processes positively correlate with the frequency of EIS use.

H14b: EIS development processes positively correlate with the internalisation of EIS use.

H15a: EIS management processes positively correlate with the frequency of EIS use.

H15b: EIS management processes positively correlate with the internalisation of EIS use.

H16a: Organisational environment positively correlates with the frequency of EIS use.

H16b: Organisational environment positively correlates with the internalisation of EIS use.

RESEARCH METHODOLOGY

Four methodologies have been identified for empirical IS research studies, namely: case studies, field studies, field tests (quasi-experimental), and laboratory studies (experimental) (Kim, 1996). That is, given the individual and organisational variables in the research model, a field study in a real setting appears more appropriate. By using a field study, data was gathered on a number of ongoing, uncontrolled situations. In addition, field study is usually deemed to be the most feasible and economical method to examine a complex phenomenon, as in this study. Furthermore, it produces relative strong effects of independent variables on dependent variables, and thus enhances the statistical conclusion of the results (Cook & Campbell, 1979; Kim, 1996).

Data Collection Method

The data collection method employed for this study was a mail survey, due to financial resources and the circumstances of the research (Kerlinger, 1986; Kim, 1996). The questionnaire for the survey was pre-tested on six colleagues, refined with feedback received and pre-tested again. Each time a consultation was made with the Statistical Consulting Service in the university where the researcher works to verify the statistical validity of the questionnaire as well. The survey questionnaire was designed following the procedures and guildelines provided by Sarantakos (2002), Babbie (2001), Dillman (1978, 2000), Wiersma (1986, 2000), and Robson (1996). Some questions were also adopted from Bergeron et al. (1995). The cover letter to the questionnaire has a statement guaranteeing the confidentiality of respondents and a statement of how the research has been reviewed by the Human Research Ethics Committee (HREC) as required in Australia. The HREC's contact for any concerns or complaints regarding the conduct of the research was provided.

Data for the pilot study were collected from CEOs, CFOs, or equivalent and two other executives in three large organisations using EIS in Australia. The questionnaire was refined with the feedback received from the pilot study to arrive at the final questionnaire for the main survey. (See Appendix B for the final questionnaire.)

Seven hundred (700) questionnaires were mailed out for the main survey to mainly CEOs and CFOs, and one other executive in 255 organizations using EIS in Australia. One hundred and forty-five (145) responses were received. Follow-up questionnaires were sent to non-respondents and 115 responses were received, giving the overall response rate of 37.14 percent, with 20.57 percent good for analysis. The organizations surveyed were identified through a database purchased from the Fairfax Business Media purposely for this study. The organizations ranged from small to very large, employing a minimum of 1,010 to a maximum of 750,000 people. The number of IT staff ranges from zero to 4,000 people in the organizations and turnover ranging from zero to greater US$1000.

Data Analysis

Preliminary evaluation of the research model and the associated hypotheses for this study involves simple analysis such as calculating the product-moment correlation coefficients (Pearson's r). A further analysis is conducted by using stepwise regression to determine the relative importance of the independent variables in explaining EIS use. Preliminary analyses were performed to ensure no violation of the assumptions of normality, linearity and homoscedasticity. The descriptive statistics for the sampled data collected are presented in Table 2. SPSS Release 11.0 for Windows was used in this process.

RESULTS AND DISCUSSIONS

Bivariate Analysis – Pearson's Product-Moment Correlation Coefficients

The results of testing the hypotheses associated with the research model, as shown in Table 3, are presented in Tables 4 and 5. Table 4 shows that the results do not support the hypothesised relationship between EIS experience and internalisation of EIS use (H1b) and the relationship between satisfaction with EIS support and frequency of EIS use (H7a). Table 5 shows that the results also do not support the hypothesised relationship between EIS satisfaction and EIS experience (H3); relationship between satisfaction with EIS support and the ability to use EIS (H4c); and the relationship between satisfaction with EIS development plans and ability to use EIS (H4d).

Table 4 shows a good explanation of the overall user behaviour to use EIS as measured by frequency of EIS use and internalisation of EIS use. Except for the hypothesised relationship between EIS experience and internalisation of EIS use (H1b) and the relationship between satisfaction with EIS support and frequency of EIS use (H7a), all the rest are significant. Table 4 shows that, overall, the results indicate there is positive correlations between the independent variables and the dependent variables as hypothesised. Table 5 however shows that, overall, the results do not indicate there is positive correlations between habits and affect (H3, H4).

Table 2. Descriptive Statistics for Variables in the Research Model

Variable	Mean	Std. Deviation
EIS Experience	2.06	1.09
Ability to Use EIS	2.67	1.03
Satisfaction with EIS Information	3.40	0.74
Satisfaction with EIS System	3.50	0.71
Satisfaction with EIS Support Services	3.47	0.85
Satisfaction with EIS Development Plans	3.02	0.70
Perceived Usefulness of EIS	3.20	2.21
Subjective Norms in Relation to EIS Use	2.38	1.82
Subjective Roles in relation to EIS Use	3.99	0.60
Subjective Values of EIS	3.71	0.73
Social Situations in relation to EIS Use	3.54	0.70
EIS Development Processes	3.44	0.67
EIS Management Processes	3.59	0.67
Organisational Environment	3.64	0.68
Frequency of EIS Use	3.64	1.18
EIS Internalisation	3.94	0.73

Table 3. Reliability Coefficients of Scales (Cronbach's Alpha) for Scaled Variables used in this Study (N = 144 Scale = 5-point Likert scale)

Variable	No. of Items	Cronbach's Alpha
Perceived Usefulness	6	0.85
Satisfaction with EIS System	7	0.88
Satisfaction with EIS Information	8	0.90
Satisfaction with EIS Support Services	5	0.92
Satisfaction with EIS Development Plans	7	0.92
Subjective Norms	4	0.81
Subjective Roles	4	0.82
Subjective Values	4	0.91
Social Situations	4	0.86
Organizational Environment	5	0.76
EIS Development Processes	5	0.74
EIS Management Processes	4	0.70
EIS Internalization	4	0.81

Regression Analysis

The bivariate analysis presented above establishes the support or otherwise of the hypotheses tested in this study. To identify the variables which are most important in explaining the variance in behaviour towards using EIS, stepwise regression analysis was further performed to measure the relative importance of the impact of changes in each explanatory variable. Preliminary analyses were first performed to ensure no violation of the assumptions of normality, linearity and homoscedasticity. The results of the stepwise regression analysis are shown in Tables 6 and 7 for frequency of EIS use and internalisation of EIS use respectively.

Table 6 shows that nearly 45 percent of the variance in frequency of EIS use is explained by seven variables—ability to use EIS *(habits)*, subject norms relating to the IS director *(social factor)*, the reliability of the EIS system *(affect)*, interaction among business units *(facilitating conditions)*, position in the organisation *(social factor—role)*, EIS experience *(habits)*, and CBIS experience *(habits)*. Overall, the results tend to indicate that habits are most important in explaining

Table 4. Pearson's Product-Moment Correlation Between the Independent Variables, Frequency of Use and Internalisation of Use (N = 144)

Independent Variable (Hypothesis)	Frequency of EIS use		Internalisation of EIS use	
	r	p	r	p
EIS Experience (H1a, b)	0.231**	0.006	0.119	ns
Ability to Use EIS (H2a, b)	0.400**	0.000	0.413**	0.000
Satisfaction with EIS Information (H5a, b)	0.329**	0.000	0.311**	0.000
Satisfaction with EIS System (H6a, b)	0.312**	0.000	0.389**	0.000
Satisfaction with EIS Support (H7a, b)	0.160	ns	0.205*	0.016
Satisfaction with EIS Development Plan (H8a, b)	0.208*	0.014	0.250**	0.003
Perceived Usefulness of EIS (H9a, b)	0.259**	0.002	0.600**	0.000
Subjective Norms in Relation to EIS Use (H10a, b)	0.373**	0.000	0.383**	0.000
Subjective Roles Relation to EIS Use (H11a, b)	0.413**	0.000	0.569**	0.000
Subjective Values of EIS (H12a, b)	0.283**	0.001	0.497**	0.000
Social Situations Relation to EIS Use (H13a, b)	0.176*	0.036	0.377**	0.000
EIS Development Processes (H14a, b)	0.249**	0.003	0.298**	0.000
EIS Management Processes (H15a, b)	0.285**	0.001	0.388**	0.000
Organisational Environment (H16a, b)	0.281**	0.001	0.573**	0.000

*Note: Significant at **p < 0.01, *p < 0.05*

Table 5. Pearson's Product-moment Correlation Between the Independent Variables, EIS Experience and Ability to Use EIS

Independent Variable (Hypothesis)	EIS Experience		Ability to use EIS	
	r	p	r	p
Satisfaction with EIS Information (H3a, H4a)	-0.001	ns	0.166*	0.048
Satisfaction with EIS System (H3b, H4b)	0.033	ns	0.232**	0.005
Satisfaction with EIS Support (H3c, H4c)	-0.010	ns	-0.005	ns
Satisfaction with Development Plan (H3d, H4d)	0.029	ns	0.017	ns

*Note: Significant at **p < 0.01, *p < 0.05*

frequency of EIS use: with EIS experience, CBIS experience and ability to use EIS variables uniquely contributing to this explanation. This is followed by the unique contributions of the variables for the social, facilitating conditions and affect factors, as mentioned above.

It is interesting to note that *position* and *CBIS experience* have not been included in the research model but in the survey questionnaire to check respondents' position and CBIS experience prior to using EIS. As the results indicate, they turned out to be important variables in explaining frequency of EIS use.

Table 7 shows that a little over 64 percent of the variance in internalisation of EIS use is explained by five variables — pace of change of business environment

Table 6. Stepwise Regression Analysis – Frequency of EIS Use

R = 0.668
R^2 = 0.447
F = 14.649 : Sig. F = 0.000

Variables Entered	From Construct	Beta	Sig.
Ability to use EIS	Habits	0.244	0.001
Because of my role, IS director thinks I should use EIS	Social Factors – Subjective norms	0.215	0.003
EIS system always reliable	Affect – EIS features	0.229	0.001
Interaction among business units encourages EIS use	Facilitating conditions	0.264	0.000
Position	Social Factor – Subjective roles	-0.166	0.024
EIS experience	Habits	0.379	0.000
CBIS experience	Habits	-0.301	0.001

Table 7. Stepwise Regression Analysis – Internalisation of EIS Use

$R = 0.801$ $R^2 = 0.642$ $F = 38.317 : Sig. F = 0.000$			
Variables Entered	**From Construct**	**Beta**	**Sig.**
Pace of change of business environment encourages EIS use	Facilitating conditions	0.362	0.000
Perceived usefulness of EIS	Consequences	0.264	0.000
Ability to use EIS	Habits	0.214	0.000
Productive value of EIS	Social Factor – Subjective values	0.161	0.009
Because of my role, colleagues think I should use	Social Factor – Subjective norms	0.152	0.020

(facilitating conditions), perceived usefulness *(consequences),* ability to use EIS *(habits),* subjective productive values of EIS *(social factor),* and subject norms relating to colleagues *(social factor).* Overall, the results tend to indicate that facilitating conditions are most important in explaining internalisation of EIS use, with the pace of change of business environment variable uniquely contributing to this explanation. This is followed by the unique contributions of the variables for the social, consequences and habits factors, as mentioned above.

In summary, the results tend to indicate that internalisation of EIS use is a more appropriate measure of user behaviour than frequency of EIS use. However, the contributions of both variables in explaining user behaviour towards EIS use are quite significant and worth taking into consideration, in deciding on the development, implementation and use of EIS in organisations.

CONTRIBUTIONS AND LIMITATIONS
OF THIS STUDY

The contributions of this study are threefold, namely, theoretical, methodological and practical. Theoretically, EIS use as a behaviour has been established and confirmed by this study using Triandis Framework. Methodologically, the approach for studying EIS as a behaviour using Triandis Framework has been established. The framework and the methodology could also be applied to other information systems to investigate factors explaining user behaviour towards those other systems.

Practically, the findings of this study have some implications for EIS development, implementation and use in organisations. EIS developers and implementers need to be award of the social, affect, consequences, and facilitating conditions factors that contribute the behaviour of EIS users towards using the systems. Proper education and training might be necessary for experience and ability to use EIS for habits to use EIS to be entrenched.

In summary, the findings of this study lend themselves to:

- Improving the development and implementation of EIS;
- Better education and training for EIS users;
- Improving EIS usage leading to the success of EIS in organisations;
- Better allocation of scarce resources for EIS;
- Provision of further research into EIS usage factors; and
- Provision of further research into usage factors for other information systems.

It is however worth mentioning that there are certain limitations to this study. First, the database purchased purposely for this study could not highlight the level of sophistication of EIS in the organisations surveyed. This might result in some of the respondents responding to the questionnaire who were using systems that might not qualify to be the EIS this study expected. Despite this, the findings have some implications for EIS and other systems in the workplace. Future research should thus include questions of levels of sophistication of EIS in the organisations surveyed.

Second, although necessary steps were taken in designing the survey questionnaire to ensure the right responses as much as possible, it is difficult to guarantee the right responses. In addition, in an attempt to get a good response rate, all the questions in the survey questionnaire were closed-ended. Although the response rate (37.14 percent) is reasonable, the percentage of usable responses (20.57 percent) after eliminating the unusable ones might suggest some respondents did not treat the questionnaire with the attention it deserved. However, some useful written comments and suggestions were provided by some respondents, as requested at the end of the questionnaire. In addition telephone calls were made to some selected respondents to seek verifications to some responses and further questions were asked to gain more insight to responses. Both the written and oral comments and suggests were very helpful in providing some more insight into the analysis and discussions of the results.

Third, due to time and resource constraints, this study adopted a cross-sectional study approach. Since cross-sectional study addresses issues at only one point in time, it does not capture the complex interrelationships between variables that come into effect over time. Although this study sought to explain behaviour but not to predict it, a longitudinal study might be more appropriate to capture such details.

Future research should thus adopt a longitudinal study approach and include open-ended questions in the data collection. More variables should also be included in the research model for the social, habits and facilitating conditions to capture the broad range of variables for these factors that might contribute to the variance in user behaviour.

CONCLUSION

This study set out to provide answers to:

1. What are the major social, cultural, and organisational factors that explain the behaviour of executives towards using EIS in organisational settings?
2. What is the relative importance of these factors in determining EIS use by executives in organisational settings?

The results of this study indicate that, theoretically, both internalisation of EIS use and frequency of EIS use variables significantly contribute to behaviour towards using EIS. However, relatively, the results of this study indicate that internalisation of EIS use is a more appropriate measure of user behaviour than frequency of EIS use. The variables that explain the variance in these two variables are worth taking note of in the development, implementation and use of EIS.

REFERENCES

Adams, D. A., Nelson, R. R., & Todd, P. A. (1992). Perceived Usefulness, Ease of Use, and Usage of Information Technology: A Replication. *MIS Quarterly*, 16(2), 227-247.

Ajzen, I. & Fishbein, M. (1980). *Understanding Attitudes and Predicting Social Behaviour*. Prentice-Hall.

Amoako-Gyampah, K. & White, K.B. (1993). User involvement and user satisfaction. *Information & Management*, 25, 1-10.

Anthony, R.N. (1965). *Planning and Control System: A framework of Analysis*. Harvard University Press.

Babbie, E. (2001). *The Practice of Social Research*, 9th ed. Wasworth.

Bajwa, D.S., Rai, A., & Brennan, I. (1998). Key antecedents of Executive Information System success: a path analytic approach. *Decision Support Systems*, 22, 31-43.

Bashein, B.J. & Markus, M.L. (2000). *Data Warehouses: More than just mining.* Financial Executives Research Foundations, Inc.

Bergeron, F., Raymond, L., & Lagorge, M. (1991). Top Managers Evaluate the Attributes of EIS. *DSS-91 Transactions,* (Ilze Zigur edition), 6-14.

Bergeron, F., Raymond, L., Rivard, S. & Gara, M. (1991). Determinants of EIS use: Testing a behavioral model. *Decision Support Systems,* 14, 131-146.

Beynon-Davies, P. (1995). Information systems 'failure': The case of the London Ambulance Service's Computer Aided Dispatch Project. *European Journal of Information Systems,* 4, 171-184.

Bidgoli, H. (1998). *Intelligent Management Support Systems.* Quorum Books.

Blackler, F., Crump, N., & McDonald, S. (1999). Managing experts and competing through innovation: an activity theoretical analysis. *Organization,* 6 (1), 5-31.

Carisson, S.A. & Widmeyer, G.A. (1990, January). Towards a Theory of Executive Information Systems. *HICSS-23 Proceedings.* Kailua-Kona, Hawaii, Jan. 2-5.

Carlson, P.J. & Davis, G.B. (1998). An investigation of media selection among directors and managers: From "self" to "other" orientation. *MIS Quarterly,* 22(3), 335-362.

Carte, T.A. (1999). *The Impact of "Publicness" on Executive Information Systems Development (Organizational Theory, Systems Development).* Doctoral Dissertation. University of Georgia, Georgia.

Choo, C.H. (1998) *The Knowing Organization: How Organizations Use Information to Construct Meaning, Create Knowledge and Make Decisions.* Oxford, UK: Oxford University Press.

Compeau, D., Higgins, C.A. & Huff, S. (1999). Social cognitive theory and individual reactions to computing technology: A longitudinal study. *MIS Quarterly,* 23(2), 145-158.

Compeau, D.R. & Higgins, C.A. (1995a). Computer self-efficacy: Development of a measure and initial test. *MIS Quarterly,* 19(2), 189-211.

Compeau, D.R. & Higgins, C.A. (1995b). Application of social cognitive theory to training for computer skills. *Information Systems Research,* 6(2), 118-143.

Compeau, D.R. & Meister, D.B. (1997, December 13). Measurement of perceived characteristics of innovating: A reconsideration based on three empirical studies. Presented at a workshop of the *Diffusion Interest Group on Information Technology.* Atlanta, GA.

Cook, T.D. & Campbell, D.T. (1979). *Quasi-Experimentation: Design and Analysis Issues for Field Settings.* Boston, MA: Houghton Mifflin Co.

Currie, W. (1995). *Management Strategies for IT. An International Perspective.* London: Pitman.

Davis, F.D. (1989). Perceived usefulness, perceived ease of use, and user acceptance of information technology. *MIS Quarterly*, 13(3), 319-340.

Davis, F.D., Bagozzi, R.P., & Warshaw, P.R. (1989). User acceptance of Computer Technology: A Comparison of two theoretical models. *Management Science*, 35(8), 982-1003.

Davis, G.B., Lee, A.S., Nickles, K.R., Chatterjee, S., Hartung, R. & Wu, Y. (1992). Diagnosis of an Information System Failure: A Framework and Interpretive Process. *Information & Management*, 23(5), 293-318.

Dillman, D.A. (1978). *Mail and Telephone Surveys — The Total Design Method.* John Wiley & Sons.

Dillman, D. A. (2000). *Mail and Internet Surveys — The Tailored Design Method.* 2nd ed. John Wiley & Sons.

Elam, J.J. & Leidner, D.G. (1995). EIS adoption, use, and impact: the executive perspective. *Decision Support Systems*, 14(2) 89-103.

Elkordy, M.M. (2000). An Integrated Model of EIS Use. In *Proceedings of 2000 Information Resources Management Association International Conference* (pp. 624-627), Anchorage, Alaska.

Elkordy, M.M. & Khalil, O.E.M. (2002). EIS Information: Use and Quality Determinants. In *Proceedings of 2002 IRMA International Conference* (pp. 1156-1157). Seattle, WA.

Engeström, Y. (1999). Activity theory and individual and social transformation. In Y. Engeström, R. Miettinen, & R.-L. Punamaki-Gitai (Eds.), *Perspectives on activity theory* (pp. 19-38). New York: Cambridge University Press.

Engeström, Y. & Escalante, V. (1996). Mundane tool or object of affection? The Rise and Fall of the Postal Buddy. In B.A. Nardi (Ed.), *Context and consciousness: activity theory and human-computer interaction* (pp. 325-374). Cambridge, MA: MIT Press.

Fishbein, M. & Ajzen, I. (1975). *Belief, Attitude, Intention and Behavior: An introduction to Theory and Research.* Addison-Wesley.

Frolick, M. & Robichaux, B.P. (1995). EIS information requirements determination: Using a group support system to enhance the strategic business objectives method. *Decision Support Systems*, 14, 157-170.

Frolick, M.N., Parzinger, M.J., Rainer, R.K., Jr., & Ramarapu, N.K. (1997). Using EISs for Environmental Scanning. *Information Systems in Management*, 14(1), 35-40.

Glover, H. Watson, H.J. & Rainer, K. (1992, Winter). 20 Ways to waste an EIS investment. *Information Strategy: The Executive's Journal*, 11-17.

Handzic, M. (1997). The impact of information reliability on utilisation and effectiveness of executive information systems. In the *Proceedings of the 8th Australasian Conference on Information Systems.*

Hill, T., Smith, N.D., & Mann, M.F. (1986). Communicating innovations: Convincing computer phobics to adopt innovative technologies. In R.J. Lutz (Ed.), *Advances in Consumer Research*, (vol. 13) (pp. 419-422). Provo, UT: Association for Consumer Research.

Hill, T., Smith, N.D., & Mann, M.F. (1987). Role of efficacy expectations in predicting the decision to use advanced technologies: The case of computers. *Journal of Applied Psychology*, 72(2) 307-313.

Hoven, J. (1996, March/April). Executive Support Systems. *Journal of Systems Management*, 48-55.

Johansen, R. & Swigart, R. (1996). *Upsizing the individual in the downsized organization: Managing the wake of reengineering, globalization, and overwhelming technological change.* Addison-Wesley.

Kelly, J.N. (1998). *Executive Information Systems.* Patricia Seybold's Office Computing Report, 11(2).

Kerlinger, F.N. (1986). *Foundations of Behavioral Research.* 3rd ed. Holt, Rinehart & Winston.

Kim, J. (1996). *An Empirical Investigation of Factors Influencing the Utilization of Executive Information Systems.* Doctoral Dissertation. University of Nebraska.

Kohn, M.L. (1969). *Class and Conformity: A Study in Values.* The Dorsey Press.

Kumar, A. & Palvia, P. (2001). Key Data Management Issues in a Global Executive Information System. *Industrial Management and Data Systems,* 101(4), 153-164.

Kuutti, K. (1996). Activity Theory as a Potential Framework for Human-Computer Interaction Research. In B. Nardi (Ed.), *Context and Consciousness: Activity Theory and Human-Computer Interaction* (pp. 17-44). Cambridge, MA: MIT Press.

Kuutti, K. (1999) Activity theory, transformation of work, and information systems design. In Y. Engeström, R. Miettinen, R. Miettinen and R.L. Punamäki-Gitai (Eds.), *Perspectives on activity theory* (pp. 360-376). Cambridge University Press.

Leidner, D.G. & Elam, J.J. (1994a, Winter). Executive Information Systems: Their Impact on Executive Decision making. *Journal of MIS,* (1993–94), 139-155.

Leidner, D.G. & Elam, J.J. (1994b). Senior and Middle Management Use of EIS:

A Descriptive Study. In the *Proceedings of the 27th Annual Hawaii International Conference on System Sciences* (pp. 135-144).

Li, G.K.H. & Jordan, E. (1998). Executive Information Systems (EIS) Development: The Role of Management Accountants. In the *Proceedings of 1998 Information Resources Management Association International Conference* (pp. 390-398). Boston, MA.

Martin, J.H., Carlisle, H.H. & Tren, S. (1973). The User Interface for Interactive Bibliographic Searching and Analysis of the Attitudes of Nineteen Information Scientists. *Journal of the American Society for Information Science,* 24(2), 47-66.

Mathieson, K. (1991). Predicting user intentions: Comparing the technology acceptance model with the theory of planned behaviour. *Information Systems Research,* 2(3), 173-191.

McBride, N. (1997). The rise and fall of an executive information system: a case study. *Information Systems Journal,* 7, 277-287.

Mintzberg, H. (1973). *The Nature of Managerial Work.* Harper & Row Publishers.

Mitev, N. (1996). Social, organizational and political aspects of information systems failure: the Computerised Reservation System at French Railways. In *Proceedings of the 4th European Conference on Information* Systems. Lisbon, Portugal.

Moore, G.C. & Benbasat, I. (1991). Development of an Instrument to Measure the Perceptions of Adopting an IT Innovation. *Information Systems Research,* 2(3), 192-222.

Nandhakumar, J. (1996). Design for success?: Critical success factors in executive information systems development. *European Journal of Information Systems,* 5, 62-72.

Nandhakumar, J. & Jones, M. (1997, December 15-17). Designing in the dark: the changing user-development relationship in information systems development. In *Proceedings of the Eighteenth International Conference on Information Systems* (pp. 75-87). Atlanta, GA.

Nardi, B.A. (1996). Some reflections on the application of activity theory. In B.A. Nardi (Ed.), *Context and Consciousness: Activity Theory and Human-Computer Interaction* (pp. 235-245). Cambridge, MA: MIT Press.

Nord, J.H. & Nord, G.D. (1995). Executive information systems: A study and comparative analysis. *Information & Management,* 29, 95-106.

Oz, E. (1994). When professional standards are lax: the Confirm failure and its lessons. *Communications of the Association of Computing Machines,* 37, 29-36.

Pervan, G. & Phua, R. (1997). A Survey of the State of Executive Information Systems in Large Australian Organisations. *Information Technology,* 29(2) 65-73.

Poulymenakou, A. & Holmes, A. (1996). A contingency framework for the investigation of information systems failure. *European Journal of Information Systems,* 37, 34-46.

Rainer, R.K., Jr. & Watson, H.J. (1995). What it does it take for successful executive information systems? *Decision Support Systems,* 14, 147-156.

Raymond, L. (1988). The impact of computer training on the attitudes and usage behaviour of small business managers. *Journal of Small Business Management,* 26(3), 8-13.

Raymond, L. & Bergeron, F. (1992). Personal DDS success in small enterprises. *Information & Management,* 22, 301-308.

Rivard, S. & Huff, S.L. (1988). Factors of success for end-user computing. *Communications of the ACM,* 31(5), 552-561.

Robson, C. (1996). *Real World Research: A Resource for Social Scientists and Practitioner-Researchers.* Blackwell.

Rockart, J.F. (1979). Chief Executives Define Their Own Needs. *Harvard Business Review,* 5(1), 81-93.

Rockart, J. F. & DeLong, D. (1992). Moments of Executive Enlightenment. In H.J. Watson,, R.K. Rainer, and G. Houdeshel (Eds.), *Executive Information Systems: Emergence, Development, Impact* (pp. 315-335). John Wiley & Sons.

Sanders, G.L. & Courtney, J.F. (1985). A field study of organizational factors influencing DSS success. *MIS Quarterly,* 9(1), 77-93.

Sarantakos, S. (2002). *Social Research,* 2nd ed. Macmillan Publishers Australia Pty. Ltd.

Sauer, C. (1993). *Why Information Systems Fail: A Case Study Approach.* UK: Alfred Waller.

Schenk, K.D. (1992). *Executive Use of Information Sources and the Impact of Executive Information Systems.* Doctoral Dissertation. University of California, Irvine.

Schneiderman, B. (1998). *Designing the User Interface: Strategies for Effective Human-Computer Interaction,* 3rd ed. Addison-Wesley.

Scholz, A. (2000). Problems and Conflicts While Developing an Executive Information System. In the *Proceedings of 2000 Information Resources Management Association International Conference* (pp. 1002-1003). Anchorage, Alaska.

Seddon, P.B. (1997). A respecification and extension of the Delone and McLean model of IS success. *Information Systems Research,* 8(3), 240-253.

Seeley, M. & Targett, D. (1999). Patterns of senior executives' personal use of computers. *Information & Management,* 35, 315-330.

Singh, S.K., Watson, H.J. & Watson, R.T. (2002). EIS Support for the Strategic Management Process. *Decision Support Systems,* 33, 71-85.

Swanson, E.B. (1974). Management Information Systems: Appreciation and Involvement. *Management Science,* 20, 178-188.

Tafti, M.H. (1992). A Three-dimensional Model of User Satisfaction with Information Systems, *International Journal of Information Resource Management,* 3(2), 4-10.

Taylor, S. & Todd, P.A. (1995). Understanding information technology usage: A test of competing models. *Information Systems Research,* 6(2), 144-176.

Thierauf, R.J. (1991). *Executive Information Systems: A Guide for Senior Management and MIS Professional.* Quorum.

Thodenius, B. (1995, April 20-22). The Use of Executive Information Systems in Sweden. In the *Proceedings of CEMS Academic Conference – Recent Developments in Economics and Business Administration.* Wien, Austria.

Thompson, R.L., Higgins, C.A., & Howell, J.M. (1991). Personal Computing: Toward a Conceptual Model of Utilisation. *MIS Quarterly,* 15(1) 125-143.

Triandis, H.C. (1971). *Attitudes, and Attitude Change,* Wiley & Sons Inc.

Triandis, H.C. (1980). Values, Attitudes, and Interpersonal Behavior. In *1979 Nebraska Symposium on Motivation: Beliefs, Attitudes, and Values* (pp. 195-259). University of Nebraska Press.

Triandis, H.C., Vassiliou, V. & Nassiakou, M. (1968). Three Cross-cultural Studies of Subjective Culture. *Journal of Personality and Social Psychology Monograph Supplement,* 8(4), part 2, 1-42.

Trice, A.W. & Treacy, M.E. (1988, Fall-Winter). Utilization As a Dependent Variable in MIS Research. *Database,* 33-41.

Turban, E. (1993). *Decision Support and Expert Systems: Management Support Systems,* 3rd ed. Macmillan Publishing.

Vandenbosch, B. (1999). An empirical analysis of the association between the use of executive support systems and perceived organizational competitiveness. *Accounting, Organization and Society,* 24, 77-92.

Vandenbosch, B. & Huff, S.L. (1999, March). Searching and Scanning: How Executives obtain information from Executive Information Systems. *MIS Quarterly,* 81-107.

Venkatesh, V. (1999). Creation of favorable user perceptions: Exploring the role of intrinsic motivation. *MIS Quarterly,* 23(2), 239-260.

Venkatesh, V. & Davis, F.D. (1996). A model of the antecedents of perceived ease of use: Development and test. *Decision Sciences*, 27(3), 451-482.

Venkatesh, V. & Morris, M.G. (2000). Why don't men ever stop to ask for directions? Gender, social influence, and their role in technology acceptance and usage behavior. *MIS Quarterly,* 24(1) 115-130.

Volonino, L., Watson, H.J. & Robinson, S. (1995). Using EIS to respond to dynamic business conditions. *Decision Support Systems,* 14, 105-116.

Vroom, V. (1964). *Work and Motivation.* Wiley and Sons Inc.

Wallis, L. (1992). Power Computing at the Top. In H.J. Watson, R.K. Rainer, and G. Houdeshel (Eds.), *Executive Information Systems: Emergence, Development, Impact* (pp. 81-105). New York: John Wiley & Sons.

Watson, H.J. & Carte, T.A. (2000). Executive Information Systems in Government Organizations. *Public Productivity & Management Review,* 23(3), 371-382.

Watson, H.J., Houdeshel, G. & Rainer, R. K. (1997). *Building Executive Information Systems and other Decision Support Applications.* New York: John Wiley & Sons.

Watson, H.J., Rainer, R. K., & Houdeshel, G. (Eds.). (1992). *Executive Information Systems: Emergence, Development, Impact.* New York: John Wiley & Sons.

Watson, H.J., Rainer, R. K., & Koh, C. (1992). Executive Information Systems: A Framework for Development and a Survey of Current Practices. In H.J. Watson, R.K. Rainer, and G. Houdeshel, (Eds.), *Executive Information Systems: Emergence, Development, Impact* (pp. 81-105). New York: John Wiley & Sons.

Weiner, L.R. (1993). *Digital woes: Why we should not depend on software.* Reading, MA: Addison-Wesley.

Weter, T.R. (1988, November 21). Tools at the Top. *Industry Week,* 41-44.

Wetherbe, J.C. (1991, March). Executive Information Requirements: Getting It Right. *MIS Quarterly,* pp. 51-61.

Wheeler, F.P., Chang, S.H. & Thomas, R.J. (1993). Moving from an executive information system to everyone's information system: lessons from a case study. *Journal of Info Technology,* 8(3), 177-183.

Wiersma, W. (1986). *Research Methods in Education: An Introduction* (4th ed.). Allyn and Bacon.

Wiersma, W. (2000). *Research Methods in Education: An Introduction* (7th ed.). Allyn and Bacon.

Young, D. & Watson, J.W. (1995). Determinates of EIS acceptance. *Info & Management,* 29, 153-164.

APPENDIX A
Operationalisation of Constructs and Measurement Scales for Research Variables

Suggested operationalisation of constructs by Triandis (1980) as defined in his framework has been used to measure the variables in the research model. In addition, relevant studies (e.g., Thompson et al., 1991; Bergeron et al., 1995) are also referenced to in the operationalisation. In the following paragraphs the various measures used are described. A five-point Likert scale is used throughout, except where otherwise stated. This is done to facilitate good response rate, following Wiersma (1986).

Habits

From Triandis' (1980) theoretical framework, habits can be measured by the past experience an individual has with an act and the ability of the individual to perform the given act. Previous IS research studies also found computer experience to relate to successful implementation of end-user computing (Rivard & Huff, 1988) and personal DSS applications (Raymond & Bergeron, 1992). An earlier IS research also found that users learn experientially (Martin et al., 1973). Accordingly, habits are operationalised by assessing the number of years of an executive's experience in using EIS and his or her ability to use the systems.

Computer system users can be classified by computer experience (ability to use the system) into novice users, knowledgeable intermittent (casual) users, and frequent or expert users (Shneiderman, 1998). The ability to use EIS is therefore measured by assessing the executive's class.

Consequences

As stated earlier, perceived consequences is the same as perceived usefulness in the technology acceptance model, and perceived usefulness is defined as the extent to which a person believes that using a particular technology will enhance his or her job performance. As in Triandis' model, perceived consequences of a behaviour (or subjective utility) is the product of the individual's beliefs (P_c) that such consequences (usefulness) will occur and the value (V_c) attached to the usefulness. Triandis suggests some methods for the measurement of (P_c) such as "asking the person to indicate his or her certainty that the consequence will or will not follow an act" (p. 202), or using a rating scale in which a the middle point is labeled "uncertain" and the ends points labeled "certain it will happen" and "certain it will not happen." Another method he suggests is to "provide individuals with a list of conceivable consequences and ask them to select the consequences they consider to be most likely to follow the act. Then a P_c of 1.00 can be assigned to the consequences that are selected and P_c of 0.00 to the remaining consequences" (p. 202). A method of measuring V_c, Triandis suggests, is to "use a set of prescaled, affectively positive or negative stimuli (e.g., going to a good movie or being told by one's boss that one is doing a poor job) and ask the subject to match a particular consequence, on the 'pleasant-unpleasant dimension,' with one of these prescaled stimuli" (p. 203).

This study adopts and adapts Triandis' methods together with the steps suggested by Ajzen and Fishbein (1980, pp. 261-263), which is also used by Bergeron et al. (1995), to measure the perceived usefulness of EIS. Similar to Bergeron et al. (1995), perceived usefulness was measured by evaluating the extent of the executive's beliefs and attached values of EIS use on their managerial (interpersonal, informational, and decisional) roles. Six five-point Likert scales adapted from Bergeron et al. (1995) were used to ascertain the beliefs of EIS use, and multiplying each score by a second six five-point Likert scales ascertained the value attached to the first six consequences of EIS use. The resulting score was obtained by averaging on the six scales similar to Bergeron, Raymond, Rivard and Gara (1995). The scales were found to be reliable, with a Cronbach's alpha equal to 0.85.

Affect

As mentioned earlier, this construct refers to an individual's feelings (satisfaction-dissatisfaction) associated with a given behaviour. In this study, it is operationalised through four variables. The first variable measured the executive's satisfaction with the EIS system, using seven five-point Likert scales. The second measured the satisfaction with information derived from the EIS system, using eight five-point Likert scales. The third measured the satisfaction with the EIS support services, using five five-point Likert scales. And the fourth measured the executive's satisfaction with the EIS system plan, using seven five-point Likert scales. All scales were adapted from Bergeron et al. (1995) and Amoako-Gyampah and White (1993). The scales were found to be reliable, with a Cronbach's alpha equal to 0.88, 0.90, 0.92, and 0.92 respectively.

Social Factors

As stated earlier, this construct consists of the reference group's subjective culture, which influences an individual member of the group's notion of appropriate or desirable behaviour. In the present context, this refers to the influence of the executive's work group (peers, superiors, subordinates, IS director) upon his or her use of EIS. Subjective culture consists of norms, roles, and values. In addition, the social situations also evoke particular behaviours. In this study, this construct was therefore operationalised through four variables. The scales and procedures for the four variables were adapted from Triandis, Vassiliou and Nassiakou (1968), Kohn (1969) and Bergeron et al. (1995). The first variable measured the subjective norms (self-instructions to do what is perceived to be correct and appropriate by the work group) by obtaining the executive's assessment of the influence of the work group upon his or her behaviour in general, using four five-point Likert scales (-2: strongly disagree, +2: strongly agree) and multiplied by their evaluation of the probability that the work group does in fact want them to use EIS, using four five-point Likert scales (0: strongly disagree, 4: strongly agree). The resulting score was obtained by averaging on the six scales similar to Bergeron et al. (1995). The scales were constructed from the steps suggested by Ajzen and Fishbein (1980, pp. 74-75, pp. 261-263), which was also used by Bergeron et al. (1995) to measure the subjective norms of EIS users. The scales were found to be reliable, with a Cronbach's alpha equal to 0.81.

The second variable measured the subjective roles (expected correct behaviours associated with the executive's use of EIS), using four five-point Likert scales. The third measured the subjective values (the broad tendencies of the work group to prefer certain states of affairs over others in relation to the executive's use of EIS), using four five-point Likert scales. And the fourth measured the social situations in the workplace settings by obtaining the executive's assessment of the interpersonal relationships with peers, superiors, subordinates, the IS director and the EIS support group in using the EIS. This was measured using five five-point Likert scales. The scales were constructed following Bergeron et al. (1995) and they were found to be reliable, with a Cronbach's alpha equal to 0.81, 0.91 and 0.86 respectively.

Facilitating Conditions

This construct is operationalised through three variables. The first variable measured the degree to which the organisational environment facilitates executives' use of EIS using five questions derived from Nandhakumar (1996), Nandhakumar and Jones (1997), and McBride (1997) with five-point Likert scales. The second measured the degree to which the EIS development processes facilitate executives' use of EIS using five questions derived from Nandhakumar (1996), and Nandhakumar and Jones (1997) with five-point Likert scales. The third measured the degree to which the EIS management processes facilitate executives' use of EIS using four questions derived from Nandhakumar (1996), and Nandhakumar and Jones (1997) with five-point Likert scales. The scaling followed those by Bergeron et al. (1995) and they were found to be reliable, with a Cronbach's alpha equal to 0.76, 0.74 and 0.70 respectively.

Behaviour

This construct is operationalised through two variables. The first variable measured the frequency at which executives use the EIS. Similar to Leidner and Elam (1994b), the value for this variable was obtained by asking executives to indicate the average number of terminal sessions per month they initiate in using the EIS. The second variable measured the internalisation of EIS use by ascertaining the executive's probabilities and values associated with the use of the system.

According to Bergeron et al. (1995), "one of the fundamental aspects of behaviour which can be measured is its intensity, i.e., the degree to which it is 'internalized' by the actor" (p. 138). Three relevant aspects of internalisation in terms of system use are identified by Trice and Treacy (1988). The first relates to the user's level of dependence upon the system. The second is the extent of system ownership felt by the user. And the third refers to the routinisation of system usage. These suggestions were followed by Bergeron et al. in their studies. This study also followed these suggestions and use a measure which consists of four five-point Likert scales, which characterised the extent to which the system has become the integral part of the executive's work activities. The scales were found to be reliable, with a Cronbach's alpha equal to 0.81.

APPENDIX B: SURVEY QUESTIONNAIRE

Department of Information Systems

University of Wollongong

Executive Information Systems Use Survey

This questionnaire is part of a study of Executive Information Systems (EIS) use in organisations. EIS are Computer-based Information Systems (CBIS) specifically designed to provide the necessary and critical information managers need to perform their managerial roles. They may go by other names in your organisation such as Enterprise-wide Information Systems, Enterprise Business Intelligence Systems, Balanced Scorecard or simply Scorecard, but their primary purpose may remain the same—to provide the necessary and critical information for managerial roles.

A.   CBIS and EIS Experiences

The following questions are about your experiences with CBIS and EIS, your ability to use EIS, and how frequently you use EIS.

1   *Your Experience with CBIS*
How many years have you personally been using CBIS? *(Please tick one)*
☐ 0 - 4   ☐ 5 - 9   ☐ 10 - 14   ☐ 15 - 19   ☐ 20 or more years

2   *Your Experience with EIS*
How many years have you personally been using EIS? *(Please tick one)*
☐ 0 - 4   ☐ 5 - 9   ☐ 10 - 14   ☐ 15 - 19   ☐ 20 or more years

3   *Your Ability to use EIS*
In which class of EIS users would you place yourself? *(Please tick one)*
Novice casual (intermittent) user   ☐
Novice frequent user   ☐
Expert (knowledgeable) casual user   ☐
Expert (knowledgeable) frequent user   ☐

4   *Your Frequency of using EIS*
On average, how many times do you logon to use an EIS? *(Please tick one)*
Several times a day   ☐
Once a day   ☐
1 - 4 times a month   ☐
Once a month   ☐
Less than once a month   ☐

B.   Perceived Usefulness and Inclination to Use EIS

Below are some statements about your personal **opinion about the usefulness of EIS** to an organisation and your **inclination** to use EIS. Please **circle** your response to each of these statements.

1   *Based on my experience with EIS I have observed that an EIS:*

Strongly Agree	Agree	Uncertain	Disagree	Strongly Disagree

Increases an organisation's performance

SA	A	U	D	SD

Provides an organisation with a competitive advantage

SA	A	U	D	SD

Provides a greater level of control over managerial activities

    SA   A   U   D   SD

Provides information that allows problems to be detected

    SA   A   U   D   SD

Improves the quality of decision-making in an organisation

    SA   A   U   D   SD

Increases the speed of decision-making in an organisation

    SA   A   U   D   SD

2   *I believe using EIS in an organisation has the potential to:*
Increase the organisation's performance

    SA   A   U   D   SD

Provide the organisation with a competitive advantage

    SA   A   U   D   SD

Provide a greater level of control over managerial activities

    SA   A   U   D   SD

Provide information that allows problems to be detected

    SA   A   U   D   SD

Improve the quality of decision-making in the organisation

    SA   A   U   D   SD

Increase the speed of decision-making in the organisation

    SA   A   U   D   SD

3   *Using an EIS helps me personally to:*
Accomplish my usual tasks

    SA   A   U   D   SD

Identify trends and obtain critical information

    SA   A   U   D   SD

Make strategic decisions

    SA   A   U   D   SD

Not using EIS any more would disadvantage me

    SA   A   U   D   SD

C.   Satisfaction with EIS

An information system user's satisfaction with the system can be measured by some attributes of the system. Below are some statements about your **satisfaction** with the **EIS system** itself, the **information** you need from the EIS, the **support services** for the EIS, and the **development plans** for the EIS. Please **circle** your response to each of these statements.

1   *The **EIS system** I use is always:*

	Strongly Agree	Agree	Uncertain	Disagree	Strongly Disagree
available	SA	A	U	D	SD
reliable	SA	A	U	D	SD
effective	SA	A	U	D	SD
flexible	SA	A	U	D	SD
easy-to-use	SA	A	U	D	SD
fast	SA	A	U	D	SD
overall satisfactory	SA	A	U	D	SD

2   *The **information** I need from my EIS is always:*

available	SA	A	U	D	SD
reliable	SA	A	U	D	SD
accurate	SA	A	U	D	SD
timely	SA	A	U	D	SD
precise	SA	A	U	D	SD
adequate	SA	A	U	D	SD
meaningful	SA	A	U	D	SD
overall satisfactory	SA	A	U	D	SD

3   *The **support services** provided by the information systems personnel for the EIS I use are always:*

	Strongly Agree	Agree Disagree	Uncertain	Disagree	Strongly
adequate	SA	A	U	D	SD
relevant	SA	A	U	D	SD
provided within an acceptable time	SA	A	U	D	SD
provided with a positive attitude	SA	A	U	D	SD
overall satisfactory	SA	A	U	D	SD

4   *Development plans for the EIS systems in my organisation are always:*

available	SA	A	U	D	SD
reliable	SA	A	U	D	SD
complete	SA	A	U	D	SD
flexible	SA	A	U	D	SD
attainable	SA	A	U	D	SD

| future-oriented | SA | A | U | D | SD |
| overall satisfactory | SA | A | U | D | SD |

D.   Norms, Roles and Values in Relation to the EIS Use

Some people use information systems as a result of self-instructions to do so because it is perceived to be correct and appropriate by some members of the organisation (**organisational norms**). And some people, by virtue of their **roles** in the organisation, may be expected by some members of the organisation to use particular systems. Further, some broad tendencies in the organisation to prefer certain states of affairs over others (**values**) may dictate that some systems are used. Below are some statements about norms, roles and values in relation to the use of EIS. Please **circle** your response to each of these statements.

1   *The following people think that I should use an EIS:*

	Strongly Agree	Agree	Uncertain	Disagree	Strongly Disagree
My colleagues	SA	A	U	D	SD
My superiors	SA	A	U	D	SD
The IS director	SA	A	U	D	SD
My subordinates	SA	A	U	D	SD

2   *Generally, I want to do what the following people think I should do:*

My colleagues	SA	A	U	D	SD
My superiors	SA	A	U	D	SD
The IS director	SA	A	U	D	SD
My subordinates	SA	A	U	D	SD

3   *By virtue of my roles in the organisation, the following people expect that I will use an EIS:*

My colleagues	SA	A	U	D	SD
My superiors	SA	A	U	D	SD
The IS director	SA	A	U	D	SD
My subordinates	SA	A	U	D	SD

4   *The use of EIS is generally considered in my organisation to be:*

Productive	SA	A	U	D	SD
Rational	SA	A	U	D	SD
Efficient	SA	A	U	D	SD
Effective	SA	A	U	D	SD

E.   Social Working Relationship and Organisational Environment in Relation EIS Use

The **social working relationships** among workers in an organisation may make it easier to use information systems. The **organisational environment** may also encourage people in the organisation to use information systems. Below are some statements about the social working relationships and the organisational environment in relation to EIS use. Please **circle** your response to each of these statements.

1   *The social working relationships between me and the following make it easier for me to use an EIS:*

	Strongly Agree	**Agree**	**Uncertain**	**Disagree**	**Strongly Disagree**
My colleagues	SA	A	U	D	SD
My superiors	SA	A	U	D	SD
The IS director	SA	A	U	D	SD
My subordinates	SA	A	U	D	SD

2   *The following aspects of my organisation encourage me to use an EIS:*

The organisational culture

SA	A	U	D	SD

The pace of changing business environment

SA	A	U	D	SD

The interactions among the business units

SA	A	U	D	SD

The power and politics of the organisation

SA	A	U	D	SD

The commitment of the organisation to EIS

SA	A	U	D	SD

F.   EIS Development and Management Processes

Some aspects of a **system's development processes** and the **management processes** associated with the system may encourage people in organisations to use the system. Below are some statements about aspects of development processes and management processes in relation to EIS use. Please **circle** your response to each of these statements.

1   *The following aspects of the EIS development processes in my organisation encourage me to use EIS:*

Strongly Agree	Agree	Uncertain	Disagree	Strongly Disagree

Executive sponsorship

SA	A	U	D	SD

My involvement and participation in the development

SA	A	U	D	SD

The availability of technical and other resources

SA	A	U	D	SD

The use of a development plan

SA	A	U	D	SD

Follow-ups made after the implementation of an EIS

SA	A	U	D	SD

2   *The following aspects of the EIS management processes in my organisation encourage me to use EIS:*

Management policies and rules

SA	A	U	D	SD

Data management

SA	A	U	D	SD

Availability of support

SA	A	U	D	SD

The availability and accessibility of the system

SA	A	U	D	SD

G.   Personal Information

We are requesting the following personal information about you that will help us in our analysis of the data we are collecting. No participant will be identified with any information provided. Please **tick** the appropriate box for your response.

1   Sex: ☐ Female   ☐ Male
2   Age: ☐ 18 - 25   ☐ 26 - 35   ☐ 36 - 45   ☐ 46 - 55   ☐ over 55
3   Highest educational level attained:
   ☐ School Cert.   ☐ Higher School Cert.   ☐ TAFE Qualification
   ☐ Bachelor Degree   ☐ Postgraduate Degree   ☐ Other *(please specify)*
4   Current position in organisation:
   ☐ Senior Manager   ☐ Middle-level Manager
   ☐ Lower-level Manager   ☐ Other *(please specify)*

Thank you once again for your time and effort in responding to this questionnaire. We appreciate very much your valuable contribution to this study. We will also appreciate it very much if you could provide us with any further comments about your use information systems for managerial work and about this survey.   Please provide your comments below or e-mail us on **george_ditsa@uow.edu.au**. *Thank you.*

Chapter IX

Culture and Anonymity in GSS Meetings

Moez Limayem
City University of Hong Kong, Hong Kong

Mohamed Khalifa
City University of Hong Kong, Hong Kong

John Coombes
City University of Hong Kong, Hong Kong

ABSTRACT

Anonymity is an important aspect of group support systems (GSS). However, as to the overall effectiveness of the use of anonymity, findings have been inconclusive. Some studies show positive effects in the number of ideas generated, quality of ideas, and uniqueness of ideas, whereas other studies show negative or neutral effects. An examination of social psychology literature indicates that the effect of public self-awareness on evaluation apprehension in different cultural groups may play a crucial role. Thus, social psychology and Hofstede's model of cultural differentiation are used in this chapter to explain the different effects of anonymity on the behavior of Hong Kong and Canadian groups during GSS sessions. It is hoped that understanding the effects of anonymity in different cultural contexts will better inform the design and facilitation of GSS in increasingly diverse global settings.

INTRODUCTION

Group support systems (GSS) are an increasingly popular means of aiding decision-making in a variety of organizational settings, by combining the computer, communication, and decision technologies to improve the decision-making process (Briggs, Nunamaker & Sprague, 1998). Such technologies make use of anonymity as a key tool to improve the quality of decisions (Nunamaker et al., 1991; Pinsonneault & Heppel, 1997; Postmes & Lea, 2000). However, with globalization, it is becoming increasingly important to adapt this tool to the cultural background of the organization or group that intends to use it effectively.

Group work is often inefficient and unproductive, suffering from a number of process losses. Inhibition and evaluation apprehension are considered as among the biggest problems that are known to hamper the active participation of group members. By allowing anonymous communication, GSSs are expected to reduce inhibition and evaluation apprehension, leading to process gains and better performance outcomes.

However, the findings from empirical studies into the use of anonymity in decision making show conflicting results (Pinsonneault et al., 1999; Chun & Park, 1998). It seems that anonymity is appropriate in some contexts, whereas it is not appropriate in others. The objective of this chapter, therefore, is to examine the effects of anonymity on specific cultural groups during activities using GSS, as this may help to clarify some of the inconsistencies in GSS research.

BACKGROUND

GSSs are usually employed with the intention to increase the effectiveness of groups by alleviating aspects of group dysfunction, and improving heuristics of individuals and groups when solving problems. Group dysfunction can be divided into process dysfunction and social dysfunction. Process dysfunction includes production blocking due to unequal participation, which is the result of unequal air time. Social dysfunctions may hinder group productivity through undesirable social processes that are present in the group. Examples of these are free riding, cognitive inertia, socialising, and domination due to status imbalance, groupthink, and incomplete analysis.

Managers spend a considerable part of their work in meetings and participating in group decisions. Anonymity is generally believed to create an environment that improves group participation, communication, and the objective evaluation of ideas, enhancing the productivity of groups and their decision-making process. Anonymity, as a distinct aspect of GSS, was expected to increase productivity by reducing the level of social or production blocking, increasing the number of interpersonal exchanges, and reducing the probability of any one member dominating the meeting. However, some studies, for example, George, Easton, Nunamaker and Northcraft (1990), found that anonymity had no effects on inhibition, group communications, and group performance. It is believed that these inconclusive results can be attributed to the fact that the effects of anonymity might depend on some contextual and group factors such as the degree of evaluation apprehension and conformance pressure experienced by group members (Pinsonneault & Heppel, 1997).

Issues, Controversies, and Problems

Quite a number of empirical findings have suggested that the use of anonymity and process structure in electronic brain-storming (EBS) generally promote a positive effect on the number of ideas generated (Jessup, Connolly & Galegher, 1990; Gallupe, Bastianutti & Cooper, 1991), and quality of ideas achieved in decision making (Zigurs & Buckland, 1998). However, the anonymity function inherent in multi-workstation GSS has been found to heighten conflict as members tend to communicate more aggressively because they tended to be more critical (Connolly, Jessup & Valacich, 1990; Jessup et al., 1990; Valacich et al., 1992), to have no effects on inhibition (Valacich, Dennis & Connoly, 1994; Valacich et al., 1992), and to have no effects on group performance (Valacich et al., 1994). Other empirical findings show that, in terms of effectiveness, nominal brainstorming may be equal to (Gallupe et al., 1991; Gallupe, Cooper & Bastianutti, 1990; Cooper, Gallupe, Pollard & Cadsby, 1998) or sometimes less (Valacich et al., 1994; Dennis & Valacich, 1993) than electronic brainstorming, indicating that at least as far as laboratory studies are concerned, empirical investigations have proved inconclusive. A summary of these results can be seen in Table 1.

The controversy surrounding the effectiveness of GSS has drawn attention to the practical usefulness of EBS over nominal brainstorming. Dennis & Valacich (1999) concluded that EBS is not likely to surpass nominal brainstorming for small groups, but with groups of over nine members, EBS offers clear performance benefits over nominal brainstorming as well as verbal brainstorming (Pinsonneault, Barki, Gallupe & Hoppen, 1999). Pinsonneault et al. (1999) concluded that existing theoretical and empirical evidence does not provide sufficient justification for the establishment of EBS' superiority over nominal brainstorming, even for large groups.

It is clear that the empirical findings of research into the effectiveness of GSS are unsatisfactory. Therefore, contextual issues, such as culture, will be required to make GSS research more meaningful and enable effective use of GSS.

Table 1. Studies on Anonymity and GSS (Adapted from Pinsonneault &
Heppel, 1998)

Study	Subjects	Independent variables	Findings
Connolly et al. (1990)	Students	Anonymity (no identification)	Number of comments (+) Quality of ideas (=) Criticalness (+)
Gallupe et al. (1997)	Students	Anonymity (no identification)	Number of unique ideas (+)
George et al. (1990)	Students	Anonymity (no identification)	Number of comments (=) Decision quality (=) Consensus (=) Inhibition (=) Equality of participation (=)
Hiltz et al. (1989)	Managers	Anonymity (pen name)	Number of comments (=)
Jessup & Tansik (1991)	Students	Anonymity (no identification)	Number of comments (=) Criticalness (=) Satisfaction (=) Equality of participation (=)
Jessup et al. (1990)	Students	Anonymity (no identification)	Number of comments (+) Criticalness (=)
Pinsonneault et al. (1997)	Students	Anonymity and established group with non-controversial topic	Number of unique ideas (-)
Shepherd et al. (1996)	Students	Anonymity and social comparison	Number of unique ideas (+)
Wilson & Jessup (1995)	Students/ Managers	Anonymity (no identification)	Number of comments (+) Number of unique ideas (+) Number of rare ideas (+)
Scott (2000)	Students	Anonymity	Number of Comments (=)

*(=) No effects of anonymity on the dependent variable; (i.e. the quality of ideas from
anonymous groups was not different from the quality of ideas generated by the non-
anonymous groups)*
*(+) Anonymity had a positive effect on the dependent variable (e.g. anonymous
groups generated a greater number of comments than the non-anonymous groups)*
*(-) Anonymity had a negative effect on the dependent variable (e.g. established
groups working on a non-controversial topic generated fewer comments when
working anonymously than when identified)*

Culture has been defined as the collective programming of the mind, which
distinguishes the members of one group or category of people from another
(Hofstede, 1991; Tan, Watson & Wei, 1995). Culture involves the beliefs, value
system, and norms of a given organization or society, and can exist at national,
regional, and corporate levels. In fact, even information systems theories and
research are heavily influenced by the culture in which they developed, and a theory

grounded in one culture may not be applicable in other countries (Tan et al., 1995; Triandis, 1987). The theories explaining the effects of GSS have come mainly from a North American perspective, and may need adjustment for appropriate explanation of the same phenomena in different contexts. Therefore, in order to incorporate a global dimension, theories and models that attempt to explain the effectiveness of technology will need to take into account the cultural background of the group being examined.

Culture was not specifically considered as an important dimension in the early studies of GSS. In fact, DeSanctis and Gallupe (1987) identified only three dimensions for the study of GSS appropriation: group size, member proximity, and task type. Watson, Ho and Raman (1994) later provided empirical support for the inclusion of culture as a dimension of GSS to add to DeSanctis and Gallupe's (1987) dimensions of group size, member proximity, and task type. Their study examined U.S. and Singaporean cultures using GSS, and the findings suggested that Singaporean groups tended to have a higher pre-meeting consensus and less change in consensus than the U.S. group. This may be explained with reference to the collectivist nature of Singaporean culture, as collectivists have a tendency towards group consensus (Meijas, Shepherd, Vogel & Lasaneo, 1997).

Tan et al. (1995) suggested ways that different cultures can be studied with other important variables such as task type and group size. The study focused on finding a way to examine the robustness of previous and current GSS research across different cultures and to add a cultural perspective to existing GSS knowledge. Hofstede's dimension of power distance was examined in relation to GSS and the possible impacts of GSS intervention in both high and low power distance countries were explored.

In studies examining only Singaporean groups (Tan et al., 1995), the use of GSS resulted in a decreased impact of status and normative influences on decision-making. These findings showed that change in consensus was greater in U.S. than Singaporean groups, and influence was more equal in Singaporean groups than U.S. groups. The higher power distance of Singaporean groups may explain the differences between these two meeting outcomes, and the study supports the proposition that GSS can overcome the effect of high power distance on group meetings.

A study comparing North American and Mexican groups participating in GSS sessions showed differences in terms of perception of consensus and satisfaction levels of group members (Meijas et al., 1997). U.S. and Mexican groups were also studied for GSS' effects on participation equity, with Mexican groups reporting higher participation equity levels than U.S. GSS groups (Meijas et al., 1997). It was suggested that high power distance cultures benefit from GSS, and that these findings indicate that culture has a significant bearing on crucial aspects of GSS meeting outcomes.

In sum, studies into the use of GSS by different cultures have indicated that there are differences between different cultures using GSS, and that cultural dimensions, such as those proposed by Hofstede (1991), have some relevance in explaining these differences. However, there is still uncertainty as to the specific impacts of culture on the performance of groups in anonymous GSS sessions, and therefore, more must be done to clearly understand how different cultures respond to anonymity.

Solutions and Recommendations

To better understand the impact of culture on anonymity in GSS, it is useful to conduct a study comparing two culturally different groups while using the anonymity function of GSS. Therefore, a cross-cultural laboratory experiment was undertaken to examine the effect of anonymity on the performance of homogeneous groups of managers in Canadian and Hong Kong cultures using anonymous GSS and non-anonymous GSS.

To provide a theoretical basis for this laboratory experiment, literature from social psychology and Hofstede's (1980) model of cultural differentiation are used as a conceptual framework for explaining effects of culture on anonymous GSS meetings. According to these areas of research, it is proposed that anonymity will have different effects depending on the culture of the group using the GSS.

In the social psychology literature, public self-awareness, involving accountability and awareness of one's own appearance in a group (Pinsonneault & Heppel, 1997), can explain how individuals from certain backgrounds and cultures can be strongly influenced by the evaluation of others. When public self-awareness is raised, concerns with social standards and conformity are also increased, and can lead to inhibition when participating during group meetings. Likewise, when punishment is not expected, individuals can become uninhibited (Pinsonneault & Heppel, 1997), leading to higher participation. Therefore, when public self-awareness is high, a correspondingly high level of anonymity will be required in order to liberate people from social evaluation. That is, when people fear social evaluation, disinhibition will occur only when they feel fully protected from it by anonymity. Thus, the Hong Kong and Canadian group's reaction to anonymity will depend on the degree of evaluation apprehension experienced by participants in the group interaction.

The Hong Kong Chinese culture is rooted in the social ethic advocated by Confucius (Oh, 1991). Unlike the North American culture, which promotes the importance of individuals (rather than the groups), Confucianism promotes status hierarchies, loyalty to people, norms of conformance, mutual obligation, and reciprocity. In the Hong Kong Chinese culture, group interactions tend to emphasize harmony, conformance, and reciprocal respect rather than openness and spontaneity. In this case, the participants will be inhibited from submitting comments that deviate from the norm (uncertainty avoidance), are against their superior's ideas (power distance), or may break harmony with the group (collectivism). Anonymity will enable the participants to submit ideas and comments without being identified, which may reduce the perceived threat of punishment. Therefore, as Hong Kong's culture usually exhibits these three influences, the Hong Kong group will benefit from anonymity as it causes disinhibition, leading to improved performance.

However, the Canadian group's culture, which frequently exhibits openness and spontaneity, will usually allow individuals to deviate from the norm. Therefore, there will be no significant level of inhibition in the Canadian GSS group, and anonymity will not significantly induce disinhibition. Consequently, there should be no positive effect on performance or perceived participation. Therefore, the Hong Kong groups will respond more positively to anonymity than the Canadian group.

The theory outlined above regarding culture's effects on GSS groups leads us to hypothesize:

H1: Anonymity will have a higher significant positive effect for Hong Kong groups than Canadian groups in terms of number of ideas generated.

H2: Anonymity will have a higher significant positive effect for Hong Kong groups than Canadian groups in terms of quality of ideas.

H3: Anonymity will have a higher significant positive effect for Hong Kong groups than Canadian groups in terms of perceived level of participation.

A 2X2 factorial design was used to test these hypotheses. As depicted in Figure 1, the two independent variables were *anonymity* and *culture*, resulting in four treatment conditions. The initial assignment of subjects to groups within their own culture was randomly determined.

In all, 144 subjects participated. The Canadian sample consisted of 72 subjects who were managers on a post-graduate course in information systems. The Hong Kong sample also consisted of 72 subjects who were managers on an identical post-graduate course in Hong Kong. In each location, 18 groups of four individuals each were given two business cases to analyze. All of the subjects performed under non-anonymous conditions for the first task and anonymously for the second task (see Figure 1).

The respective parts of the experiment took place in identical group decision support system laboratories at each site (Hong Kong and Canada), with tables

Figure 1. Research Methodology

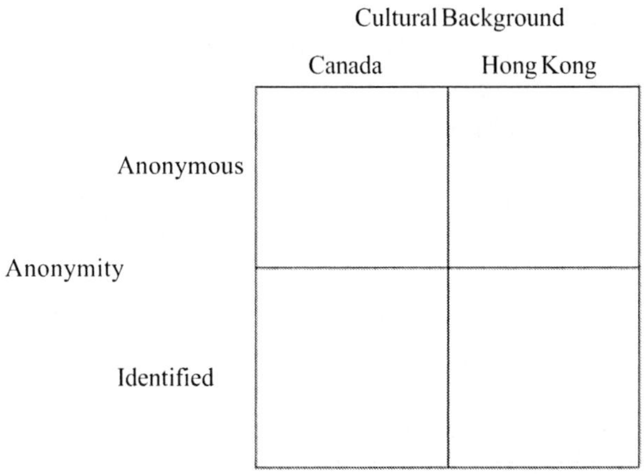

arranged in a U-shaped pattern, a computer terminal in front of each chair, and a projection facility at the front of the tables that constituted a public viewing screen. Each group member was first asked to read a background statement for the Case Analysis Tasks and to submit ideas and comments, based on his or her personal judgment. They then were given training in the use of the GSS. Group members then worked together using the GSS to analyze the first business case with submitted comments in anonymous conditions, and then the second case submitting comments in non-anonymous conditions. The instructions, facilitators, procedure, and conditions were identical for each culture. At the end of each analysis, each group member filled out a post-meeting questionnaire to measure the perceived level of participation during the group task. Thus, group performance was measured according to the number of ideas generated, idea quality, and perceived level of participation.

The results of the field studies verified our hypothesis. Anonymity was found to have more significant positive effects for Hong Kong groups. With anonymity, the performance of the Hong Kong group improved significantly in terms of number of contributions, quality of contributions, and perceived level of participation. No significant differences in the performance measures were found for the Canadian groups, except for the quality of contributions, which deteriorated with anonymity. A qualitative analysis of this negative effect revealed social loafing and lack of accountability as possible causes.

Future Trends

As we move into the world of virtual organizations and electronic commerce, the use of GSS by groups of different cultures becomes an irreversible trend. For practitioners or user of GSS, groupware applications, or other electronic communication systems, the implications are important. We cannot simply think of anonymity as a concept that is good or bad in itself. The use of anonymity should depend on the culture in which it is applied. For example, it is probably not a good idea to use anonymity in some cases where the culture of the group does not emphasize status hierarchies, conformance, mutual obligation, and reciprocity. In these situations, anonymity could even lead to negative outcomes such as social loafing due to the reduction in motivation and effort that occurs when individuals work in anonymous groups. Conversely, it may be beneficial to use anonymity for GSS-supported groups with cultures that normally exhibit higher levels of conformance pressure and evaluation apprehension.

In a broader sense, GSS and groupware designers and developers should pay special attention to the implementation of anonymity features. For example, they could make it easier for users to turn these features on and off to accommodate the culture of the groups using the systems. Finally, facilitators should remember that studies suggest that culture influences participation in the GSS environment (Tung & Quaddus, 2002). Therefore, facilitators should study the culture of the group using the technology before blindly using anonymity to generate or evaluate ideas.

Conclusion

Culture is clearly an important factor affecting a group's response to anonymity in the GSS context. Therefore, culture's influence on group structure and evaluation apprehension are important considerations for designers, facilitators, and users of GSS. Considering the lack of research on the effects of culture on GSS, further research in this field would appear to be worthwhile. This may be conducted on other interactions associated with cultures using the anonymous function of GSS. This research also has fascinating implications for technology's effect on other cultures. An interesting line of research for the future will be to isolate the relative impact of anonymity with different cultures engaged in different tasks and situations. The knowledge gained from this and other continuing studies, will assist in the effective application of GSS increasingly diverse and global contexts.

ACKNOWLEDGMENT

The work described in this chapter was fully supported by a grant from the Research Grants Council of the Hong Kong Special Administrative Region, China. (Project no. 9040564).

REFERENCES

Briggs, R.O., Nunamaker J.F., & Sprague, R.H. (1998). 1001 Unanswered Research Questions in GSS. *Journal of Management Information Systems, 14*(3), 3-21.

Chun, K. J., & Park, H. K. (1998). Examining the conflicting results of GDSS research. *Information and Management*, 33, 313 -325.

Connolly, T., Jessup, L.M., & Valacich, J.S. (1990). Effects of Anonymity and Evaluative Tone on Idea Generation in Computer-Mediated Groups. *Management Science, 36*(6), 689-703.

Cooper, W. H., Gallupe, R.B., Pollard, S., & Cadsby, J. (1998, April). Some liberating effects of anonymous electronic brainstorming. Small Group Research. *Thousand Oaks, 29*(2), 147-178.

Dennis, A.R., & Valacich, J.S. (1993). Computer brainstorms: More heads are better than one. *Journal of Applied Psychology, Washington, 78*(4), 531-538.

Dennis, A.R., & Valacich, J.S. (1999). Electronic brainstorming: Illusion and patterns of productivity. *Information Systems Research, 10*(4), 305-319.

DeSanctis, G. L., & Gallupe, R. B. (1987). A foundation for the study of group decision support systems. *Management Science, 33*(5) 589-609.

Gallupe, R.B, Bastianutti, L., & Cooper, W.H. (1991). Unblocking Brainstorms. *Journal of Applied Psychology*, 76, 137-142.

Gallupe, R.B, Cooper, W.H., & Bastianutti, L. (1990). *Why is electronic brainstorming more productive than traditional brainstorming?* An experimental study. Whistler, British Columbia, Canada: Proc. Admin. Sciences Association of Canada (Information Systems Division).

Gallupe, R.B., Cooper, W.H., Pollard, S., & Cadsby, J. (1997). *Electronic Brainstorming, anonymity and deviance*. Working Paper. Queen's University, Kingston Ontario.

George, J. F., Easton, G. K., Nunamaker, J. F. Jr., & Northcraft, G. B. (1990). A study of collaborative group work with and without computer-based support. *Information Systems Research, 1*(4), 394- 415.

Hiltz, S.R. (1978). Controlled Experiments with Computerized Conferencing: Results of a Pilot Study. American Society for Information Science. *Bulletin of the American Society for Information Science, 4*(5), 11-15.

Hiltz, S.R., Turoff, M., & Johnson, K. (1989) Experiments in group decision making: disinhibition, deindividuation, and group process in pen name and real name computer conferences. *Decision Support Systems, 5*(2), 217–232.

Hofstede, G. (1980). *Culture's Consequences: International Differences and Relaxed Values.* Beverly Hills, CA: Sage.

Hofstede, G. (1991). *Cultures and Organisations; Software of the Mind.* London: McGraw-Hill.

Jessup, L.M., & Tansik, D.A. (1991). Group Problem Solving in an Automated Environment: The Effects of Anonymity and Proximity on Group Process and Outcome with a Group Decision Support System. *Decision Sciences, 22*(2), 266-279.

Jessup, L.M., Connolly, T. & Galegher, J. (1990). The Effects of Anonymity on GDSS Group Process with an Idea-Generating Task. *MIS Quarterly, 14*(3), 312-321.

Jessup, L. M., Connolly, T., & Tansik, D.A. (1990). Toward a theory of automated group work: The deindividuating effects of anonymity. *Small Group Research, 21*(3), 333-348.

Mejias, R.J., Shepherd, M.M., Vogel, D.R. & Lasaneo, L. (1997). Consensus and perceived satisfaction levels: A cross cultural comparison of gss and non-gss outcomes within and between the United States and Mexico. *Journal of Management Information Systems*, 13, 137-161

Nunamaker, J.F., Dennis, A.R., Valacich, J.S., Vogel, D.R., & George, J.F. (1991). Electronic meeting systems to support group work. *Comm. ACM, 34*(7), 40-61.

Oh, T.K. (1991). Understanding managerial values and behaviour among the gang of four: South Korea, Taiwan, Singapore, and Hong Kong. *Journal of Management Development, 10*(2), 44-56.

Pinsonneault, A., & Heppel, N. (1997). Anonymity in Group Support Systems Research: A New Conceptualization, Measure, and Contingency Framework. *Journal of Management Information Systems, 14*(3), 89-108.

Pinsonneault, A., Barki, H., Gallupe, R.B., & Hoppen, N. (1999). Electronic Brainstorming: The Illusion of Productivity. *Information Systems Research, 10*(2), 216-130.

Postmes, T., & Lea, M. (2000). Social processes and group decision making: anonymity in group decision support systems. *Ergonomics, 43*(8), 1252-1274.

Scott, C.R. (2000). The impact of physical and discursive anonymity on group members' multiple identifications during computer-supported decision making. *Western Journal of Communication, 63*(4), 456-487.

Shepherd, M.M., Briggs, R.O., Riening, B.A., Yen, J. & Nunnamaker, J.F. (1996). Invoking social comparison to improve electronic brainstorming: Beyond anonymity. *Journal of Management Information Systems, 12*(3), 155-170.

Tan, B.C.Y., Watson, R.T, & Wei, K.K. (1995). National culture and group support systems: Filtering communication to damped power differentials. *European Journal of Information Systems,* 4, 82-92.

Triandis, H.C. (1987). Individualism and social psychological theory. In C. Kagitcihbasi, (Ed.), *Growth and Progress in Cross-Cultural Psychology* (pp. 78-83) Lisse, The Netherlands: Swets and Seitlinger.

Tung, L.L., & Quaddus, M.A. (2002). Cultural differences explaining the differences in results in GSS: implications for the next decade. *Decision Support Systems*, 33, 177-199.

Valacich, J. S., Dennis, A. R., & Connolly, T. (1994). Idea generation in computer based groups: a new ending to an old story. *Organizational behavior and Human Decision Processes,* 57(3), 448-468.

Valacich, J. S., Dennis, A. R., & Nunamaker, J. F., Jr. (1992). Group size and anonymity effects on computer-mediated idea generation. *Small Group Research,* 23, 49-73.

Valacich, J. S., Jessup, L. M., Dennis, A. R., & Nunamaker, J. F., Jr. (1992). A conceptual framework of anonymity in group support systems. *Group Decision and Negotiation*, 1, 219-241.

Watson, R.T., Ho, T.H., & Raman, K.S. (1994, October). A fourth dimension of group support systems. *Communications of the ACM,* 37(10), 45-55.

Wilson, J., & Jessup, L.M. (1995). A field experiment on GSS anonymity and group member status. *Proceedings of the 28th Annual Hawaii International Conference on Systems Sciences*, (pp. 212-221).

Zigurs, I., & Buckland, B. K. (1998, September). A theory of task/technology fit and group support systems effectiveness. *MIS Quarterly, 22*(3), 313-334.

Chapter X

Asynchronous and Distributed Multi-Criteria Decision Making Using a Web-Based Group Support System

Sajjad Zahir
University of Lethbridge, Canada

Brian Dobing
University of Lethbridge, Canada

ABSTRACT

A detailed model for designing a Web-based Multi-Criteria Group Support System (MCGSS) is presented. The model is based on the Analytic Hierarchy Process (AHP) and uses the intensity of preferences of group members rather than simple voting procedures. This approach offers several advantages over simple voting mechanisms, including a much richer picture of both individual and group positions and more equitable decision-making. A prototype system, with a user-friendly graphical user interface (GUI), has been developed and used to analyze an experimental group decision process over the Internet.

This permits a wider range of users, including those with limited typing skills, asynchronous communication across many time zones, and a larger number of participants than conventional systems. An agenda for further research is outlined.

INTRODUCTION

Groups have no doubt been making decisions since prehistoric times. From early diagrams in mud or sand, groups have moved to flip charts and erasable white boards. But these innovations have not really changed the process. Group Support Systems (GSS) offer the potential of new ways for groups to work together, but most reported usage is still for systems that simply supplement face-to-face meetings. The computer screen has replaced lines in the sand, and enforced structures (e.g., facilitators, agendas, brainstorming, and voting) that well-organized groups have always used. But there is no fundamental difference in the process.

Hammer (1990, p. 104) argues that we need to re-engineer the workplace, not simply automate existing procedures. "Instead of embedding outdated processes in silicon and software, we should obliterate them and start over." The same argument can be applied to the group decision-making process. There is a clear need for GSS that can effectively support larger groups working asynchronously. This type of system does not need to be more effective than face-to-face meetings to be valuable (Fjermestad & Hiltz, 1998). Because of the high costs of bringing people together, and the time lost in doing so, a system that allows them to be consulted remotely offers considerably more value than most GSSs studied so far.

Research in GSS has concentrated on two main streams: (1) the design and evaluation of features and technology; and (2) the effects of the technology on group decision outcomes and processes (Williams & Wilson, 1997). This paper belongs to the first of these categories, providing a more theoretically sound and richer voting procedure that should be well-suited to decision-making over the Internet. Our main focus is the design issues of the GSS, which must be addressed before more meaningful research on the decision-making process can be undertaken (Fjermestad & Hiltz, 1998). An Internet-based asynchronous GSS, allowing global participation and using the intensity of preferences, operates in a profoundly different way from traditional face-to-face meetings. The more sophisticated voting mechanism should help address the communication and cultural issues that face global virtual teams (Dubé & Paré, 2001). Participants can articulate their positions in considerably more detail, allowing consensus to be measured on more levels than simply the preferred alternative. Some future research opportunities are outlined in this paper.

BACKGROUND

A recent survey of GSS research (Fjermestad & Hiltz, 1998) found that the systems most frequently studied are quite unlike those needed by many organizations. Organizations are increasingly global and contain "virtual" components. Previous research has generally occurred in Decision Room environments using LANs, but time zones and the pressures of other commitments mean systems must run asynchronously on the Internet. But only about 10% of research has studied asynchronous meetings. The GSS must support larger groups, because participation is no longer limited by room size and more input is needed. But 80% of past research limited group size to 10 or fewer. The decisions they support are often complex, requiring many types of expertise and taking considerable time for deliberation. But over half of past studies imposed a one-hour maximum. This may work with student groups, whose members have little attachment to the decision being made. It does not seem realistic for organizational decision-making. In addition, most of the groups studied had no leader and no facilitator. This is also partly due to the types of student groups often studied. The interfaces used in the studies were often simple, limited by early personal computer technology to text-based interaction. Today, because of the wide variety of potential users, GSSs need graphical interfaces that are easier to use and follow standardized formats. Finally, most studies have used GSSs that permitted only simple voting procedures or none at all. (Some tasks involved allocation of funds to projects and thus permitted a limited form of proportional voting.) But these voting mechanisms are insufficient to adequately capture everyone's position with larger groups and complex issues.

A meta-analysis of GSS that considered virtual teams concluded that "distributed virtual teams made worse decisions than the control groups working without GSS" (Dennis & Wixom, 2002). They also found that GSS lowered satisfaction with the decision-making process. However, most of these studies involved simulated virtual teams composed of students. In many cases, the only practical alternative to virtual team decision-making is centralized decision-making. Satisfaction is also likely to be higher when participants recognize this and are also aware of how much it would cost, in dollar terms and in time and personal inconvenience, to hold face-to-face meetings. Furthermore, a recent study using graduate business students making a product development decision found that virtual teams were actually the most effective (Schmidt, Montoya-Weiss & Massey, 2001).

As noted, most GSSs offer a simple voting mechanism (Williams & Wilson, 1997) and this can be used to make decisions (majority rule). However, group leaders and facilitators are often more interested in knowing where members stand and, most critically, why. With face-to-face meetings, simple voting mechanisms are often sufficient. Participants likely know where most of their colleagues stand through their comments and body language, and can probably anticipate many positions before the meeting begins. As the number of participants increases, their backgrounds become more diverse, they represent a wider range of locations and business functions, and the media is less rich (i.e., no longer face-to-face). Obtaining a picture of where group members stand and how they might be clustered becomes more difficult. But this information is essential in guiding the decision-making process.

There is also an implicit assumption through much of the GSS literature that one-person, one-vote democracy is how organizations are run, or at least should be run. In practice, managers frequently seek input but do not feel bound by majority rule voting. They may not even want such voting to occur. Multicriteria voting greatly improves the quality of input and helps managers with the more important tasks of analyzing alternatives and building consensus around the one chosen.

Saaty (1989, 1990) introduced the idea of using the AHP to support group decisions. Many other authors have also investigated group decision-making within the same framework (e.g., Forman & Peniwati, 1996; Ramanathan & Ganesh, 1994; Zahir, 1999a; Zahir, 1999b). The AHP computes preference intensities for decision alternatives after aggregating preference measurements with respect to their chosen criteria. Aggregate preferences are no longer determined by counting the number of votes. AHP provides a richer data set that more fairly represents the positions taken by all parties, data that leaders and facilitators can use to facilitate the consensus building process. Traditional "yes-no" voting provides very little information on options except for the one chosen; there is no room for expressing the degree or intensity of preferences. In the conventional AHP, group aggregations can be done either by arithmetic mean or geometric mean approach (Saaty, 1990). But the geometric mean aggregation has been shown to violate the Pareto optimality condition, one of the axioms of Social Choice Theory (Ramanathan & Ganesh, 1994).

Zahir (1999a, 1999b) extended the AHP to the Euclidean vector space (VAHP). He proposes a simple aggregation procedure (based on vector addition of preferences) that, unlike the geometric mean approach of the conventional AHP, satisfies most Social Choice Theory axioms (Zahir, 1999c). The VAHP also enables us to compute group coherence in a straightforward manner (see Eq. 3 of Section 2). In this paper, we use the VAHP formalism just for the sake of illustration; we could have used the arithmetic mean method of aggregation within the traditional AHP group decision procedures without any loss of generality.

Some existing GSS already incorporate intensity of preferences. One of them is Team Expert Choice™(1999), based on the AHP, but designed for decision-making by a group connected by a local area network (LAN). These basic PC and LAN hardware configurations are now clearly dated (Mandviwalla & Gray, 1998). With increasing globalization and virtual organizations, groups need to meet and make decisions remotely. The Internet already has most of the building blocks in place or under development (e.g., video conferencing) and allows participants to be separated in space and/or time to a much greater degree than conventional LAN-based systems. Indeed, one of the limitations on GSS usage is that these systems simply supplement face-to-face meetings. The advantages of using them are not always clear (Chun & Park, 1998) and groups can easily revert to conventional meeting structures. Furthermore, past research has found that "positive effects of GSS use were noted more often in ... asynchronous settings" (Ramsden, 2000).

Thus, more research is needed to find ways to utilize the Internet to create effective distributed decision-making tools. Internet-based systems are still in the early stages. In a recent review of the status of Multi-Criteria Decision Support Systems (MCGSS), Internet-based systems were not mentioned (Siskos & Spyridakos, 1999). INSPIRE, a Web-based negotiation system shows the potential of this technology (Kersten & Noronha, 1999). However, INSPIRE is not designed for GSS applications. Web-HIPRE is a recent Web-based tool that provides a common platform for individual and group decision-making (Mustajoki & Hamalainen, 2000). It also facilitates multi-criteria decision analysis by implementing both multiattribute value theory (MAVT) (Keeney & Raiffa, 1976) and the Analytic Hierarchy Process (Saaty, 1980) along with its variations (Saaty, 1996). Our MCGSS is a prototype system in which we use the framework of VAHP for group aggregation and also present a visual aid for pairwise comparison of two objects using a pair of adjustable sliders. Using the VAHP facilitates computation of group coherence that is not supported in Web-HIPRE.

THE AHP AND GROUP PREFERENCES

The Web-based MCGSS presented here is designed so that users can enter their preferences in an easily understood and user-friendly interface through a Web browser (e.g., Netscape Communicator or Microsoft Internet Explorer). Easy-to-learn and user-friendly interfaces are essential if GSSs are to become more commonly used in organizational decision-making. While Team EC™ uses an aggregation rule that asks users to enter the ratio of comparisons directly, MCGSS uses more intuitive slider controls. The system uses intensity of preferences as defined by the VAHP. The proposed system will not only collect more detailed attitudes from participants and aggregate them, but also incorporate tools for sophisticated analysis that should help produce a better understanding of individual and subgroup positions. The result is a multi-criteria decision model that enables and enhances communication, information sharing, and consensus building among group participants in distributed settings.

We assume that our group typically consists of five to 20 members, covering the sizes of most groups studied to date (Fjermestad & Hiltz, 1998), who have sufficient time to share information and negotiate positions. However, the MCGSS has no absolute limit on the number of participants. Although there is no guarantee that the group will arrive at a consensus, the decision-making environment and the time given are expected to bring some level of "homogeneity" to their knowledge and information base in order to move towards that end. Only a limited level of "homogeneity" can be achieved through a group discussion process, because the true information base of an individual includes lifelong experiences. Each individual processes information and synthesizes knowledge in a unique way, as characterised by each individual's value system, so each member can hold varying preferences for the decision alternatives spanning the decision space.

In our system, the aggregation of group preferences is done according to the Euclidean version of the AHP (Zahir, 1999a, 1999c). The VAHP provides a simple construct to define groups of individuals in the context of any particular decision problem. The model is outlined below.

Let $\mathbf{V}^i$ ($i = 1 \ldots N$) be the grand preference vector of the ith individual in a group consisting of N decision-makers. The preference vectors are defined in an n-dimensional alternative space such that $(V_j^i)^2$ is the aggregate intensity of preference (i.e., relative priority) of the ith voter assigned to the jth decision alternative, $j = 1$, ..., n. Each individual is assumed to compute his or her own hierarchy, which will depend on the set attributes or criteria chosen by each voter, although everybody will decide among the same set of decision alternatives. The judgements (i.e., the preference operators) can be different and are independently constructed.

The thinking patterns of group members can be roughly grouped into one of three categories:
1.   All of them think alike; i.e., we have a consensus.
2.   The members' opinions vary, but with most clustered into two or more subgroups.
3.   Members' opinions differ considerably so there is little consensus.

Groups of the first type can successfully use any voting mechanism, if one is even needed. But for groups in the second category, the MCGSS can provide considerable insight into both the level of consensus and also the key issues that are preventing a fuller consensus. For groups in the third category, the voting results are not very meaningful but the underlying data provides more insight into the areas of disagreement.

We compute the group preferences using vector addition; i.e., $\mathbf{G}^k = \sum_{i=1}^{N} \mathbf{V}^i$.

$\hat{\mathbf{G}}^k$ is the normalized unit vector along such that:

$$\hat{G}_j = \frac{\sum_{i=1}^{N} V_j^i}{\sqrt{\sum_{j}^{n} \left(\sum_{i=1}^{N} V_j^i \right)^2}} \tag{1}$$

This guarantees $(\hat{\mathbf{G}})^T \hat{\mathbf{G}} = 1$. The preference for alternative i for the group is:

$$\Pi_i = (\hat{G}_i)^2 \tag{2}$$

such that $\sum_i \Pi_i = 1$. Hence, Π_i is the relative intensity of preference of the entire group corresponding to alternative i. Thus, the most preferred alternative has the maximum of all Π_i.

The coherence of the group is given by:

$$r = <\mathbf{V}^{i} \cdot \mathbf{V}^{j}> = <(\mathbf{V}^i)^T \mathbf{V}^j> \quad (i,j = 1.. N, i \neq j)$$

$$= \frac{2}{N(N-1)} \sum_{\substack{i=1, j=1 \\ i \neq j}}^{N} v^i v^j \tag{3}$$

The intensity-based decision process allows us to clearly picture where members stand on all alternatives and why. This information is much more meaningful than simple vote counts. The MCGSS enables each decision-maker to select his or her decision hierarchy, enter his or her judgements into the pairwise comparison matrices, and have his or her grand preference vector calculated and saved in the database. Then, the "facilitator" will use the analysis tools to compute the final aggregate intensity of group preferences (i.e., Π_i) before presenting the collective views to the group.

OVERVIEW OF THE MULTI-CRITERIA GROUP SUPPORT SYSTEM (MCGSS)

Conventional GSSs include tools to facilitate processes such as exchange of information, brainstorming, consensus building, and negotiations. In the MCGSS, the exchange of information takes place over the Internet or Intranet using e-mail, video-conferencing, and advanced data/information sharing tools. Consistent with the simplicity and user-friendliness of typical graphical interfaces (e.g., the Windows or Apple operating systems), we propose that users enter the relative preference for each alternative via a "bar graph" (using a slider control), for which the height of each bar (which can be dragged by the mouse to any height within the control) would represent the preference assigned to each alternative. Although every individual will provide relative overall preferences for the same decision alternatives, not everyone will arrive at that preference using the same number and type of attributes. Hence, the system must allow each decision-maker to select the relevant set of criteria reflecting their values and to make judgments with respect to various value-based criteria. Such a set of value-based criteria can be agreed upon prior to a group choice process in consultation with the participants of the group.

The system has two types of users and, hence, two types of interface and dialogues. The decision-makers (i.e., the group members) are the main users and the system enables them to make, enter, and record their preferences about a given list of decision alternatives evaluated under a selected set of criteria. They first select the criteria from a given set reflecting their personal values and beliefs. The decision-makers then enter their pairwise judgments regarding the alternatives using the slider controls mentioned above. They also perform a pairwise comparison of the criteria they chose to judge the alternatives. Although all members consider the same alternatives, their choice of criteria can vary. Once they are confident about their preferences, they submit the data for recording. The other user is the group "facilitator" who analyzes the database of individual preferences using aggregating methodologies. The facilitator also reports the final results of any group choice process. The final results show the intensity of group preferences assigned to each alternative.

The outline of the MCGSS conceptualised in this paper is preliminary in nature and further research is needed before a full-fledged version is developed. We have developed a prototype system and this paper presents the results of an experiment involving a public policy decision scenario. In addition to those features in the prototype, the data security, identity verification, data storage, computation, aggregation and display of results are all important, required components of the system.

THE ARCHITECTURE OF THE SYSTEM

A traditional Group Decision Support System (GDSS) (DeSanctis & Gallupe, 1989; Gray & Nunamaker, 1989; Sauter, 1997) integrates two concepts: Groupware and DSS. The Groupware component takes care of such functions as information exchange among the group members. Because the MCGSS is Internet-based, synchronous and asynchronous exchanges can occur through e-mail, discussion groups, and chat rooms. Files (documents, data, analysis, etc.) can be attached. The DSS component, particularly the alternative selection process, was designed with two interfaces, one for the members of the group and the other for the facilitator.

The modular structure of the MCGSS architecture is shown in Figure 1. The major DSS components are Databases, Model Bases, and Dialogues. The supporting components are a DBMS (Data Base Management System) and an MBMS (Model Base Management System) that provide the links between the Dialogues and the Database and Model Base respectively. Group members and the facilitator access the system through two different dialogues or interfaces. Each component is described in further detail below.

Database

The voting preferences database may or may not be the same database that contains data specific to the task. One table contains information about each decision-maker belonging to the group. Each decision-maker will have a unique ID along with other pertinent information such as postal address, e-mail address, phone number, position in the organization, etc. Other tables contain the data needed by the VAHP model to calculate decision-makers' grand preference vectors. This data is entered through the user dialog.

Model Base

The model base of the MCGSS consists of three types of models. The VAHP/AHP model is accessed by decision-makers while entering their relative preferences for the criteria and the decision alternatives subject to each criterion. For each

Figure 1. Components of the MCGSS

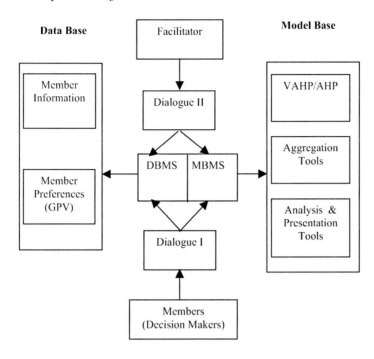

Legend:
GPV: Grand Preference Vector (part of VAHP)
MBMS: Model Base Management Systems

member, this model will compute the preference vectors, aggregate them with the criteria weights, and finally calculate each member's grand preference vector. The squares of the elements of this vector are the aggregate relative priorities of the decision alternatives according to the voter being considered. This information will be utilized by the second model base that consists of tools for group aggregation (see equations 1 to 3), leading to the final intensity of preferences for the decision alternatives as the verdict of a group decision process. Other analysis tools can generate further results if desired.

Dialogues

The system provides two dialogues, one for the group members and the other for the facilitator. Members enter their preferences through the Member Dialogue discussed in the next section. The Facilitator's Dialogue is similar to other GSS, allowing access to the databases and model bases as needed. This dialog includes "switchboard" screens that provide quick and simple access to various results from the analysis. In some situations, the group might also prefer that everyone have access to some (or even all) of the data normally available only to the facilitator. The system should be able to support any degree of openness.

A CONCEPTUAL DESIGN OF THE USER INTERFACE

The user interface is the key to usability, and this is most applicable to the group member interface in a GSS system. Group members may be anyone in the organization, and occasionally from outside the organization. Their technical skills and, in particular, their typing skills can range from those of beginners to very experienced users. The member interface has been designed with this in mind. A very easy-to-learn and easy-to-use interface can have a tremendous impact on the eventual success of the system.

One of the main interface design issues is determining the mechanism by which members express their judgments while comparing any two objects (i.e., criteria or alternatives). In decision-making applications of the AHP, decision-makers compare only reasonably similar alternatives because humans cannot differentiate one object from another by a factor greater than nine (Saaty, 1980). Thus, the ratio scale suggested by Saaty (1980, 1990) takes values from one to nine and their reciprocals. When members have a widely varying set of objects to compare, they must be regrouped into more homogeneous clusters, with one common object being shared between two clusters. For the type of group decisions we are interested in, the alternatives are already known and the group members must now compare them with each other. With AHP, decision-makers enter the judgments into a pairwise comparison matrix using either numerical or verbal modes. In the latter case, verbal judgments are translated into numeric values according to the following suggested scheme (Saaty, 1996):

Finer judgments falling within any two consecutive points of the scale can also be accommodated. One advantage of the verbal mode is that it can be implemented through voice-recognition technology. However, distinctions among the different text labels and the levels they represent may not be as clear as they should be.

For the MCGSS, preferences are entered through the slider controls described earlier. Bar heights can be adjusted dynamically by dragging the mouse or some similar device. The heights of the bars are measured in pixels and thus present an almost continuous variation. However, the minimum height cannot be zero, as division by zero cannot be permitted in the model. Therefore, the minimum height of any preference bar will be set to h_0 pixels. If h_1 and h_2 are the heights of two side-by-side bars selected by a group member while comparing any two objects, then

Figure 2. Opening Screen

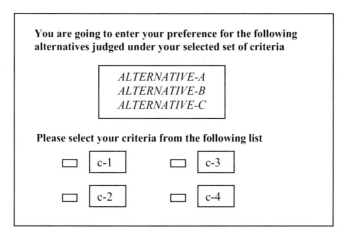

the corresponding entry p_{12} into the preference operator **P** will be given by $(h_1/h_2)^{1/2}$ (Zahir, 1999a). This may lead to situations where the value of the ratio exceeds nine. In that case, we suggest that whenever a judgment exceeds nine, we assign a large value (H_0) to the ratio in order to reflect an overwhelming preference. The reciprocals will be interpreted likewise. It is well-known (Saaty, 1990; Zahir, 1999a) that in the limit $H_0 \rightarrow \infty$ we get "Boolean" results that very much mimic "yes-no" voting results.

Another matter that is important to the decision-maker is "consistency." A simple example would be transitive consistency – if alternative A is ranked higher than B and B is ranked higher than C, then A should also rank higher than C. The system can report back to the decision-makers about the consistency of their judgments, giving them an opportunity to review their preference inputs, and can also report to the facilitator. Ideally, inconsistent decisions will be avoided and, if not, easily detected. Based on these discussions, a sequence of possible dialogues for an imaginary decision-maker is presented below. Only the most important components of the dialogue are included; other parts can be added as desired or needed. Figure 2 is the opening screen.

The user can select as many of the criteria as desired (or none at all) by clicking in the choice boxes adjacent to the left of each criteria stub. If no criteria are selected, the decision alternatives (i.e., the candidates) will be judged under the goal objective called "best alternative." This leads us to the screen shown in Figure 3.

Once a criterion stub (in Figure 3) is clicked, another window (Figure 4) opens up with stubs for each pairwise comparison to be made. Having n alternatives means $n(n-1)/2$ comparison data have to be entered for each criteria. A matching preference bar window opens up whenever the user clicks on any of the stubs in

Figure 3.   Selecting Criteria for Entering Relative Preferences for the Alternatives

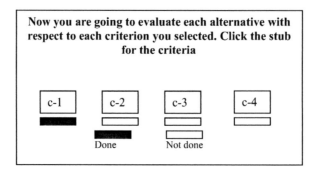

Figure 4. In each window, there are also buttons to accept the input or cancel the screen and return to the previous one.

The bars in each preference window are different colors with appropriate labels. Both the bars should have the same width, so their relative heights imply the relative dominance of one to the other. If desired, all the preference windows can remain open at the same time to give users a complete picture of their judgments. Another screen similar to the one in Figure 4 allows users to enter relative preferences for their selected criteria. This screen generates the weights for the criteria. As discussed earlier, the preference of Alternative-A with respect to Alternative-B is the ratio of the heights of the corresponding bars and is automatically determined by the system using the slider control positions.

IMPLEMENTATION OF A PROTOTYPE SYSTEM

Although the prototype system developed is based on the conceptual design described above, we made some simplifications in the screen design for the prototype version. Instead of having a sequence of screens (Figure 2 to 4), we combine them into one with multiple segments. The prototype system is designed and implemented to perform an experiment using a particular decision scenario as presented in Figure 5.

While the decision statement is arguably biased, this does not affect its use in this situation. Indeed, decision-makers are often faced with leading statements that they can either accept or question. The important aspect of case is that it is a public policy issue relevant to the university community. A group of 10 students was formed as part of the experiment using the prototype system. The hierarchy of the decision process is shown in Figure 6. This was also given in the Web page to enable the users to structure their decision-making exercise. The system (called Decision

Figure 4: Selecting Pairwise Comparison Options for Criterion c-1

**You are now going to pairwise compare the alternatives
in respect of Criteria:**   c-1

1	2	3

Alternative-A   Alternative-A   Alternative-B
vs   vs   vs
Alternative-B   Alternative-C   Alternative-C

*< to enter the relative preference information about the candidates,
please click stub 1, 2 or 3>*

Forum) was developed in Java and posted as an applet on one of the authors' Web sites. This provided group members with easy access while taking part in the experiment. The decision scenario and instructions for using the system were also given online.

The members of the group were allowed to exchange information among themselves via e-mail and they also accessed information about vending machines on the Web. The author acted as the facilitator as members' responses were forwarded to the author as e-mail. Each member had an ID that was required for the system to forward the data to the facilitator. The ID was only used for tagging members' responses. Both the intensity-based preferences and the direct voting responses were recorded for each participant. Figures 7 and 8 show some relevant snap shots of the user interface. As can be seen from Figure 7, group members used scroll bars to express their relative preferences about any two objects being compared. Then, the final aggregate preferences for each user are displayed along with the overall consistency index in both graphical and numeric forms.

The consistency index allows users to re-evaluate their pairwise comparisons before they finally choose to record them. Section B (Figure 8) of the interface deals with direct voting and is enabled using a standard HTML form. Each member of the group received an introduction to AHP and Decision Forum before they entered their preferences. However, in the prototype system, the set of criteria was the same for all in order to keep the system simple. For the same reason, the successive windowing feature of the interface was ignored; all were integrated into one screen. First, users had to pairwise compare the criteria (see Figure 7). Since there are only two criteria, only one comparison (hence two comparison bars) was needed. Then, under each criterion, three comparisons (involving three pairs of comparison bars) were needed. Finally, pressing the button 'Calc. Aggregate' produced the aggre-

Figure 5. The Decision Scenario of the Experiment

Vending Machines: Our Choices

Vending Machines (VM) are all over. They sell items like candy, drinks and condiments. Except drinks, they can be called junk foods. Still we use them occasionally and buy them frequently at exorbitant prices. Their presence encourages their use and naturally generates a lot of trash. Vending Machines are convenient but their use comes with a cost that includes inflated prices, pollution and unhealthy habits. Let us assume that as a group we have an option to make a choice. The choices are:

1) Have Vending machines without any control on them **(NoControlVM),**

2) Have Vending Machines with controls on the prices, locations and items **(ControlledVM)**

3) No Vending Machines (any type) on campus **(NoVM).**

You have to judge them under two criteria: ***Net Cost*** and ***Convenience***.

In Section A, you judge the alternatives (i.e., the choices) under each criteria through pairwise comparisons using a visual scale, then the system gives you the intensity of preferences for each choice after aggregating the inputs from a user. The individual choices are then taken into account to obtain a social choice, i.e., the best choice elected by a group.

In Section B, you will simply vote for the best choice.

Figure 6. Hierarchy of the Decision Scenario

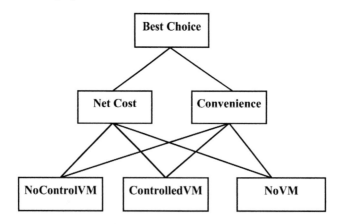

Figure 7. Section A - Decision Forum© Screen for AHP-Based Intensity of Preferences

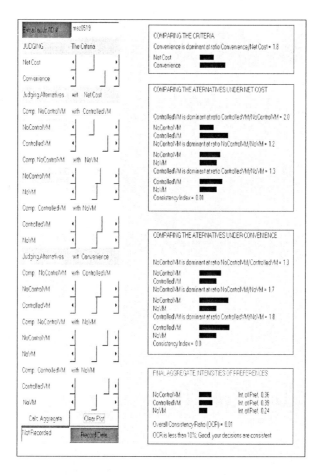

gate intensity of preferences in both numeric and graphical form. The "Clear Plot" and "Record Data" buttons erased the final output and sent the data to the facilitator for recording.

ANALYSIS OF THE DATA: COMPARISON WITH DIRECT VOTING

Table 1 shows the data of the grand preference vectors of 10 participants in the group decision experiment. The indices 1, 2, 3 correspond to 'NoControlVM' (NC), 'ControlledVM' (CV), and 'NoVM' (NV) respectively.

Figure 8: Decision Forum© Screen for Voting Preferences

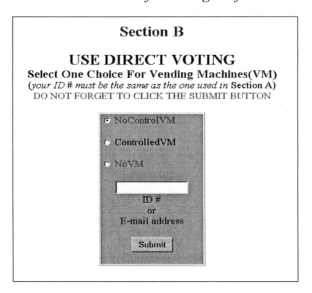

Then, the group aggregation rule of (1) gives the normalized group preference vector $\hat{\mathbf{G}}$:

$$\hat{\mathbf{G}} = \begin{bmatrix} \hat{G}_1 \\ \hat{G}_2 \\ \hat{G}_3 \end{bmatrix} = \begin{bmatrix} .5717 \\ .6057 \\ .5534 \end{bmatrix}$$

We used MS Excel as the analysis tool (see Figure 1). The intensities of preferences Π_i are calculated using (2). They are:

Table 1. Grand Preference Vectors of the Group Members ($V_1^2 + V_2^2 + V_3^2 = 1$)

DM #	Vote	V1	V2	V3
1	CV	0.5568	0.7348	0.3873
2	CV	0.5196	0.6782	0.5196
3	CV	0.3317	0.6557	0.6782
4	NC	0.9592	0.2000	0.2000
5	CV	0.5385	0.7000	0.4690
6	CV	0.4690	0.7141	0.5196
7	CV	0.4796	0.4583	0.7483
8	CV	0.5745	0.5916	0.5568
9	NC	0.6928	0.5657	0.4472
10	CV	0.3606	0.5099	0.7810

$$\Pi_1 = (\hat{G}_1)^2 = 0.3269, \quad \Pi_2 = (\hat{G}_2)^2 = 0.3669, \quad \Pi_3 = (\hat{G}_3)^2 = 0.3062$$

That means the relative priorities of the entire group as a whole are about 32% for NC, 37% for CV, and 30% for NV. On the other hand, if we count the votes, NC received 20%, CV received 80%, and NV received 0%. The coherence of the group can be calculated using (3) as follows:

$$\rho = <\mathbf{V}^i \cdot \mathbf{V}^j> = <(\mathbf{V}^i)^T \mathbf{V}^j> \quad (i,j = 1.. \ 10, \ i \neq j)$$

$$= \frac{1}{45}(\mathbf{V}^1 \cdot \mathbf{V}^2 + \mathbf{V}^1 \cdot \mathbf{V}^3 + ... + \mathbf{V}^2 \cdot \mathbf{V}^3 + ... + \mathbf{V}^8 \cdot \mathbf{V}^{10} + \mathbf{V}^9 \cdot \mathbf{V}^{10}) = .9107$$

We used a module written in C++ to compute the coherence. This module is a part of the model base in Figure 1. The prototype system does not integrate all model bases. Therefore, we used the MS Windows multitasking feature as the interface to integrate Decision Forum, MS Excel, MS Outlook and the module to compute the coherence. As expected, the experiment shows that intensity-based procedures produce a "softer" winning picture than the voting method. In addition, the MCGSS provides information about the coherence of the group. Thus, it may be a better method for consensus building.

POTENTIAL USES OF THE SYSTEM AND FUTURE RESEARCH

While groups are called on to make a wide variety of decisions, our primary interest is in strategic decision-making by smaller groups (five to 20 members) within organizations. These decisions generally offer a wide range of possible alternatives and the participants typically come from different functional backgrounds (e.g., production, accounting, marketing) and possibly geographic locations as well. Improved strategic decision-making can easily offer sufficient benefits to justify the costs. Thus, the key issue is whether the MCGSS can actually improve the decision-making process not so much over face-to-face meetings, which are usually impractical, but rather over some less structured method of obtaining input from a variety of stakeholders.

The MCGSS allows us to classify groups based on two dimensions as shown in Table 2. The first dimension is the level of consensus on the decision itself, which all voting mechanisms gather (although often imperfectly). The second dimension is the level of consensus on the underlying factors that support the decision. This is a dynamic classification system, with groups moving among the quadrants over time.

We illustrate how this model works by considering an IS Project Committee, responsible for approving project proposals, allocating resources, and monitoring their progress. Few organizations have the resources to handle all system requests. Moreover, the proposals may well include some overlap (where different proposals seek to address a problem in similar ways) and some conflict (where the proposed systems would move the organization in different directions).

The MCGSS provides some benefits over simple voting procedures for all groups, regardless of quadrant. Consider first the "Shared Values" quadrant, where group members agree on the decision criteria but not the decision itself. For example, there could be widespread agreement that improved customer service is the most critical issue, but no agreement on what system strategy would best address it. Simple voting would show only the disagreement, while the criteria data collected from the VAHP procedure would more clearly show the substantial level of consensus on the customer service issue. Group leaders can use this information to build on areas of consensus or to address areas of conflict.

Groups in the "Coalition" quadrant have achieved a reasonable level of consensus on the decision that would be easily demonstrated by a simple vote. However, the criteria data would show that the consensus does not have a common base. Changing circumstances may cause some members to withdraw their support. While this can also affect groups with True Consensus, they will tend to move more as a group because their underlying values are consistent. Coalitions can be fragile, leading to problems during implementation.

Once a group has achieved "True Consensus" they have less to gain from the MCGSS, except for the reassurance that they are in full agreement and not a potentially temporary coalition. The voting procedure adopted is unlikely to impact the decision at this point, but it may have played an important role in helping the group arrive at this state.

Table 2. Decision Consensus Matrix

	Decision Alternative Consensus	
Criteria Consensus	Low	High
Low	No Consensus	Coalition
High	Shared Values	True Consensus

Finally, groups in the "No Consensus" quadrant will be aware of the sharp divisions among members that apply to both the decision and the criteria for making it. No voting procedure is going to resolve the level of conflict that is present, but MCGSS will provide members with a fuller and deeper understanding of where the conflicts are and what subgroups might possibly exist.

For traditional face-to-face groups, members can perceive the degree of consensus through the ongoing discussions. Simple body language (nods, frowning, etc.) lets everyone know where people stand. But for distributed groups interacting asynchronously over the Internet, assessing consensus on criteria can be much more difficult. The data collected by the MCGSS could be more helpful in this situation. In particular, research is needed to measure the utility and effectiveness of the MCGSS with "virtual teams" versus "face-to-face" teams (Warkentin, Sayeed & Hightower, 1997).

The use of VAHP rather than simple voting suggests several interesting research questions. First, will group members (and particularly group leaders) interpret the results correctly? As shown in the example in Section 7, simple voting can produce a much higher apparent preference (80%) than VAHP (37%). We would expect that most people overestimate the degree of consensus obtained through simple voting, while perhaps underestimating the consensus produced through VAHP. An experiment could be designed where subjects watch tapes of group decision-making exercises and are then asked to estimate both simple vote and VAHP results.

Another issue is how group members will react to an 80% simple vote result compared to a 37% VAHP result. We would expect the 80% result to seem decisive and be quickly adopted as the final decision. But a 37% consensus may leave the group much less comfortable. The results of this are difficult to predict. Additional time could be wasted in an effort to raise the 37%, but even if the dissenters join the majority the consensus could remain under 50%. Alternatively, recognizing that the alternatives are not widely separated might encourage further debate and result in a different (perhaps better) solution. Groups given both pieces of information might initially find them confusing and even contradictory. Experiments could measure the effect of voting methods on both decision-making time and group satisfaction. Comparing decision quality is obviously desirable, but usually impractical given the nature of problems that are addressed by groups.

Second, and related to the first question, will people accept a voting mechanism that they do not fully understand? Tabulating votes is a very simple process and easily verified if need be. Will participants accept the preference scores? Or will they revert to simple voting? How will participants react to the more elaborate voting process? The process will require more time and effort, which again could be good (forcing more rigorous thinking) and bad (taking longer to reach the same outcome). How should the richer data set be used and who should have access to it? Should the analysis be left only to the facilitator or should everyone be able to make his or her own interpretation of the results? Group members will need to trust the process and, if the VAHP results seem contrary to their perceptions, this could be difficult to achieve.

Regarding the user interface, experimental results regarding the proposed visual mode of eliciting preference judgments are not available in the literature. Therefore, further research is needed for its validation. The positioning, size, and orientation of the bars (i.e., horizontal vs. vertical) should be considered. In addition, we need further research to determine what kind of screen management (multiple windows versus successive screens on a single window) will be more acceptable to users. Is this form of data entry faster than typing numerical scores? Do the entries better reflect the feelings of the group members? Are there cultural differences that need to be considered?

Finally, a different research approach is needed to study distributed GSS. There is limited value in comparing performance to face-to-face meetings, because the latter are so often impractical. Instead, researchers may wish to acknowledge that global teams need an Internet-based GSS and focus on the desired features and interface.

CONCLUSIONS

We have built a Web-based MCGSS that enables users to enter their intensity of preferences using a visual interface. The underlying decision model is the Analytic Hierarchy Process (AHP). The result is a more enriched input that uses the power of computers, the ease of use of a Graphical User Interface (GUI), and the global reach of the Internet to provide decision-making tools that really do offer much more power than diagrams in the sand.

This system takes advantage of Internet technology and enables a novel procedure to aggregate intensities of preferences. A new visual scale for expressing relative comparative judgments has been proposed for the VAHP/AHP, a multi-criteria decision-making tool providing the model base for the MCGSS. The scale was implemented using controls available through a standard Web browser. The prototype system was used in a group decision-making scenario and the results have been presented.

Once a system like this is made fully functional, we have to determine how acceptable such a system will be to corporate users. How effective the MCGSS will be and how the users will react to the new cognitive issues associated with the system will be interesting research issues. Will it reduce the time taken by group members to come to a final decision? Will it change the path or process they follow? Will it increase or decrease group conflicts? This may depend upon the skill of the facilitator, who will now have much more data with which to work in locating conflict and understanding their underlying causes. "Yes-no" voting systems are simple and allow easier manipulation of voting results. But the MCGSS requires more detailed input from participants, making it harder to manipulate the final outcome. MCGSS is guided more by analytic thinking than gut feelings. Thus, changing the voting procedure can have profound consequences for Internet-based GSS systems.

REFERENCES

Chun, K.J. & Park, H.K. (1998). Examining the conflicting results of GDSS research. *Information & Management, 33*(6), 313-325.

Dennis, A.R. & Wixom, B.H. (2002). Investigating the Moderators of the Group Support System Use with Meta-Analysis. *Journal of Management Information Systems, 18*(3), 235-257.

DeSanctis, G. & Gallupe, B. (1989). Group Decision Support Systems: A New Frontier. In R.H. Sprague, Jr. and H.J. Watson (Eds.), *Decision Support Systems: Putting Theory into Practice*, 2nd ed. (pp. 259-271). Englewood Cliffs, NJ: Prentice Hall.

Dubé, L. & Paré, G. (2001). Global Virtual Teams. *Communications of the ACM, 44*(12), 71-73.

Fjermestad, J. & Hiltz, S.R. (1998). An Assessment of Group Support Systems Experimental Research: Methodology and Results. *Journal of Management Information Systems, 15*(3), 7-149.

Forman, E.H. & Peniwati, K. (1996). Aggregating Individual Judgements and Priorities with the Analytic Hierarchy Process. *Proceedings of the Fourth International Symposium on the Analytic Hierarchy Process* (pp. 383-391). Vancouver, Canada.

Gray, P. & Nunamaker, J.F. (1989). Group Decision Support Systems. In R.H. Sprague, Jr. and H.J. Watson (Eds.), *Decision Support Systems: Putting Theory into Practice*, 2nd ed. (pp. 272-287). Englewood Cliffs, NJ: Prentice Hall.

Hammer, M. (1990). Reengineering Work: Don't Automate, Obliterate. *Harvard Business Review, 68*(4), 104-112.

Keeney, R.L. & Raiffa, H. (1976). *Decisions with Multiple Objectives: Preferences and Value Tradeoffs*. New York: John Wiley & Sons.

Kersten, G. & Noronha, S. (1999). Negotiation via the World Wide Web: A Cross-cultural Study of Decision Making. *Group Decision and Negotiation, 8*(3), 251-279.

Mandviwalla, M. & Gray, P. (1998). Is IS Research Relevant? *Information Resources Management, 11*(1), 7-15.

Mustajoki, J. & Hamalainen, R.P. (2000). Web-HIPRE: Global Decision Support by Value Tree and AHP Analysis. *INFOR, 38*(3), 208-220.

Ramanathan, R. & Ganesh, L.S. (1994). Group Preferences Aggregation Method Employed in AHP: An Evaluation and an Intrinsic Process for Deriving Members' Weightages. *European Journal of Operational Research, 79*(2), 249-265.

Ramsden, D. (2000). Groups that Work Apart: Implications of Computer-Mediated Communications. *Proceedings of the ASAC-IFSAM 2000 Conference, 21*(4), 174-188. Montreal, Canada.

Saaty, T.L. (1980). *The Analytic Hierarchy Process*. New York: McGraw-Hill.

Saaty, T.L. (1989). Group Decision Making and the AHP. In B.L. Golden, E.A. Wasil & P.T. Harker (Eds.), *The Analytic Hierarchy Process: Application and Studies* (pp. 59-67). New York: Springer-Verlag.

Saaty, T.L. (1990). *Multicriteria Decision Making: The Analytic Hierarchy Process*. Pittsburgh, PA: RWS Publications.

Saaty, T.L. (1996). *The Analytic Network Process*. Pittsburgh, PA: RWS Publications.

Sauter, V. (1997). *Decision Support Systems*. New York: John Wiley & Sons.

Schmidt, J.B., Montoya-Weiss, M.M. & Massey, A.P. (2001). New Product Development Decision-Making Effectiveness: Comparing Individuals, Face-to-Face Teams, and Virtual Teams. Decision Sciences, 32(4), 575-600.

Siskos, Y. & Spyridakos, A. (1999). Intelligent Multicriteria Decision Support: Overview and Perspectives. *European Journal of Operational Research,* 113(2), 236-246.

Team Expert Choice.™(1999). *Group Decision Support Software*. Pittsburgh, PA: Expert Choice, Inc.

Warkentin, M.E., Sayeed, L., & Hightower, R. (1997). Virtual Teams versus Face-to-Face Teams: An Exploratory Study of a Web-based Conference System. *Decision Sciences, 28*(4), 975-996.

Williams, S.R. & Wilson, R.L. (1997). Group Support Systems, Power, and Influence in an Organization: A Field Study. *Decision Sciences, 28*(4), 911-937.

Zahir, S. (1999a). Geometry of Decision Making and the Vector Space Formulation of the Analytic Hierarchy Process. *European Journal of Operational Research, 112*(2), 373-396.

Zahir, S. (1999b). Clusters in a Group: Decision Making in the Vector Space Formulations of the Analytic Hierarchy Process. *European Journal of Operational Research, 112*(3), 620-634.

Zahir, S. (1999c). Synthesizing Intensities of Group Preferences in Public Policy Decisions Using the AHP: Is It the Time for the 'New Democracy'? *Canadian Journal of Administrative Sciences, 16*(4), 353-366.

Chapter XI

Activity Theory as a Theoretical Foundation for Information Systems Research

George Ditsa
University of Wollongong, Australia

ABSTRACT

Theoretical models from social psychology have been widely used by information systems (IS) researchers as theoretical foundations to explain and predict information systems use. Unfortunately, most of these models used ignore the social context in which IS is used, but rather focused mainly on the individual and the technology. History and time are as well ignored in most cases. The set of philosophical concepts presented by Activity Theory makes it possible to marry the human aspects and the technological aspects of information systems into a more holistic research approach in information systems. This chapter presents the basic concepts of Activity Theory and its potential as a theoretical foundation for information systems use research.

INTRODUCTION

The field of information systems continues the search for appropriate approaches to information systems research that would marry the social and technological aspects in information systems. There has been the "war" between the quantitative and qualitative research camps, which, fortunately, was just recently declared to be over. Qualitative research is said to be now welcomed in almost all IS journals (Myers, 1999). Indeed, an increasing number of IS research is turning to qualitative research in IS. However, the search for a unifying theoretical foundation for IS research seems to be far from over. As the information technology advances so rapidly and the use of IS increases by the day, cracks in some earlier IS researches are beginning to appear. History, time, the socio-technical nature of IS and, perhaps most importantly, the absence of strong and unifying theoretical foundations may have contributed to these cracks (Markus, 2000).

Debates about the nature of the field of information systems still rages on in the IS community. IS researchers have suggested the use of social psychology models as potential theoretical foundations for research on the determinants of user behaviour and system use (e.g., Christie, 1981; Burton, Chen & Grover, 1993; Szajna & Scamell, 1993; Davis, Bagozzi & Warshaw, 1989; Netemeyer & Bearden, 1992, Bagozzi, Baumgartner & Yi, 1992; Martocchio, 1992; Nataraajan, 1993; Kelloway & Barling, 1993; Mykytyn & Harrison, 1993; Wishnick & Wishnick, 1993; Saga & Zmud, 1994). Among the most commonly used theories for research in this area are the Theory of Reason Action (TRA), the Technology Acceptance Model (TAM), the Expectancy Theory, the Theory of Planned Behaviour (TPB), and the Social Cognitive Theory (SCT).

Despite the large amount of research surrounding the area of IS use, studies (Franklin, Pain, Green & Owen, 1992; Hornby et al., 1992; Hovmark & Norel, 1993; Williams, 1994; Markus & Keil, 1994) suggest that most systems fail to meet the objectives and aspirations held for them, not because they are not technically sound, but because psychological and organisational issues were not well-addressed during the development, implementation and use of the systems.

This chapter aims at presenting Activity Theory as an alternative theoretical foundation for IS research to address some of the shortcomings of the current theoretical approaches. The chapter first takes a brief look at some commonly used social psychology theories in IS research. The chapter then presents an overview of the concept of Activity Theory, followed by a discussion of Activity Theory as a theoretical framework for information systems research supported by one practical example of a work activity and an Activity Theory framework for a research work currently being carried out by the authors. The chapter continues by pointing out some problems and limitations in applying Activity Theory in IS research before concluding.

SOME COMMONLY USED THEORIES IN INFORMATION SYSTEMS RESEARCH

A variety of theoretical perspectives have been used by IS researchers to study different aspects of the individual's reactions to information technology. These including Diffusion of Innovations (e.g., Compeau & Meister, 1997; Moore & Benbasat, 1991); the Technology Acceptance Model (TAM), which is an adaptation of the Theory of Reason Action (TRA) (e.g., Davis, 1989; Davis, Bagozzi & Warshaw, 1989; Venkatesh & Davis, 1996); the Theory of Planned Behaviour (TPB) (e.g., Mathieson, 1991; Taylor & Todd, 1995); and Social Cognitive Theory (SCT) (e.g., Compeau & Higgins, 1995a, 1995b; Hill, Smith & Mann, 1986, 1987). It has been acknowledged this body of research has produced some useful insights into the cognitive, affective, and behavioural reactions of individuals to technology, and into the factors that influence these reactions (Compeau, Higgins & Huff, 1999).

According to Compeau et al. (1999, p. 1), in each of the theories noted above, behaviour (e.g., the use of computers) is viewed as the result of a set of beliefs about technology and a set of affective responses to the behaviour. The beliefs are represented by the perceived characteristics of innovating in Innovation Diffusion research, by perceived usefulness and perceived ease of use in TAM, by behavioural beliefs and outcome evaluations in TPB, and by outcome expectations in SCT. Seddon (1997) refers to these as the net benefits (realised or expected) accruing from the use of a system. Affective responses are typically measured by attitudes towards use, an individual's evaluation of the behaviour as either positive or negative. These commonalities in the models reflect a belief in the cognitive basis of behaviour.

Compeau et al. (1999, p. 1) suggest, however, that, while TAM and the Diffusion of Innovations perspectives focus almost exclusively on beliefs about the technology and the outcomes of using it, SCT and the TPB include other beliefs that might influence behaviour, independent of perceived outcomes. The TPB model incorporates the notion of Perceived Behavioural Control (PBC) as an independent influence on behaviour, recognising that there are circumstances in which a behaviour might be expected to result in positive consequences (or net benefits), yet not be undertaken due to a perceived lack of ability to control the execution of the behaviour. PBC encompasses perceptions of resource and technology facilitating conditions, similar to those measured by Thompson, Higgins and Howell (1991), as well as perceptions of ability, or self-efficacy (Taylor & Todd, 1995). However, none of the above theoretical frameworks addresses explicitly the interpersonal, social, and situational factors that may influence the user's behaviour and use of IT. This is the potential we believe Activity Theory holds.

OVERVIEW OF ACTIVITY THEORY

Activity Theory originates from the former Soviet Union, and has its root in the German philosophy of Kant and Hegel. Activity Theory treats the individual's personality as an outgrowth of social forces rather than the autonomous being of the Western rationalist Cartesian model (Bødker, 1991). Scandinavian researchers, such as Engeström (1987, 1990), Bødker (1991, 1996), Kuutti (1992, 1996), and Karpatschof (1992) studied, applied and extended the concepts of the theory. Other western psychologists to study the theory in detail include Nardi (1996a, 1996b, 1996c), Draper (1993), Raeithel (1992), Cole and Maltzman (1969), Cole (1988) and Tolman (1988). Tolman (1988) produced a useful dictionary of English terms for the theory, as well as the origin of some words in both Russian and German. Researchers, such as Wertsch (1981, 1985, 1987, 1994), introduced the approach in the West, but due to the relative abstractness and unfamiliarity of the concepts it was not well-received in the West.

But, perhaps, Yjrö Engeström's (1987) ground-breaking work has provided more insight and understanding into Activity Theory. His extended model of the theory has established activity theory as a theoretical framework for IS research. Engeström critically examined three classical lineages (the semiotic and epistemological lineage from C. S. Peirce to K. Popper; the lineage from symbolic interactionism of G. H. Mead to modern interactionist developmental psychology of Trevarthen; and the lineage of cultural-historical psychology from L. S. Vygotsky to A. N. Leont'ev) before extending the cultural-historical conceptions of Vygotsky and Leont'ev into the unifying human activity model. Engeström used quotations extensively from his theoretical sources throughout his book in his analysis and discussions. The quotations, he said, he used as "windows into the innermost movement and dynamics of my theory construction" Engeström (1987, p. 22). Engeström's (1987) unifying human activity model has become Activity Theory as we know it today.

To bring more understanding of the theoretical basis on which Activity Theory is established, the following sections will present an overview of Engeström's

(1987) work leading to the extended Activity Theory model from Vygotsky. Before the overview, some definition of terms will come first.

Definitions of Terms

When considering the term *activity*, the underlying concept on which Activity Theory is based, it is important to realise that in English the term *activity* does not carry the essential connotation of "doing in order to transform something," as do the corresponding German or Russian terms *(tätigheit* and *dejatel'nost)* from which the theory has evolved.

An activity is a form of doing directed to an object, and activities are distinguished from each other according to their objects. Transforming the object into an outcome motivates the existence of an activity. An object can be a material thing, but it can also be less tangible (such as a plan) or totally intangible (such as a common idea) as long as it can be shared for manipulation and transformation by the participants of the activity (Kuutti, 1996, p. 27).

Engeström, in the preface of his (1987) book, defines *human activity* as "a systemic formation unifying the process of production, distribution, exchange and consumption as transitions between subject, object, instrument, community, rules, and division of labor" (Engeström, 1987).

From now on in this chapter, any reference to Engeström refers to Engeström (1987) unless otherwise stated.

The Three Lineages Leading to the Unifying Human Activity Model

The Triangles of Activity

Drawing on the fundamental conceptual and methodological breakthroughs experienced in philosophy, biology, and social sciences in the 19th century, which have some profound meaning for humans and society, Engeström examined three lineages of thought in the 20th century that have taken seriously the idea of man as a systemic and historical being. These lineages have produced attempts at modeling the basic structure of human activity. Engeström restrained his search for a viable root model of human activity with the following initial delimitations.

First, activity must be pictured in its simplest, genetically original structural form, as the smallest unit that still preserves the essential unity and quality behind any complex activity.

Second, activity must be analysable in its dynamics and transformations in its evolution and historical change. No static or eternal models will do.

Third, activity must be analysable as a contextual or ecological phenomenon. The models will have to concentrate on systemic relations between the individual and the outside world.

Fourth, specifically human activity must be analysable as culturally-mediated phenomenon. No dyadic organism-environment models will suffice. This requirement stems from Hegel's insistence on the culturally-mediated, *triadic* or *triangular* structure of human activity.

Engeström established that the prerequisites for a theory of human activity that fulfill these four requirements could be found in three broad research traditions. The first one is the theorising on signs, meanings, and knowledge, beginning with Peirce and extending through Ogden and Richards all the way to Popper's evolutionary epistemology. The second one is the study of the genesis of intersubjectivity, founded by G. H. Mead and finding continuity in studies of infant communication and language development. And the third one is the cultural-historical school of psychology, starting with Vygotsky and maturing in Leont'ev. In all these theories, the concept of mediation, of thirdness or triangularity, is seen as the constitutive feature of human activity. This idea is frequently expressed, developed, and applied in the form of graphical models.

The First Lineage: From Peirce to Popper

In this lineage, Engeström examined theories from Peirce to Popper and concludes that these theories provide the idea of activity as individual construction of knowledge. The theories narrow human activity down to individual intellectual understanding and provide little cues for grasping how material culture is created in joint activity.

C. S. Peirce, one of the founders of semiotics, built his theory of mediation on the idea of a triadic relationship between an object, a mental interpretant, and a sign. Because of Peirce's rather excessive and often opaque work, Engeström discussed his work through the concise but balanced interpretation of Parmentier (1985).

> *A* Sign, *or* Representamen, *is a First which stands in such a genuine triadic relation to a Second, called its Object, as to be capable of determining a Third, called its* Interpretant, *to assume the same triadic relation to its object in which it stands itself to the same Object (Peirce, 1902, cited in Parmentier, 1985, p. 27).*

Engeström contends that the triadic relation is not reducible to independent dyads. Otherwise, the dynamic character of the triad is destroyed and "there is no interpretation or representation by the resultant moment of the earlier moment; no symbolic or conventional relations exist among the elements; and no thought, idea, or meaning is embodied and transmitted in the process" (Parmentier 1985, p. 26).

According to Engeström, there are two vectors in this dynamism. First, there is the vector of *representation* pointing from the sign and interpretant towards the object. Second, there is the vector of *determination* pointing from the object towards both sign and interpretant.

This interlocking of the vectors of representation and determination implies that the three elements in the sign relation are never permanently object, representamen, and interpretant, but rather each shifts roles as further determinations and representations are realized.... Semiosis is, thus, an 'infinite process' or an 'endless series' in which the interpretant approaches a true representation of the object as further determinations are accumulated in each moment" (Parmentier 1985, p. 29).

In Engeström's view, besides purely logical and linguistic entities, Peirce applied his conception to human actions too and supported this with a quote.

In all action governed by reason such genuine triplicity will be found; while purely mechanical actions take place between pairs of particles. A man gives a brooch to his wife. The merely mechanical part of the act consists of his laying the brooch down while uttering certain sounds and her taking it up. There is no genuine triplicity here; but there is no giving either. The giving consists in his agreeing that a certain intellectual principle shall govern the relations of the brooch to his wife. The merchant in the Arabian Nights threw away a datestone which struck the eye of a Jinnee. This was purely mechanical, and there was no genuine triplicity. The throwing and the striking were independent of one another. But had he aimed at the Jinnee's eye, there would have been more than merely throwing away the stone. There would have been genuine triplicity, the stone being not merely thrown, but thrown *at* the eye. Here, *intention,* the mind's action, would have come in. Intellectual triplicity, or Mediation, is my third category" (Peirce, 1902, cited in Parmentier, 1985, p. 41).

Engeström perceives this citation reveals the first fundamental problem in Peirce's conception. The mediating sign is here, in the context of human action, treated as something purely mental and intentional. It thus loses its potentially, anti-Cartesian, cultural quality and reverts to individualism and rationalism.

Although Peirce often made clear that his notion of representation included everything, mental as well as nonmental, that possesses attributes, he gave little attention to the sensible or material qualities of signs in the nonmental category, or what he later termed the representamen. In fact, the need for some 'medium of outward expression' is admitted only as something that may be necessary to translate a 'thought-sign' to another person; and these material qualities are, in

Figure 1. Meaning as the Triad of Thoughts, Words and Things (Ogden & Richards, 1923, p. 11)

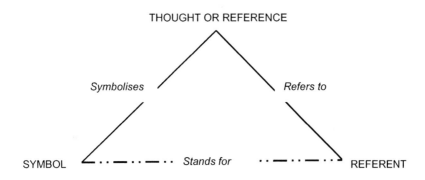

THOUGHT OR REFERENCE

Symbolises   *Refers to*

SYMBOL   *Stands for*   REFERENT

themselves, only a residue of nonsemiotic properties of the sign that play no positive role in the sign's representative function (Parmentier, 1985, p. 33).

The second problem in Peirce's thought, Engeström perceives, is the strict separation of the form from the content of the signs and the exclusive interest in the pure form. According to Engeström, the contents in no way contributed to the determination of the form, and sign forms became "blind vehicles for communicating meanings that they do not influence" (Parmentier, 1985, p. 45).

Engeström then points to Ogden and Richards' (1923) seminal work on the meaning of meaning in which they present the diagram (Figure 1) as their point of departure.

The specific nature of the bottom line of the triangle is pointed out by the authors, i.e., the relation between symbol (word) and referent (thing).

> *Between the symbol and the referent there is no relevant relation other than the indirect one, which consists in its being used by someone to stand for a referent. Symbol and Referent, that is to say, are not connected directly … but only indirectly round the two sides of the triangle (Ogden & Richards, 1923, pp. 11-12).*

Engeström interprets this to mean that there is no direct correspondence between the symbol and the thing it symbolizes, or between words and things. Their relation is always *constructed* by humans and, thus, historically changing. Engeström concludes that such meanings are constructions and the construction of meaning is a specifically human type of activity.

Engeström then examines Karl Popper's (1972) conception of three worlds, among modern epistemological theories, which he says is certainly the most well-known version of triplicity. Popper's basic position is the following.

First, there is the physical world - the universe of physical entities ...; this I will call 'World 1.' Second, there is the world of mental states, including states of consciousness and psychological dispositions and unconscious states; this I will call 'World 2.' But there is also a *third* such world, the world of the contents of thought, and, indeed, of the products of the human mind; this I will call 'World 3' ... (Popper & Eccles, 1977, p. 38).

According to Engeström, in Popper's World 3, Popper includes stories, explanatory myths, tools, scientific theories, scientific problems, social institutions, and works of art. These entities, according Engeström, may and often do exist in material form. But the material aspect is not essential. World 3 entities can also exist in a nonmaterial, unembodied form. The prime examples of such entities are scientific and other *problem situations*, Engeström added. Problem situations, according to Popper, exist objectively within the mass of knowledge, regardless of whether people have become conscious of them or not. The task is to discover them and Popper contends that grasping World 3 objects is totally independent of the material embodiments of those objects.

The Second Lineage: From Mead to Trevarthen

While the first lineage provides the idea of activity as individual construction of knowledge, Engeström's examination of theories from Mead to Trevarthen in the second lineage reveals that these theories provide the social, interactive, symbol-mediated construction of reality. But this construction is still conceived of as construction-for-the-mind, not as practical material construction.

According to Engeström, the second lineage towards the theory of activity was initiated by G. H. Mead's "social behaviorism." Mead's theory was aimed at overcoming individualism and intellectualism. "We are not, in social psychology, building up the behaviour of the social group in terms of the behaviour of the separate individuals composing it; rather, we are starting out with a given social whole of complex group activity, into which we analyse (as elements) the behaviour of each of the separate individual composing it ..." (Mead, 1934, p. 7).

That is, the individual's behaviour is influenced by that of the social group, and according to Mead, this social, interactive construction of physical objects takes place through symbols.

Symbolisation constitutes objects not constituted before, objects which would not exist except for the context of social relationships wherein symbolisation occurs. Language does not simply symbolise a situation or object which is already there in advance; it makes possible the existence or appearance of that situation or object, for it is a part of the mechanism whereby that situation or object is created. The social process relates the responses of one individual to the gestures of another, as the meanings of the latter, and is thus responsible for the rise and existence of new objects in the social situation, objects dependent upon or constituted by these meanings (Mead, 1934, p. 78).

Thus, Mead presents a triadic definition of meaning as:

> *This threefold or triadic relation between gesture, adjustive response, and resultant of the social act which the gesture initiates is the basis of meaning; for the existence of meaning depends upon the fact that the adjustive response of the second organism is directed toward the resultant of the given social act as initiated and indicated by the gesture of the first organism. The basis of meaning is thus objectively there in social conduct, or in nature in its relation to such conduct (Mead, 1934, p. 80).*

Engeström deduced that there are four basic elements in Mead's reasoning about activity: the individual, the other(s), the symbol, and the object. The intriguing question that Engeström posed is that of the origin of symbols, which, according to Mead, grow out of gestures.

Leont'ev and Tran Duc Thao agree with Mead on the constructed nature of objects, but disagree with him on the interpretation of construction as mere communication and symbolisation. For them, the construction of objects is above all sensuous, material construction by means of tools, i.e., production. Communication and symbolisation are seen as derivative, though organically intertwined, aspects of production. According to Leont'ev, conscious gestures originate as people experience that even when a work movement does not lead to its practical result for some reason or other, it is still capable of affecting others involved in production. It could, for example, draw them into the fulfillment of a given action.

Movements thus arose that preserved the form of the corresponding work movements but lacked practical contact with the object, and consequently also lacked the effort that converted them into real work movements. These movements, together with the vocal sounds that accompanied them, were separated from the tasks of acting on an object, and separated from labour activity, and preserved in themselves only the function of acting on people, the function of speech intercourse. In other words, they were converted into gestures. A gesture is nothing else than a movement separated from its result, i.e., not applied to the object at which it is aimed (Leont'ev, 1981, p. 219).

According to Engeström, both Leont'ev and Tran Duc Thao stress the genetic connection of gestures and tool-mediated work on material objects. Their point of departure is the original unity of instrumental and communicative aspects of activity. Therefore, signs and symbols are seen as derivative instruments of productive activity, which necessarily has an interactive, communicative form. For Mead, the original situation is that of interaction, of a "social process" with only secondary and abstract presence of material objects. For him, symbols are not primarily instruments for mastering tool-mediated procedures on objects.

The Third Lineage: From Vygotsky to Leont'ev

While the second lineage provides the social, interactive, symbol-mediated construction of reality, the third lineage, from Vygotsky to Leont'ev, according to Engeström, gave birth to the concept of activity based on material production, mediated by technical and psychological tools as well as by other human beings. And this is the lineage from which Engeström derived the model of the structure of human activity through genetic analysis. In grounding the model, Engeström used the works of Vygotsky and some of his followers — A. N. Leont'ev, E. V. Il'enkov, V. P. Zinchenko, L. A. Radzikhovskii, D. B. El'konin, M. Wartofsky, and A. Meshcheryakov — with some references to the first and second lineages.

According to Engeström, the third lineage began in 1930 when L. S. Vygotsky, the founder of the Soviet cultural-historical school of psychology, sketched his idea of mediation as follows.

Every elementary form of behavior presupposes *direct* reaction to the task set before the organism (which can be expressed with the simple S - R formula). But the structure of sign operations requires an intermediate link between the stimulus and the response. This intermediate link is a second order stimulus (sign) that is drawn into the operation where it fulfills a special function; it creates a new relation between S and R. The term 'drawn into' indicates that an individual must be actively engaged in establishing such a link. The sign also possesses the important characteristic of reverse action (that is, it operates on the individual, not the environment).

Figure 2. The Structure of the Mediated Act (Vygotsky, 1978, p. 40)

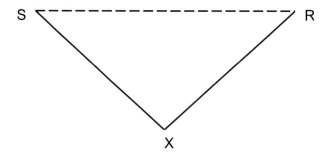

Consequently, the simple stimulus-response process is replaced by a complex, mediated act, which we picture as show in Figure 2.

In this new process the direct impulse to react is inhibited, and an auxiliary stimulus that facilitates the completion of the operation by indirect means is incorporated. (Note Vygotsky's use of the word facilitate here to mean mediate)

Careful studies demonstrate that this type of organisation is basic to all higher psychological processes, although in much more sophisticated forms than that shown above. The intermediate link in this formula is not simply a method of improving the previously existing operation, nor is a mere additional link in an S-R chain. Because this auxiliary stimulus possesses the specific function of reverse action, it transfers the psychological operation to higher and qualitatively new forms and permits humans, by the aid of extrinsic stimuli, to *control* their *behaviour* from the *outside*. The use of signs leads humans to a specific structure of behaviour that breaks away from biological development and creates new forms of a culturally-based psychological process (Vygotsky, 1978, pp. 39-40).

Vygotsky distinguished between two interrelated types of mediating instruments in human activity: tools and signs. The latter belonged to the broader category of "psychological tools." "The *tool's function is to serve as the conductor* of human influence on the object of activity; it is externally oriented; it must lead to changes in objects. It is a means by which a human external activity is aimed at mastering, and triumphing over, nature" (Vygotsky, 1978, p. 55) (italics added).

According to Vygotsky, psychological tools have a different character.

> *They are directed toward the mastery or control of behavioural processes—someone else's or one's own—just as technical means are directed toward the control of processes of nature.*

The following can serve as examples of psychological tools and their complex systems: language; various systems for counting; mnemonic techniques; algebraic symbol systems; works of art; writing; schemes, diagrams, maps, and mechanical drawings; all sorts of conventional signs; etc. (Vygotsky, 1981b, p. 137).

And according to Vygotsky, both technical tools and psychological tools mediate activity. But only psychological tools imply and require reflective mediation, consciousness of one's (or the other person's) procedures. Vygotsky (1978, p. 54) describes these two types of instruments as *parallel,* as "subsumed under the same category" of mediated activity. However, a little later in the same text he characterises their relation in *hierarchical* terms.

The use of artificial means, the transition to mediated activity, fundamentally changes all psychological operations just as the use of tools limitlessly broadens the range of activities within which the new psychological functions may operate. In this context, we can use the term *higher* psychological function, or *higher behaviour* as referring to the combination of tool and sign in psychological activity (Vygotsky, 1978, p. 55).

In Engeström's interpretation, we may actually distinguish between two levels of mediation: the primary level of mediation by tools and gestures *dissociated from one another* (where gestures are not yet real psychological tools), and the secondary level of mediation by tools *combined with* corresponding signs or other psychological tools. The acquisition and application of new tools *broadens* the sphere of influence. The acquisition and application of new psychological tools *elevates* the level of influence (potentially; the result is actually achieved only when the tool and the psychological tool meet each other).

In Engeström's view, the essence of psychological tools is that they are originally instruments for cooperative, communicative and self-conscious shaping and controlling of the procedures of using and making technical tools (including the human hand). He sees this original function being well-demonstrated in Tran Duc Thao's (1984) analysis of the emergence of developed indicative gestures and first representations among prehominids. Engeström contends that this formation of psychological tools (= secondary instruments) through the combination of previously separate gestures and technical tools (= primary instruments) is actually the essence of what Mead called the emergence of "significant gestures" or "significant symbols" and of what Trevarthen calls "secondary intersubjectivity." And according to Engeström, this idea of primary and secondary instruments is clearly expressed by Marx Wartofsky.

> . . . *what constitutes a distinctively human form of action is the creation and use of artifacts as tools, in the production of the means of existence and in the reproduction of the species. Primary artifacts are those directly used in this production;* secondary *artifacts are those used in the preservation and transmission of the acquired skills or modes of action or praxis by which this production is carried out. Secondary artifacts are therefore* representations *of such modes of action, and in this sense are* mimetic, *not simply of the* objects *of an environment which are of interest or use in this production, but of these objects as they are acted upon, or of the mode of operation or action involving such objects. Canons of representation, therefore have a large element of convention, corresponding to the change or evolution of different forms of action or* praxis, *and thus cannot be reduced to some simple notion of 'natural' semblance or resemblance. Nature, or the world*

*becomes a world-for-us, in this process, by the mediation of such
representations . . . (Wartofsky, 1979, p. 202).*

Wartofsky calls secondary artifacts "reflexive embodiments." He points out
that their mode may be gestural, oral, or visual, but "obviously such that they may
be communicated in one or more sense-modalities." These representations "are not
'in the mind', as mental entities"; they are 'externally embodied representations'"
(Wartofsky, 1979, p. 202).

For Engeström, Wartofsky's secondary artifacts and Vygotsky's psychological tools are essentially the same things. According to Engeström, Vygotsky's
intellectualist bias led to a somewhat one-sided emphasis on signs and word
meanings. The broader category of psychological tools, as well as the exciting
relations between technical and psychological tools, was not elaborated concretely
by Vygotsky. Engeström recognises that, ironically, the activity-oriented approach
in Soviet psychology after Vygotsky tried to get rid of Vygotsky's intellectualism
by neglecting the problem of signs and psychological tools in general. "If the polemic
with concrete works of Vygotsky on the problem of the sign was necessary and
natural, the removal of this problematic - in principle - led only to a substantial
'narrowing' of the theory of activity" (Davydov & Radzikhovskii, 1985, p. 60).
Engeström further acknowledged that in the recent revival of Vygotskian studies,
signs may again be treated too much "on their own," separated from the spectrum
of psychological tools and their relations with primary tools. This danger,
Engeström points out, seems to lure even in outstanding analysis, such as that of
Wertsch's (1985b) on Vygotsky's concept of semiotic mediation.

According to Vygotsky, the instrumentally mediated act "is the simplest
segment of behaviour that is dealt with by research based on elementary units"
(Vygotsky, 1981b, p. 140). On the other hand, V. P. Zinchenko (1985)
demonstrates Vygotsky used another basic unit of analysis, namely that of meaning
or word meaning.

Engeström continues by looking at V. P. Zinchenko's (1985, p. 100) argument
that meaning "cannot be accepted as a self-sufficient analytic unit since in meaning
there is no 'motive force' for its own transformation into consciousness." Only the
cognitive aspect of thinking is fixed in meaning; the affective and volitional aspect
is left unexplained. The author then suggests that the adequate unit is tool-mediated
action, which is actually the same thing as Vygotsky's instrumental act. Furthermore, as V. P. Zinchenko (1985, p. 103) correctly states, "one can consider tool-
mediated action as being very close to meaning as unit of analysis" because "of
necessity, tool-mediated action gives rise both to object meaning and to categorical
meaning."

Engeström, however, sees V. P. Zinchenko's failure to demonstrate how the suggested unit of tool-mediated action will overcome the limitations inherent in the unit of meaning. Engeström contends tool-mediated action in no way solves the problems of motivation, emotion, and creation. To the contrary, it seems that both meaning and tool-mediated action are formations of the same structural level. This is the level of goal-directed, individual cognition, the "rational level" of human functioning. According to Engeström, the problems of motivation, emotion, and creation seem to be unanswerable on this level. They belong to a higher, collective and — paradoxically — less conscious level of functioning. Shoots of this line of analysis, Engeström points out, are visible in Vygotsky's insistence on the concept of *higher* psychological functions. But this hierarchical aspect of Vygotsky's conception is left undeveloped by V. P. Zinchenko.

The problem of levels in human functioning was theoretically worked out by A. N. Leont'ev, a collaborator and pupil of Vygotsky. He demonstrated this by his, now famous, example of primaeval collective hunt.

When a member of a group performs his labour activity he also does it to *satisfy one of his needs*. A beater, for example, taking part in a primaeval collective hunt, was stimulated by a need for food or, perhaps, by a need for clothing, which the skin of the dead animal would meet for him. At what, however, was his activity directly aimed? It may have been directed, for example, at frightening a herd of animals and sending them toward other hunters, hiding in ambush. That, properly speaking, is what should be the result of the activity of this man. And the activity of this individual member of the hunt ends with that. The rest is completed by the other members. This result, i.e., the frightening of game, etc., understandably does not in itself, and may not, lead to satisfaction of the beater's need for food, or the skin of the animal. What the processes of his activity were directed to did not, consequently, coincide with what stimulated them, i.e., did not coincide with the motive of his activity; the two were divided from one another in this instance. Processes, the object and motive of which do not coincide with one another, we shall call 'actions'. We can say, for example, that the beater's activity is the hunt, and the frightening of game his action (Leont'ev, 1981, p. 210) (italics added).

> . . . *what unites the direct result of this activity with its final outcome? Obviously nothing other than the given individual's relation with the other members of the group, by virtue of which he gets his share of the bag from them, i.e., part of the product of their joint labor activity. This relationship, this connection is realised through the activity of other people, which means that it is the activity of other people that constitutes the objective basis of the specific structure of the human individual's activity, means that*

historically, i.e., through its genesis, the connection between the motive and the object of an action reflects objective social connections and relations rather than natural ones (Leont'ev, 1981, p. 212).

These lines, originally published in 1947, according to Engeström demonstrate the insufficiency of an individual tool-mediated action as a unit of psychological analysis. Without consideration of the overall collective activity, the individual beater's action seems "senseless and unjustified" (Leont'ev, 1981, p. 213). Engeström contends that, human labour, the mother form of all human activity, is cooperative from the very beginning. According to him, we may well speak of the activity *of the individual,* but never of *individual activity;* only actions are individual.

Engeström continues to argue that what distinguishes one activity from another is its object. According to Leont'ev, *the object of an activity is its true motive.* Engeström contends that, thus, the concept of activity is necessarily connected with the concept of motive and under the conditions of division of labor, the individual participates in activities mostly without being fully conscious of their objects and motives. The total activity seems to control the individual, instead of the individual controlling the activity. (A good example is the total activity of a university system.)

According to Engeström, activities are realised by goal-directed actions, subordinated to conscious purposes. These are the typical objects of the cognitive psychology of skills and performances, whether they are motor or mental. But human practice is not just a series or a sum of actions. In other words, "activity is a molar, not an additive unit" (Leont'ev, 1978, p. 50). "Correspondingly, actions are not special 'units' that are included in the structure of activity. Human activity does not exist except in the form of action or a chain of actions" (Leont'ev, 1978, p. 64).

Engeström's interpretation of this is that one and the same action may accomplish various activities and may transfer from one activity to another. One motive may obviously find expression in various goals and actions. And finally, actions are carried out in variable concrete circumstances. The methods with which the action is accomplished are called *operations.* Actions are related to conscious goals; operations to *conditions* not often consciously reflected by the subject. He added that tools are crystallised operations.

Thus in the total flow of activity that forms human life, in its higher manifestations mediated by psychic reflection, analysis isolates separate (specific) activities in the first place according to the criterion of motives that elicit them. Then actions are isolated — processes that are subordinated to conscious goals, finally, operations that directly depend on the conditions of attaining concrete goals (Leont'ev, 1978, pp. 66-67).

Engeström alludes to the hunting example that demonstrates the development from activity to actions as the consequence of division of labour. Engeström contends that there is also the opposite direction of development, often neglected in the interpretation of Leont'ev's work, and adds that actions may develop into an activity.

> *These are the ordinary cases when a person undertakes to perform some actions under the influence of a certain motive, and then performs them for their own sake because the motive seems to have been displaced to their objective. And that means that the actions are transformed into activity (Leont'ev, 1981, p. 238).*

Leont'ev's hierarchical levels of activity are currently shown as in Figure 3. Leont'ev also recognised social and communicative aspects of activity. *Another condition (besides the instrumental) is that the individual's relations with the world of human objects should be mediated by his relations with people, and that these relations should be included in a process of intercourse. This condition is always present. For the notion of an individual, a child, who is all by itself with the world of objects is a completely artificial abstraction. The individual, the child, is not simply thrown into the human world; it is introduced into this world by the people around it, and they guide it in that world (Leont'ev, 1981, p. 135).*

Only through a relation with other people does man relate to nature itself, which means that labour appears from the very beginning as

Figure 3. Hierarchical Levels of Activity

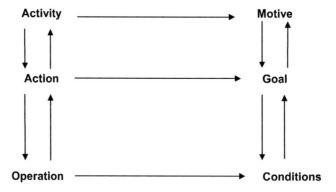

a process mediated by tools (in the broad sense) and at the same
time mediated socially (Leont'ev, 1981, p. 208.)

According to Engeström, the problem, however, is that the instrumental and the communicative aspect of activity were not brought into a unified complex model by Leont'ev. Vygotsky's model of the instrumental act (Figure 2) was not graphically superseded in Leont'ev's work.

Engeström sees this incomplete unification of the two aspects of activity in Leont'ev's work giving room for Lomov's (1980) attempt to separate activity and communication as the two spheres of the life process of the individual. According to Lomov, activity should be understood as the relation subject-object, while communication comprises the relation subject-subject. This dualistic conception was heavily criticised by A. N. Leont'ev's son, A. A. Leont'ev. According to him, activity cannot be legitimately characterised as individual; rather, it is social in all its components (A. A. Leont'ev, 1980).

Thus, when we are dealing with joint activity, we can with full
justification speak of a collective subject *or of a total subject of this*
activity, whose interrelation with the 'individual' subjects can only
be comprehended through a psychological analysis of the structure
of the joint activity (A. A. Leont'ev, 1980, p. 530).

According to Engeström, the communication for A. A. Leont'ev is an integral aspect of every activity. On the other hand, communication may also differentiate into its own specialised activity system — very clearly in various forms of mass communication, for example. But in this case, according to Engeström, it retains all the basic elements of activity (including the aspect of internal communication within it).

Engeström contends that, though A. A. Leont'ev's point is convincing enough, he, too, refrained from producing a more adequate unified model of activity. In other words, the essential elements and inner relations of activity were not comprehensively analysed and modeled by either the older or the younger Leont'ev. Radzikhovskii (1984) raised this problem for discussion again in the Soviet Union.

This morphological paradigm [of A. N. Leont'ev] does not . . .
explain very well why activity should change as a consequence of
the real or imagined presence of other people; nor does it answer
the question of wherein, from the psychological point of view, lies
the qualitative difference between 'another' person and any other

physical object, e.g., questions associated with communication, interaction, etc. . . . the social nature of motives and means of activity is by no means reflected in a specific structure of activity; this social nature is invariant relative to this structure . . . (Radzikhovskii, 1984, p. 37).

According to Engeström, Radzikhovskii's most important argument is that "the genesis of activity itself is not illuminated, i.e., the structural-genetic original unit from which the structure of activity ... unfolds is not demonstrated" (Radzikhovskii, 1984, p. 40). Engeström sees Radzikhovskii proposing "social action" or "joint action" as the alternative unit of analysis.

Concretely, we are saying that the general structure of ontogenetically primary joint activity (or, more accurately, primary joint action) includes at least the following elements: subject (child), object, subject (adult). The object here also has a symbolic function and plays the role of the primary sign. In fact, the child's movement toward, and manipulation of, an object, even when he is pursuing the goal of satisfying a vital need, is also simultaneously a sign for an adult: to help, to intervene, to take part. . . . In other words, true communication, communication through signs, takes place here between the adult and the child. An objective act is built up around the object as an object, and sign communication is built up around the same object as the sign. Communication and the objective act coincide completely here, and can be separated only artificially . . . (Radzikhovskii, 1984, p. 44).

The unit defined above should be seen as genetically earlier (in ontogeny), as determining the basic internal sign structure of human activity, and, finally, as a universal unit and a component of individual activity (Radzikhovskii, 1984, p. 49).

According to Engeström, at the first glance, Radzikhovskii is merely adopting the neo-Meadian conception of activity, exemplified in Trevarthen's model of secondary intersubjectivity. However, Radzikhovskii's account of the genesis of "primary joint action," Engeström argues, differs substantially from those of Mead and Trevarthen. For Radzikhovskii, the use of the sign in the primary joint action is non-conscious and completely fused into the action on the object. For Mead, this kind of sign usage is something that precedes the specifically human stage of conscious "significant gestures." And Trevarthen's elaborate data shows that, up to nine months, the infant's gestures and object-actions are *separate,* not fused together. Their combination (not merger) is a developmental achievement, signifying a new level in the child's self-consciousness.

Engeström views Radzikhovskii's description of the "primary joint action" as corresponding to the actual structure of animal activity preceding humanity in evolutionary terms because of his nearly total neglect of the role of material production and material instruments (and their relations to signs and other "psychological tools").

Engeström concludes that, in spite of its rather regressive outcome, Radzikhovskii's attempt is a symptom of the existence of an unsolved problem in the Vygotsky - Leont'ev tradition. Engeström, however, admitted that the third lineage, from Vygotsky to Leont'ev, gave birth to the concept of activity based on material production, mediated by technical and psychological tools as well as by other human beings, and then gave himself the task of deriving a model of the structure of human activity through genetic analysis.

The Evolution of Activity

From the analysis and discussions of the third lineage, Engeström deduced that the general mode of biological adaptation as the animal form of activity might be depicted as in Figure 4.

A central tenet embedded in this model, according to Engeström, is the collective and populational character of animal activity and species development [he cited Jensen (1981) in support]. According to Engeström, species is seen as a systemic formation, as a "methodology of survival," produced to solve the contradiction between population and nature, and in this formation, the prototype and the procedure define each other in a complementary manner.

Figure 4. The General Structure of the Animal Form of Activity

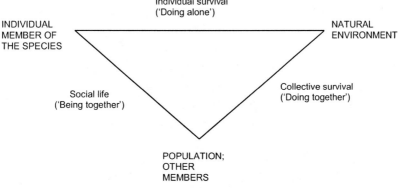

Engeström argues that the adaptive nature of animal activity does not mean passive acquiescence in the demands and pressures of nature, and made reference to Lewontin (1982), which shows that organisms and the environment always penetrate each other in several ways.

> *The importance of these various forms of dialectical interaction between organism and environment is that we cannot regard evolution as the 'solution' by species of some predetermined environmental 'problems' because it is the life activities of the species themselves that determine both the problems and the solutions simultaneously. . . . Organisms within their individual lifetimes and in the course of their evolution as species do not adapt to environments; they* construct *them (Lewontin, 1982, pp. 162-163).*

Engeström contends that on higher levels of animal evolution, we witness ruptures in each of the three sides of the triangle depicted in Figure 4. The uppermost side of "individual survival" is ruptured by the emerging utilisation of tools, most clearly demonstrated by the anthropoid apes (he cited Schurig (1976) in support). The left hand side of "social life" is ruptured by collective traditions, rituals and rules, originating at the crossing of adaptation and mating. The right hand side of "collective survival" is ruptured by division of labor, influenced by the practices of breeding, upbringing, and mating, and appearing first as the evolving division of labor between the sexes.

These ruptures, according Engeström, cannot be comprehended "simply as a linear process of higher development, but rather as a process in which, under the influence of various different evolutionary factors, differing competing lines of development may have emerged" (Keller, 1981, p. 150). Anthropoid apes, according to Engeström, are the prime example of the rupture by tools; and dolphins, with their extraordinary "capacity to organise many individuals into a system which operates as a whole" (Keller, 1981, p. 151), may be a prime example of the ruptures in "doing together" and "being together."

According to Engeström, this stage of "ruptures" is actually the dim transitional field between animal and mankind which may be depicted by Figure 5. Anthropoid apes, Engeström said, do not make and preserve tools systematically. Tool making and tool utilisation are still exceptional rather than dominant forms of their activity. The activity of dolphins, he said, may be assessed analogously. He quotes Keller (1981) in support.

> *The fact . . . that the transition from animal psyche to human consciousness is not completed in the case of the dolphins is . . . to*

Figure 5. Structure of Activity in Transition from Animal to Man

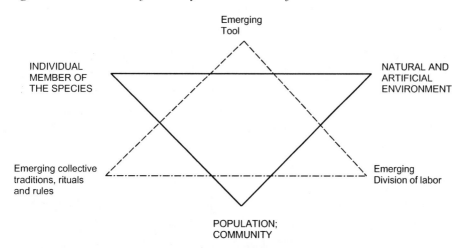

be explained by the circumstance that there is no active, instrumentally mediated, appropriation of material reality within the social behaviour of dolphins parallel to the use and preparation of external aids for the completion of operations such as is found in the phylogenetic line of the apes, and which can be seen as an anticipation of human productive (that is, mediated by tools) activity at the animal level. However complex the social life of dolphins may be, the relationships that arise within it are not coordinated by 'the activity of production', they are not determined by it and do not depend upon it (Keller, 1981, p. 153).

Engeström contends that the breakthrough into human cultural evolution—into the specifically human form of activity—requires that what used to be *separate ruptures* or emerging mediators become *unified determining factors.* And according to Engeström, at the same time, what used to be ecological and natural becomes economic and historical, and he quotes Reynolds (1982) in support.

Since intentional action is frequently cooperative and socially regulated in non-human primates, it makes more sense to derive cooperation from social interactions where it already exists than from object-using programs where it does not. Consequently, a theory of the evolution of human technology should place less emphasis on differences in the tool-using capacities between human and apes (important as they are) but ask instead how emergent tool-using capacities become integrated into the domain of intentional social action (Reynolds, 1982, p. 382; see also Reynolds, 1981).

Engeström referred to an elegant sketch of this original integration proposed by Richard Leakey and Roger Lewin in which they point out that humans are the only primate who *collect* food to be eaten later. In their mixed economy, the early humans did this both by gathering plants and by scavenging and hunting meat. However, "sharing, not hunting or gathering as such, is what made us human" (Leakey & Lewin, 1983, p. 120). Another point of integration, according to Leakey and Lewin, was the emergence of collectively organized tool-making, concentrated on steady campsites.

Engeström views the paleoanthropological ideas of Leakey and Lewin as corresponding to the philosophical point made by Peter Ruben.

> *Every social system is faced with the analytical problem of dividing the total product into necessary and surplus product. And the regulations created for distribution of these products provide the norms for 'justice' in each system. So the existence of a surplus of labour beyond necessary labour is given* a priori *in every system of labour, and one can say that sociality, in contrast to individuality, is perceivable exactly in this surplus product. . . . It is the struggle for the surplus product that constituted sociality! . . . Thus, a social mechanism that is especially a mechanism of political domination . . . does not serve as a genetical precondition for bringing about the surplus product, but as a means for its quantitative expansion (Ruben. 1981, pp. 128-129).*

Following from the analysis and discussions above, Engeström reorganised the whole structure of human activity system and presented it as shown in Figure 6 and went on to justify the model. In the model, *subject* refers to the individual or sub-group whose agency is chosen as a point of view in the analysis. The *object* refers to the "raw material" or problem space at which the activity is directed and which is molded or transformed into *outcomes* with the help of physical and symbolic, external and internal *tools* (mediating instruments and signs). The *community* comprises multiple individuals and/or sub-groups who share the same general object. The *division of labor* refers to both the horizontal division of tasks between the members of the community and to the vertical division of power and status. Finally the *rules* refer to the explicit and implicit regulations, norms and conventions that constrain actions and interactions within the activity system.

Figure 6.   The Structure of Human Activity

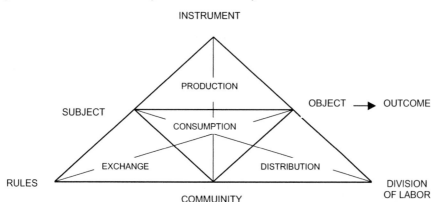

Engeström argues the model depicted in Figure 6 is a logical continuation of the transitional model depicted in Figure 5. What used to be adaptive activity is transformed into consumption and subordinated to the three dominant aspects of human activity: production, distribution and exchange (or communication). The model, he said, suggests the possibility of analysing a multitude of relations within the triangular structure of activity. He, however, warned that the essential task is always to grasp the systemic whole, not just separate connections. He then made reference to the essentials of the analysis provided by Karl Marx in the introduction to *Grundrisse*.

> *Production creates the objects which correspond to the given needs; distribution divides them up according to social laws; exchange further parcels out the already divided shares in accord with individual needs; and finally, in consumption, the product steps outside this social movement and becomes a direct object and servant of individual need, and satisfies it in being consumed. Thus production appears to be the point of departure, consumption as the conclusion, distribution and exchange as the middle . . . (Marx, 1973, p. 89).*

Marx goes on to show that things are not so simple as this. Production is always also consumption of the individual's abilities and of the means of production. Correspondingly, consumption is also production of the human beings themselves. Furthermore, distribution seems to be not just a consequence of production, but also its immanent prerequisite in the form of distribution of instruments of production and distribution of members of the society among the different kinds of production.

Finally, exchange, too, is found inside production in the form of communication, interaction and exchange of unfinished products between the producers. Marx went on to dispel any notion that the boundaries between the sub-triangles in Figure 6 are blurred and eventually given up.

> *The conclusion we reach is not that production, distribution, exchange and consumption are identical, but that they all form the members of a totality, distinctions within a unity. Production predominates not only over itself, in the antithetical definition of production, but over the other moments as well. The process always returns to production to begin anew. That exchange and consumption cannot be predominant is self-evident. Likewise, distribution as distribution of products; while as distribution of the agents of production it is itself a moment of production. A definite production thus determines a definite consumption, distribution and exchange as well as definite relations between these different moments. Admittedly, however, in its one-sided form, production is itself determined by the other moments. For example if the market, i.e. the sphere of exchange, expands, then production grows in quantity and the divisions between its different branches become deeper. A change in distribution changes production, e.g. concentration of capital, different distribution of the population between town and country, etc. Finally, the needs of consumption determine production. Mutual interaction takes place between the different moments. This is the case with every organic whole (Marx. 1973, pp. 99-100).*

Engeström deduced that Marx's notions of "the antithetical definition of production" and of production "in its one-sided form," especially when applied to the earliest simple forms of societal organisation, seem to refer to the double existence of production as *both* the whole activity system of Figure 6 *and* as the uppermost sub-triangle or action-type of that system.

In other words, each sub-triangle in Figure 6 is potentially an activity of its own. Within the total practice of the society, the sub-triangles are initially only actions since their *object* is still a relatively undifferentiated whole and the temporal, spatial, and social boundaries between them are fluid.

Inner Contradictions of Human Activity

According to Engeström, an activity system does not exist in a vacuum. It interacts with a network of other activity systems. For example, it receives rules and instruments from certain activity systems (e.g., management), and produces outcomes for certain other activity systems (e.g., clients). Thus, influences from outside "intrude" into the activity systems. However, such external forces are not a sufficient explanation for surprising events and changes in the activity. The outside influences are first appropriated by the activity system, turned, and modified into internal factors. Actual causation occurs as the alien element becomes internal to the activity. This happens in the form of imbalance. The activity system is constantly working through contradictions within and between its elements. In this sense, an activity system is a virtual disturbance and innovation-producing machine.

Engeström contends that the primary contradiction of all activities in capitalist socio-economic formations is that between the exchange value and the use value within each element of the activity system. He used the work activity of a physician in primary medical care again as an illustration. The primary contradiction in the object of the doctor's work activity takes the form of patient as person to be helped and healed versus patient as source of revenue and profit (or on the flip side, as opportunity to profit by cutting costs), and quotes Leont'ev (1981, p. 255) in support.

> *The doctor who buys a practice in some little provincial place may be very seriously trying to reduce his fellow citizens' suffering from illness, and may see his calling in just that. He must, however, want the number of the sick to increase, because his life and practical opportunity to follow his calling depend on that.*

According to Engeström, the primary contradiction can be found by focusing on any of the elements of the doctor's work activity. For example, *instruments* of this work include a tremendous variety of medicaments and drugs. But they are not just useful for healing—they are above all commodities with prices, manufactured for a market, advertised, and sold for profit. Every doctor, according to Engeström, faces this contradiction in his or her daily decision making, in one form or another.

Engeström observed that, as a new element enters into the activity system from outside, secondary contradictions appear between the elements. An example of a secondary contradiction in medical work would be that caused by the emergence of new kinds of *objects*, that is, patients and their medical problems. Conflicts emerge between the increasingly ambivalent and complex problems and symptoms of the patients and the traditional biomedical diagnostic *instruments*. Patients' problems increasingly often do not comply with the standards of classical diagnosis and classification of diseases. They require an integrated social, psychological, and biomedical approach that may not yet exist.

A tertiary contradiction, according to Engeström, appears when a culturally more advanced object and motive are introduced into the activity. Such a tertiary contradiction arises when, say, practitioners of a medical clinic, using experiences from other clinics, design and adopt a new model for their work that corresponds to the ideals of a more holistic and integrated medicine. The new ideas may be formally implemented, but they are internally resisted by the vestiges of the old activity.

According to Engeström, quaternary contradictions are those that emerge between the changing central activity and its neighbouring activities in their interaction. Suppose that a primary care doctor, working on a new holistic and integrated basis, refers the patient to a hospital operating strictly on a traditional biomedical model. Conflicts and misunderstandings easily emerge between these activity systems.

An elaboration (Figure 7) showing the four levels of contradictions placed in appropriate locations in a schematic network of activities presented in Figure 6.

Level 1: Primary inner contradiction (double nature) within each constituent component of the central activity.

Level 2: Secondary contradictions between the constituents of the central activity.

Level 3: Tertiary contradiction between the object/motive of the dominant form of the central activity and the object/motive of a culturally more advanced form of the central activity.

Level 4: Quaternary contradictions between the central activity and its neighbour activities.

Figure 7. Four Levels of Contradictions in a Network of Human Activity Systems

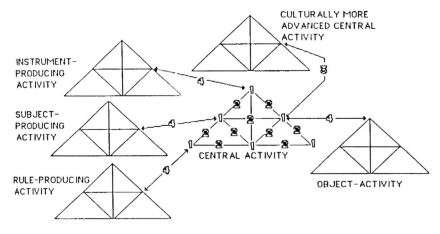

In Il'enkov, views contradictions are not just inevitable features of activity. They are "the principle of its self-movement and . . . the form in which the development is cast" (Il'enkov, 1977, p. 330). This means that new qualitative forms of activity emerge as solutions to the contradictions of the preceding form. This in turn takes place in the form of "invisible breakthroughs," innovations from below.

In reality it always happens that a phenomenon which later becomes universal originally emerges as an individual, particular, specific phenomenon, as an exception from the rule. It cannot actually emerge in any other way. Otherwise history would have a rather mysterious form.

Thus, any new improvement of labour, every new mode of man's action in production, before becoming generally accepted and recognised, first emerges as a certain deviation from previously accepted and codified norms. Having emerged as an individual exception from the rule in the labour of one or several men, the new form is then taken over by others, becoming in time a new universal norm. If the new norm did not originally appear in this exact manner, it would never become a really universal form, but would exist merely in fantasy, in wishful thinking (Il'enkov, 1982, p. 83-84).

ACTIVITY THEORY AND INFORMATION SYSTEMS RESEARCH

As can be seen from the previous sections, Activity Theory presents a research approach that learns itself more to interpretive research. The Activity Theory framework can be used to interpret actions of individuals and a community of individuals that are directed towards a desired outcome. The framework allows an explicit way of interpreting the mediating influences of the *tools* used, the *rules* that apply, and the *division of labour* that exists among a *community* people that engage in actions directed to an *object* and an *outcome*. Each individual's (*subject*) motives, actions, and goals towards the outcome can also be explicitly examined and interpreted within the framework. The Activity Theory framework presents a holistic way of examining and interpreting the social and the technological aspects of information systems. Some IS researchers (e.g., Engeström (1990, 1996a, 1996b), Engeström and Escalante (1996), Nardi (1996a), Kuuti (1991, 1999), Blackler, Crump and McDonald (1999) and Jonassen and Rohrer-Murphy (1999)) have, indeed, used the framework in investigations that involved both the social and the technological aspects of information systems.

In applying the Activity Theory framework, human activity should be viewed as an interdependent system involving the individual (*subject*), *tools*, a problem space (*object*), the *community* of people who are similarly concerned with the problem, the *division of labour* between community members aimed at the object and the outcome, and the conventions (*rules*) regarding actions. The activity of the individual (top three components of Figure 6) should not be viewed in isolation, but should be tied to the larger cultural context. And human activity should be seen as socially bound and not simply the sum of individual actions (Engeström, 1990). Furthermore, the system as a whole should be considered as dynamic and continually evolving. For example, any changes to cultural practice may inspire the creation or reworking of a tool, or any changes in the design of a tool may influence a subject's orientation toward an object, which in turn may influence the cultural practices of the community.

As well, it should be borne in mind that any perturbations at any one point in the activity system (see Figure 6) will produce ripples and, occasionally, can cause major transformations across the system. The framework thus provides a holistic view that recognises both the socially distributed nature of human activity and the transformative nature of activity systems in general. The framework also suggests ways of inducing cultural changes and also draws attention to possible points of leverage in the attempt to overcome the unique nature of IS use (Engeström, 1990). For example, changing the nature of the rules of IS use and the expected outcomes, and modifying the division of labour, or valuing tools, including IS, may create a different user behaviour towards the use of the IS.

Viewed from this perspective, research into IS use can be conceptualised as a process of manipulating the "points of leverage" in the framework, where IS is the tool. It is important, therefore, that IS researchers should not aim at isolating individual cognitive processes through controlled experimentation and survey methods, but should instead work toward understanding the organisational context in which IS is used. This notion of Activity Theory is supported by theories of situated cognition. As Salomon (1995) points out:

> *Even if we accept only the idea that some cognitions are socially distributed under some conditions (Perkins, 1993), or that distributed and "solo" cognitions mutually affect each other in an ongoing spiral of development (Salomon, 1993), then research that excludes interpersonal, social, technological, and situational factors becomes badly one-sided and constrained (p. 14).*

He continues by adding that this raises doubts about the validity of traditional experimental methodologies and argues for new forms of educational research in which individuals, and groups of individuals, are studied "in situ" (Salomon, 1995). This argument holds for research in IS use as well. Victor Kaptelinin summarises the appropriateness of Activity Theory in the study of information systems in these words:

> *One of the most important claims of activity theory is that the nature of any artifact can be understood only within the context of human activity – by identifying the ways people use this artifact, the needs it serves, and the history of its development (1996, p. 46).*

AN EXAMPLE OF WORK ACTIVITY

Engeström used the following example of a work activity to concretise the model.

Consider the work *activity* of a physician working at a primary care clinic (Figure 8). The *object* of his work is the patients with their health problems and illnesses. The *outcomes* include intended recoveries and improvements in health, as well as unintended outcomes such as possible dissatisfaction, non-compliance and low continuity of care. The instruments include such powerful *tools* as X-rays, laboratory, and medical records - as well as partially internalised diagnostic and treatment-related concepts and methods. The *community* consists of the staff of the clinic, distinguished from other competing or collaborating clinics and hospitals. The *division of labour* determines the tasks and decision-making powers of the physician, the nurses, the nurses' aides, and other employee categories. Finally, the rules regulate the use of time, the measurement of outcomes, and the criteria for rewards.

Figure 8. The Work Activity of a Primary Care Physician

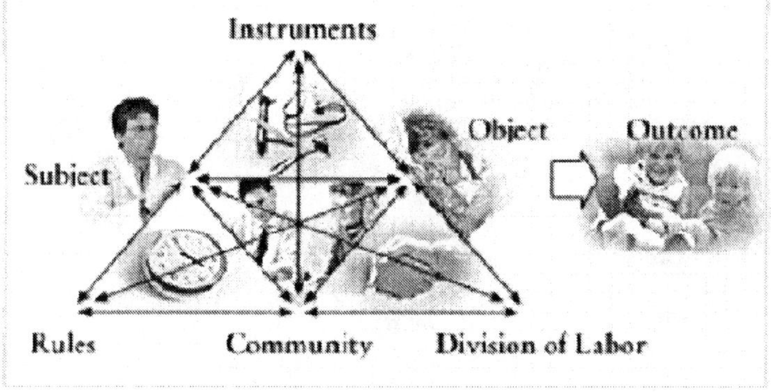

Source: http://www.helsinki.fi/~jengestr/activity/6a.htm

The same primary health care activity will look quite different if we take the point of view of another subject in the community, for instance a nurse. Yet, both subjects share the overall object — the patients and their health problems. An activity system is always heterogeneous and multi-voiced. Different subjects, due to their different histories and positions in the division of labour, construct the object and the other components of the activity in different, partially overlapping and partially conflicting ways. There is constant construction and re-negotiation within the activity system. Coordination between different versions of the object must be achieved to ensure continuous operation. Tasks are reassigned and re-divided, rules are bent and reinterpreted. And the use of a tool(s) will be influenced by all the components of the activity system.

Let us consider another example of an executive of an organisation who is to make a decision (the object) and makes the decision (outcome) by using an executive information system (EIS) as a tool (Figure 9). The executive's individual attributes such as computer literacy, age, education, skill, ability, knowledge, attitude, values, beliefs, and motivation to use the EIS will influence the use. However, like the primary care physician, the executive's use of the EIS may also be influenced by the laws, policies, regulations, standards, norms, ethical issues, and other workplace practices (rules); the staff and stakeholders (the community) of the organisation; the division of labour that goes with the decision-making (the object) and the decision made. A research framework as in Figure 9 is being used by the authors to research into executive's use of EIS.

Figure 9. Executive Use of EIS

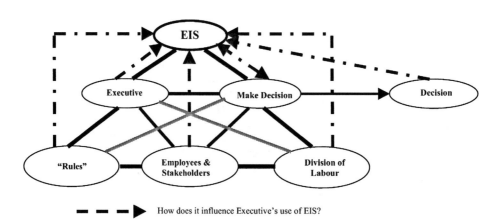

PROBLEMS AND LIMITATIONS IN APPLYING ACTIVITY THEORY IN IS RESEARCH

All research approaches have their problems and limitations. Activity Theory is no exception. A researcher who embarks on using Activity Theory has to have an in-depth knowledge and understanding of the activity system under investigation, including the dynamic interplay of all the units of the activity system. This means the researcher has to keep the system under constant and relatively long observation, and as result becomes more actively immersed in the activity process. The researcher must be very conversant with the rules, the division of labour, and the object of an activity, as well as understanding the motive and goals of the individual and the community involved in the activity. Also, some of the activities do not directly result into the desired outcome, but rather indirectly. These will undoubtedly mean there should be multiple data collection methods if one is to achieve a convincing research result using the Activity Theory approach.

The researcher would also have to keep in mind the four premises upon which Engeström derived the Activity Theory model as we know it today, as recapped below.

First, activity must be pictured in its simplest, genetically original structural form, as the smallest unit that still preserves the essential unity and quality behind any complex activity.

Second, activity must be analysable in its dynamics and transformations in its evolution and historical change. No static or eternal models will do.

Third, activity must be analysable as a contextual or ecological phenomenon. The models will have to concentrate on systemic relations between the individual and the outside world.

Fourth, specifically human activity must be analysable as culturally-mediated phenomenon. No dyadic organism-environment models will suffice. This requirement stems from Hegel's insistence on the culturally-mediated, *triadic* or *triangular* structure of human activity.

Nardi (1996c) also points out four methodological implications of Activity Theory:

1. The research time frame must be long enough to understand users' objects, including, where appropriate, changes in objects over time and their relation to the objects of others in the setting being studied.

2. Attention must be paid to broad patterns of activity rather than narrow episodic fragments that fail to reveal the overall direction and import of an activity.

3. The use of a varied set of data collection techniques, including interviews, observations, video, and historical materials, without undue reliance on any one method.
4. There must be the commitment to understand things from the users' point of view.

CONCLUSION

This chapter outlined some of the strengths and weakness of Activity Theory and advocates its use as an alternative theoretical foundation for IS research to address some of the shortcomings of the current theoretical approaches. The strength of Activity Theory is the importance of its integrating framework linking a set of theoretical principles. It is a powerful and clarifying descriptive tool rather than a strongly predictive theory. The object of Activity Theory is to understand the unity of consciousness. Activity Theory incorporates strong notions of intentionality, history, mediation, collaboration, and development in constructing consciousness (Kaptelinin, 1996). Despite some of the weaknesses outlined above, Activity Theory has a unique way of considering IS as a tool and the advantage of a methodology which considers history, time, the individual, the group of individuals, the organisation, as well as IS in a research setting.

REFERENCES

Bagozzi, R.P., Baumgartner, H. & Yi, Y. (1992). State Versus Action Orientation and the Theory of Reasoned Action: An Application to Coupon Usage. *Journal of Consumer Research,* 18(4), pp. 505-518.

Bødker, S. (1991). Through the Interface: A Human Activity Approach to User Interface Design. Hillsdale, NJ: Lawrence Erlbaum.

Bødker, S. (1996). Applying Activity Theory to Video Analysis: How to Make Sense of Video Data in HCI. In Bonnie Nardi (Ed.), *Context and Consciousness: Activity Theory and Human-Computer Interaction* (pp. 147-174) Cambridge, MA: MIT Press.

Burton, F., Chen, Y. & Grover, V. (1992-93). An Application of Expectancy Theory for Assessing User Motivation to Utilise an Expert System. *Journal of Management Information Systems,* 9 (3), pp. 183-198.

Christie, B. (1981). *Face to File Communication: A Psychological Approach to Information Systems*. New York: Wiley.

Cole, M. (1988). Cross-cultural Research in the Sociohistorical Tradition. *Human Development,* Vol. 31.

Cole, M. & Maltzman, I. (Eds.). (1969). *A Handbook of Contemporary Soviet Psychology.* New York: Basic.

Compeau, D., Higgins, C.A. & Huff, S. (1999). Social cognitive theory and individual reactions to computing technology: A longitudinal study. *MIS Quarterly,* 23(2), pp. 145-158.

Compeau, D.R. & Higgins, C.A. (1995a). Computer self-efficacy: Development of a measure and initial test. *MIS Quarterly,* 19(2), pp. 189-211.

Compeau, D.R. & Higgins, C.A. (1995b). Application of social cognitive theory to training for computer skills. *Information Systems Research,* 6(2), pp. 118-143.

Compeau, D.R. & Meister, D.B. (1997, December 13). Measurement of perceived characteristics of innovating: A reconsideration based on three empirical studies. Presented at a workshop of the *Diffusion Interest Group on Information Technology.* Atlanta, GA.

Davis, F.D. (1989). Perceived usefulness, perceived ease of use, and user acceptance of information technology. *MIS Quarterly,* 13(3), pp. 319-340.

Davis, F.D., Bagozzi, R.P., & Warshaw, P.R. (1989). User acceptance of Computer Technology: A Comparison of two theoretical models. *Management Science,* 35(8), pp. 982-1003.

Davydov, V.V. & Radzikhovskii, L.A. (1985). Vygotsky's theory and the activity-oriented approach in psychology. In J. V. Wertsch (Ed.), *Culture, communication, and cognition: Vygotskian perspectives.* Cambridge, MA: Cambridge Press.

Draper, S. (1993). Activity Theory: The New Direction for HCI? *Intl. Journal of Man Machine Studies,* 38, pp. 812-821.

Engeström, Y. (1987). *Learning by expanding: An activity-theoretical approach to developmental research.* Helsinki: Orienta-Konsultit.

Engeström, Y. (1990). *Learning, working and imagining: Twelve studies in activity theory.* Helsinki: Orienta-Konsultit Oy.

Engeström, Y. (1996a). Non scolae sed vitae discimus: Toward overcoming the encapsulation of school learning In H. Daniels (Ed.), *An introduction to Vygotsky* (pp. 151-170). London: Routledge.

Engeström, Y. (1996b). The tensions of judging: handling cases of driving under the influence of alcohol in Finland and California. In Y. Engeström and D. Middleton (Eds.), *Cognition and communication at work.* Cambridge, MA: Cambridge University Press.

Engeström, Y., & Escalante, V. (1996). Mundane tool or object of affection? The Rise and Fall of the Postal Buddy. In B.A. Nardi (Ed.), *Context and consciousness: Activity theory and human-computer interaction* (pp. 325-374). Cambridge, MA: MIT Press.

Engeström, Y., Miettinen, R., & Punamaki-Gitai, R.L. (Eds.) (1999). *Perspectives on activity theory.* New York: Cambridge University Press.

Franklin, I., Pain, D., Green, E., & Owen, J. (1992). Job Design Within a Human Centred (system) Design Framework. *Behaviour and Information Technology*, 11(3), pp. 141-150.

Hill, T., Smith, N.D., & Mann, M.F. (1986). Communicating innovations: Convincing computer phobics to adopt innovative technologies. In R.J. Lutz (Ed.), *Advances in Consumer Research*, vol. 13 (pp. 419-422). Provo, UT: Association for Consumer Research.

Hill, T., Smith, N.D., & Mann, M.F. (1987). Role of efficacy expectations in predicting the decision to use advanced technologies: The case of computers. *Journal of Applied Psychology*, 72(2), pp. 307-313.

Hornby, P., Clegg, C.W., Robson, J.I., MacLaren, C.R.R., Richardson, S.C.S. & O'Brien, P. (1992). Human and Organizational Issues in Information Systems Development. *Behaviour and Information Technology*, 11(3), pp. 160-174.

Hovmark, S. and Norell, M. (1993). Social and Psychological Aspects of Computer-aided Design Systems. *Behaviour and Information Technology*, 12(5), pp. 267-275.

Il'enkov, E. V. (1977). *Dialectical logic: Essays on its history and theory.* Moscow: Progress.

Il'enkov, E. V. (1982). The dialectics of the abstract and the concrete in Marx's *Capital.* Moscow: Progress.

Jensen, U.J. (1981). Introduction: Preconditions for evolutionary thinking. In U. J. Jensen & R. Harre (Eds.), *The philosophy of evolution* (pp. 1-22). Brighton: The Harvester Press.

Jonassen, D.H. & Rohrer-Murphy, L. (1999). Activity theory as a framework for designing constructivist learning environments. *Educational Technology, Research and Development,* 47(1), pp. 61-79.

Kaptelinin, V. (1996). Computer-Mediated Activity: Functional Organs in Social and Developmental Context. In B.A. Nardi (Ed.), *Context and Consciousness: Activity Theory and Human-Computer Interaction* (pp. 235-245). Cambridge, MA: The MIT Press.

Karpatschof, B. (1992). The Control of Technology and the Technology Control.

Multidisciplinary Newsletter for Activity Theory, Intl. Standing Conference for Research on Activity Theory (ISCRAT). Berlin, Germany.

Keller, P. (1981). Natural history and psychology: Perspectives and problems. In U. J. Jensen & R. Harre (Eds.), *The philosophy of evolution* (pp. 137-154). Brighton: The Harvester Press.

Kelloway, E.K., & Barling, J. (1993). Members' participation in local union activities: Measurement, prediction, and replication. *Journal of Applied Psychology*, 78(2), pp. 262-279.

Kuutti, K. (1991). Activity theory and its applications to information systems research and development. In H.E. Nissen, H.K. Klein, and R.A. Hirschheim (Eds.), *Information systems research: Contemporary approaches & emergent traditions* (pp. 529-549). Amsterdam: North-Holland.

Kuutti, K. (1992). HCI Research and Activity Theory Position. *Proceedings East-West Intl. Conference on Human-Computer Interaction,* ICSTI (pp. 13-22). St. Petersburg, Russia.

Kuutti, K. (1996). Activity Theory as a Potential Framework for Human-Computer Interaction Research. In Bonnie Nardi (Ed.), *Context and Consciousness: Activity Theory and Human-Computer Interaction* (pp. 17-44). Cambridge, MA: MIT Press.

Kuutti, K. (1999). Activity theory, transformation of work, and information systems design. In Y. Engeström, R. Miettinen, R. Miettinen and R.L. Punamäki-Gitai (Eds.), *Perspectives on activity theory* (pp. 360-376). Cambridge University Press.

Leakey, R. E. & Lewin, R. (1983). *People of the lake: Mankind and its beginnings*. New York: Avon Books.

Leont'ev, A. A. (1980). Tfitigkeit und Kommunikation. Sowjetwissenschaft. Gesellschaftswissenschaftliche Beitrfige 33, 522-535.

Leont'ev, A. N. (1978). Activity, consciousness, and personality. Englewood Cliffs, NJ: Prentice Hall.

Leont'ev A. N. (1981). *Problems of the development of the mind*. Moscow: Progress Publishers.

Lewontin, R. C. (1982). Organism and environment. In H. C. Plotkin (Ed.), *Learning, development, and culture* (pp. 151-169). New York: Wiley.

Lomov, B.F. (1980). Die Kategorien Kommunikation und Tätigkeit in der Psychologie. Sowjetwissenschaft. Sesellschaftswissenschaftliche Beitäge 33, pp. 536-551.

Luria, A. R. (1976). Cognitive development. Cambridge: Harvard University Press.

Markus, M. L. (2000). Conceptual Challenges In Contemporary IS Research. *Journal of Global Information Management,* 8(3), pp. 42-45.

Markus, M.L. & Keil, M. (1994). If We Build It, They Will Come: Designing Information Systems That People Want to Use. *Sloan Management Review,* 35(4), pp. 11-25.

Martocchio, J.J. (1992). The Financial Cost of Absence Decisions. *Journal of Management,* 18(1), pp. 133-152.

Marx, K. (1973). *Grundrisse: Foundations of the critique of political economy (rough draft).* Harmondsworth: Penguin Books.

Mathieson, K. (1991). Predicting user intentions: Comparing the technology acceptance model with the theory of planned behaviour. *Information Systems Research,* 2(3), pp. 173-191.

Mead, G. H. (1934). *Mind, self, and society.* Chicago, IL: The University of Chicago Press.

Moore, G.C. & Benbasat, I. (1991). Development of an instrument to measure the perceptions of adopting an information technology innovation. *Information Systems Research,* 2(3), pp. 192-222.

Myers, M.D. (1999, December 1-3). *Getting Qualitative Research Published.* The 10th Australasian Conference on Information Systems (ACIS) Panels. Wellington, New Zealand.

Mykytyn, P.P., Jr. & Harrison, D.A. (1993). The application of the Theory of Reasoned Action to senior management and strategic information systems. *Project Management Journal,* 6(2), pp. 15-26.

Nardi, B.A. (Ed.). (1996a). *Context and Consciousness: Activity Theory and Human-Computer Interaction.* Cambridge, MA: MIT Press.

Nardi, B.A. (1996b). Some reflections on the application of activity theory. In B.A. Nardi (Ed.), *Context and Consciousness: Activity Theory and Human-Computer Interaction* (pp. 235-245). Cambridge, MA: MIT Press.

Nardi, B.A. (1996c). Studying Context: A Comparison of Activity Theory, Situated Action Models, and Distributed Cognition. In B.A. Nardi (Ed.), *Context and Consciousness: Activity Theory and Human-Computer Interaction* (pp. 69-102). Cambridge, MA: MIT Press.

Nataraajan, R. (1993). Prediction of choice in a technically complex, essentially intangible, highly experiential, and rapidly evolving customer product. *Psychology & Marketing,* 10(5), pp. 367-379.

Netemeyer, R.G. & Bearden, W.O. (1992). A Comparative Analysis of Two Models of Behavioral Intention. *Journal of the Academy of Marketing Science,* 20(1), pp. 49-59.

Ogden, C. K. & Richards, I. A. (1923). *The meaning of meaning*. London: Kegan Paul, Trench, Trubner & Co.

Parmentier, R. J. (1985). Signs' place *in medias res:* Peirce's concept of semiotic mediation. In E. Mertz & R. J. Parmentier (Eds.), *Semiotic mediation: Sociocultural and psychological perspectives* (pp. 23-48). Orlando, FL: Academic Press.

Perkins, D.N. (1993). Person-plus: A distributed view of thinking and learning. In G. Salomon (Ed.), *Distributed cognitions* (pp. 88-110). New York: Cambridge University Press.

Popper, K. R. (1972). Objective knowledge: An evolutionary approach. Oxford: Clarendon Press.

Popper, K. R. & Eccles, J. C. (1977). The self and its brain. Berlin: Springer.

Radzikhovskii, L. A. (1984). Activity: Structure, genesis, and units of analysis. *Soviet Psychology* XXI1: 2, pp. 35-53.

Raeithel, A. (1992). Activity theory as a foundation for design. In C. Floyd, H. Zullighoven, R. Budde, and R. Keil-Slawik (Eds.), *Software development and reality construction* (pp. 391-415). Berlin: Springer-Verlag.

Reynolds, P. C. (1982). The primate constructional system: The theory and description of instrumental object use in humans and chimpanzees. In M. von Cranach & R. Harre (Eds.) *The analysis of action: Recent theoretical and empirical advances* (pp. 343-386). Cambridge, MA: Cambridge University Press.

Ruben, P. (1981). From moralization to class society or from class society to moralization: Philosophical comments on Klaus Eder's hypothesis. In U.J. Jensen & R. Harre (Eds.), *The philosophy of evolution* (pp. 120-136). Brighton: The Harvester Press.

Saga, V.L. & Zmud, R.W. (1994). The Nature and Determinants of IT Acceptance, Routinization, and Infusion. *Diffusion, Transfer and Implementation of Information Technology (A-45),* Elsevier Science, 67-85.

Salomon, G. (1993). No distribution without individuals' cognition: A dynamic interactional view. In G. Salomon (Ed.), *Distributed cognitions* (pp. 111-138). New York: Cambridge University Press.

Salomon, G. (1995). Real Individuals in Complex Environments: A New Conception of Educational Psychology. Draft Document.

Schurig, V. (1976). *Die Entstehung des Bewusstseins*. Frankfurt am Main-New York: Campus.

Seddon, P.B. (1997). A respecification and extension of the Delone and McLean model of IS success. *Information Systems Research,* 8(3), pp. 240-253.

Szajna, B. & Scamell, R. (1993, December). The Effects of Info Systems User Expectations on Their Performance and Perceptions. *MIS Quarterly,* 17(4), pp. 493-516.

Taylor, S. & Todd, P.A. (1995). Understanding information technology usage: A test of competing models. *Information Systems Research,* 6(2), pp. 144-176.

Thompson, R.L., Higgins, C.A., & Howell, J.M. (1991). Personal computing: Towards a conceptual model of utilisation. *MIS Quarterly,* 14, pp. 125-143.

Tolman, C.W. (1988). The Basic Vocabulary of Activity Theory in *Activity Theory,* No.1, ISCRAT. Berlin, Germany.

Tran Duc Thao. (1984). *Investigations into the origin of language and consciousness.* Dordrecht: Reidel.

Venkastesh, V. & Davis, F.D. (1996). A model of the antecedents of perceived ease of use: Development and test. *Decision Sciences,* 27(3), pp. 451-482.

Vygotsky, L. S. (1978). *Mind in society: the development of higher psychological processes.* Cambridge, MA: Harvard University Press.

Vygotsky, L. S. (1981a). The genesis of higher mental functions. In J. V. Wertsch (Ed.), *The concept of activity in Soviet psychology.* Armonk, NY: Sharpe.

Vygotsky, L. S. (1981b). The instrumental method in psychology. In J. V. Wertsch (Ed*.), The concept of activity in Soviet psychology* (pp. 134-143). Armonk, NY: Sharpe.

Wartofsky, M. (1979). *Models: Representation and scientific understanding.* Dordrecht: Reidel.

Wertsch, J.V. (Ed.). (1981). *The concept of activity in Soviet psychology.* Armonk, NY: M.E. Sharp Inc.

Wertsch, J.V. (1985). *Vygotsky and the Social Formation of Mind.* Cambridge, MA: Harvard University Press.

Wertsch, J.V. (Ed.). (1987). *Culture Communication and Cognition: Vygotskian Perspective.* Cambridge University Press.

Wertsch, J.V. (1991). *Voices of the Mind.* Harvard University Press.

Wertsch, J.V. (1994, Fall). The Primacy of Mediated Action in Sociocultural Studies. *Mind, Culture and Activity: An International Journal,* 1(1). Laboratory of Comparative Human Cognition, UCSD, CA.

Williams, T.A. (1994). Information Technology and Self-managing Work Groups. *Behaviour and Information Technology,* 13(4), pp. 268-276.

Wishnick, Y.S. & Wishnick, T.K. (1993). Relationships between school labour relations practitioners' personal and social beliefs and their propensity toward using an interest-based negotiations model in the public schools. *Journal of Collective Negotiations in the Public Sector,* 22(3), pp. 215-231.

Zinchenko, V. P. (1985). Vygotsky's ideas about units for the analysis of mind. In J. V. Wertsch (Ed.), *Culture, communication, and cognition: Vygotskian perspectives* (pp. 94-118). Cambridge, MA: Cambridge University Press.

Chapter XII

Publishing Model for Web Applications: A User-Centered Approach

Roberto Paiano
University of Lecce, Italy

Leonardo Mangia
University of Lecce, Italy

Vito Perrone
Politecnico di Milano, Italy

ABSTRACT

This chapter defines a publishing model for Web applications starting from the analysis of the most well-known modeling methodology, such as HDM, OOHDM, WebML, Conallen's method and others.

The analysis has been focused to verify the state of art about the modeling of Web application pages. In particular, the different types of elements that compose the Web page in the above models are taken into consideration.

This chapter describes the evolution of the HDM methodology starting from the first approach based on the definition of a LP concept up to the more structured and complex Conceptual page, based on the influence of "operations" on the modeling of the dynamics of navigation between pages.

INTRODUCTION

Design and development of WWW applications is quickly evolving to become more engineered products introducing powerful models of hypermedia applications. The entire lifecycle to obtain affordable outcomes must be considered as a complex process that should be supported by tools in order to help the designer in each phase.

Starting from a conceptual modeling makes it easier to manage the changes but it requires a well-engineered process to correctly drive the entire cycle from the model to the outcomes.

Our research activity is oriented to develop both a model to suit the complexity and a set of tools to support the designer from the analysis phase to a prototype of the Web application in order to have an effective test of model. These tools, based on a relational database, support also the multi-delivery feature to customize the application according to the user role (families of applications).

The main goal of this chapter is to define a publishing model for Web applications, starting from the analysis of the most well-known modeling methodology, such as HDM, OOHDM, WebML, Conallen's method and others.

The analysis has been focused to verify the state of art about the modeling of Web application *pages* and to capture the different types of elements that compose the Web page in the above models.

BACKGROUND

In 1993 the Hypermedia Design Model (HDM) (Garzotto, Paolini & Schwabe, 1993; Garzotto, Mainetti & Paolini, 1995, 1996) was published, the first modeling approach oriented to the design of multimedia application that was enhanced to support the hypermedia applications (Bochicchio, Paiano & Paolini, 1999).

In this environment a relevant aspect is represented by definition of Logic and Presentation pages. Logic pages have been introduced into the model to better design what the designer considers the unit of fruition of the specific WWW application (example: a painter and all his works, or the collection of all painters, and so on). The Presentation pages are a collection of logic pages that appear to the user into the HTML page (example: the home page and the previous logic page can appear in two frames of a unique HTML page), managing the dynamic behaviour.

In our research activity we developed the tools, starting from HDM concepts, to support the entire applications lifecycle through the prototyping using an engine that will be briefly described in the next section.

In the last months the Web environment has been oriented on the Web applications more than on Web sites, so the HDM model is evolving to its 2000 version (W2000) in order to best capture all the dynamic and navigational behaviour of WWW applications.

Adding the operation of the traditional Web sites means that the model structure and the behaviour may change dynamically and are strictly related to the user profile.

Our research is oriented to define an Information Conceptual Model and a Navigation Conceptual Model by rendering the design concept using customized UML diagrams. UML was extended to define a suitable framework for this task.

The next step is the definition of a Conceptual Publishing Model, which is the core of this chapter, which inherits the information and navigation definition and customizes the user behaviour.

Several authors are publishing interesting ideas about this problem, but they are starting from the page definition, while we start from a conceptual framework (Conallen, 1999; Ceri, Fraternali & Bongio, 2000; Schwabe & Rossi, 2000).

Although for small applications into a well-known application domain it is possible to directly design the Web page, having in mind, without any formalism, the information and navigation structure in order to realize a well-structured design it's needed to have a different approach to the design.

JWEB II NAVIGATION ENGINE: THE LOGIC PAGES APPROACH

The main requirements taken into account in the design and in the development of the JWeb II Navigation Engine (NE) are:
- Generation of hypermedia applications described in standard structures (easily maintainable).
- Management of different client devices with particular presentation/visualization technology (multi-delivering) such as the Internet, WAP, CD-Rom, etc.
- More different end-users, maintaining individual history for each session.

According to these requirements, the JWeb II NE design is structured in two different steps. In the first step, the part of the application independent from the client device presentation technology (presentation-independent module) is generated, while, in the next step, the other part that is dependent on this technology (presentation-dependent module) is built. So the generation of hypermedia applications consists of the creation of the physical pages (presentation-dependent) that will be published directly on the client device and LPs, (presentation-independent) that contain all the necessary information for the creation of the physical page (Figure 1).

Figure 1. Delivery Process

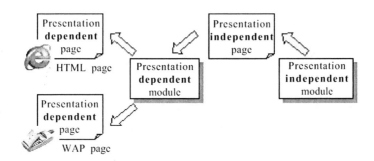

This distinction allows the complete reuse of the presentation-independent modules that represent the main design and development effort, while the presentation-dependent module must be edited according the particular presentation technology (WAP-WML, HTML, etc.).

For example, in a Web-based hypermedia application the presentation-dependent module generates HTML physical pages compatible with the Web browser. These HTML pages are created from standard logical pages that contain the right contents. In particular, the logical pages contain both all the data stored in database structures and all the information maintained by the JWeb II NE to manage the correct user navigation and the user dynamic structures (ex. shopping bag). When changing the presentation technology (ex. from HTML to WML-wap) all the modules for the logical pages generation remain valid, while the mapping on HTML physical pages must be adapted to support the WAP technology.

Besides the creation of pages, both logic and physical, the JWeb II NE manages the exchange of messages with the client device. Particularly, the presentation-dependent modules receive string format commands from the client device, according to the presentation technology, and translate these commands into standard procedure calls for the presentation-independent module

In details the logical pages structured as in Figure 2, pick up and join information about:

- item (one or more) selected (ex. an artist),
- application link for the selected item (ex. the artist's works),
- active collection (actual showed element position, link to the next and previous elements, etc.),
- centres of other collection (ex. "Web sections" collection), and
- user navigation (back, user history, etc.).

Figure 2. Logic Page Structure

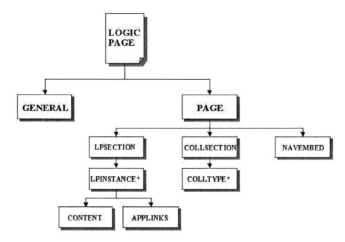

The LP contains the information in standard and abstract form, independent from the user device presentation technology. A logical page, as shown in Figure 2, is made up of some hierarchical sections that pick up in separated ways the information about selected elements (*LPSection*), collections (*CollSection*), and links for default navigation (*NavEmbed*).

In JWebII NE the LPs are XML files with a specific DTD; these LPs are built according a specific template and they pick up all the information needed to create the physical page respecting the end user request. The information for the logical pages is stored in a database with a structure independent from the specific application (named run-time database).

In the simple applications, there is almost a direct relationship between the logical page and information for the end user, while in the most complex applications it is possible you need to show the end user the information present in different logical pages.

Figure 3 shows a Web page of an e-commerce application that describes the information about a particular model of shirt, its relative application links, the active collection (all the models with available filters) and another collection (the Web application's sections).

This page has information present in four different LPs, respectively:
* LP1: information about support functionality
* LP2: information about active "models" collection
* LP3: information about "Web sections" collection
* LP4: information about selected "models" and their relative application links

Figure 3. The Logic Pages

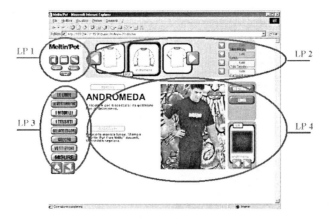

In the LP2 and LP3, the furthermost information is in the section *COLL Section*; while in the LP4, the most further information is in the section *LP Section*.

The LPs (but precisely the relative physical pages) are composed together in presentation level without a precise design methodology. In the case of Figure 3 the composition is made using the HTML technique.

This LP approach to model Web pages was used to realize an e-commerce application in a European project (Bochicchio et al., 1999). This experience has underlined that the approach is efficient to model Web application for a run-time navigation engine (such as JWeb II NE), but some problems were undefined:

- the division of the final content in different logical pages is presentation-oriented and not a result of a publishing model,
- the definition of the interaction between logic pages in the same physical page, and
- what happen when the "operations" change the contents of a logic page.

W2000: THE CONCEPTUAL PAGES APPROACH
Motivation

On the basis of the former open issues on the logical pages approach, it is clear that this kind of modeling approach is quite effective for modeling pages to be used by the engine previously described. On the other hand, taking into account our experience in Web application modeling, we realized that it is ineffective for modeling pages from the user point of view, capturing the user experience already in the modeling phase. For this reason we introduced the conceptual pages modeling that focuses on modeling Web pages just as they will be perceived by the users, introducing a user-centered semantic in defining the various aspects of the pages, modeling the interactions among pages and within the page. Based on this definition, the conceptual pages modeling should be located above the logical pages modeling (opportunely revisited) for those applications that will be executed by the JWeb engine.

The model aims to reach the following objectives:

- To define a self-standing model: to allow the designer to directly model the Web pages starting from the requirements.
- To define a model that could become part of a more complex methodology, such as HDM and its evolution, W2000 (Baresi, Garzotto & Paolini, 2001).

The first objective is due to the fact that, from the analysis of other modeling techniques, a methodology supporting the direct modeling (even from a user-centered point of view) of the Web pages does not still exist. On the other hand, such a methodology should be the most used for modeling small and well-known applications using a structured approach. In this scenario, it is very important to manage both the complexity of the structural composition of the pages (generally the pages join several different kinds of elements) and the navigation dynamics between pages. Furthermore, using a structured approach, it is possible to reuse both the model and the multimedia elements in a framework-like environment.

The second objective concerns the need to complete the model W2000 in order to have a complete methodology to design Web applications. Even though this model has been thought as a natural extension of the HDM model, it is rather general for being used to model the pages of an application designed using one of the other known methodologies like Ceri et al. (2000) and Schwabe and Rossi (2000). Generally, these methodologies split the overall application design into different phases concerning the different aspects of a Web application, that is, contents, navigational characteristics, pages and, only someone, the operations and transactions (UWA, http://www.uwaproject.org).

The W2000 model has two distinct levels:

- *Information Design:* where the *information structures* are designed. Information structures represent the contents available to the users of the application. The information is modeled from the user point of view, meaning that the designer design each object of interest for the user choosing only that information that could be of interest for a particular user. Moreover, in this design phase the *access structures* are designed. The access structure, named *collections*, provides the user with a way to explore the information contents of the application.

- *Navigation Design:* where the *navigation structures* are designed. Navigation structures re-organize contents for a navigational purpose. They define both the atomic piece of content that will be presented to the user, named *nodes*, and the way the user can pass from one piece of content to another; that is, the accessibility relationships form each node towards the other nodes. Moreover the navigation model in W2000 contains the notion of cluster, which is a way to organize the nodes for *context navigation* purposes. Each cluster represents a context of interest for a user, and the designers have to design both the contextual navigation, that is navigation within the cluster, and the infra-clusters navigation, that is navigation among the various clusters.

Like the above levels, the conceptual pages model deeply uses the notion of "type" for all its elements, allowing a more flexible page structure to better reuse components and contents. Furthermore, to satisfy the requirement to complete the W2000 model, some guidelines and rules are defined to map the Navigation level to the Page level. We have already said that a relevant aspect of the model is the possibility to model the "user experience." The way we made this possible was by the introduction of a primitive used to organize information and navigational features needs to the user to perform a certain task in a specific context. For example, some tasks could be browsing items in your shopping bag, scrolling through the pictures of a painter, exploring all book information, etc.

The Model

One of the most important aspects of a model is a precise definition of its focus. The model we are presenting in this chapter aims to reach a number of objectives that we can summarize as in the sequel:

- The main purpose of the model is the identification of the pages of the application. Due to the complexity of a Web page, we have to characterize what a Web page is.
- We model only the composition of a Web page in terms of its contents and its navigational capabilities.
- We separate the modeling of the contents from the modeling of the graphical and visualization aspects related to these contents. In this way we can define the meaning (even in terms of contents and navigational capabilities) of a Web page from a user-centered point of view independently from how it will be visualized and with which graphical solution. This way of designing should separate the designer contribution from that of the experts of graphic or visual communication.

On the other hand, we do not explicitly take into consideration temporal, spatial, and graphical aspects. For this reason both a text and a video are simple content units; events through text can be only read, while the video can be played, stopped, zoomed, etc.; that is, the user can have further interactions with it. Moreover, if a piece of content is delivered as simple HTML or as a more complex flash file, it does not matter because it is often a piece of context. We decided to neglect these aspects for having a lighter model and because of the richness of multimedia kinds of contents and the various way of rendering the same content using different graphical solutions. Anyway, we let the designer specify some temporal, spatial, and graphical aspects in an informal manner, using the comment property we added to each model primitive.

Based on the former considerations, our conceptual pages model describes the organization of information content of a hypermedia application into pages in terms of the following:

- it identifies the basic elements for presentation, i.e., publishing units,
- it organizes them into sections and pages, and
- it organizes the navigation within and across pages.

In the next sections the model primitives will be described in terms of their properties, a possible notation, and their usage. A number of examples will be shown so the reader can make himself familiar with the concepts we present and better understand both their meaning and their usage. Regarding the notation we adopted for the model, some considerations could be done. Once the semantic and properties of each primitive have been defined, whichever notation could be used, depending on who will use this notation for making the application design and who will be the reader of the diagrams and so forth. Moreover, using a graphical notation or not, which implies making sometimes an excessive number of pictures, can be influenced by the availability of a tool supporting the design phases. In our case we chose an UML-like notation that means a notation based on UML, conveniently customised and adapted. The reasons for this choice can be found in the spread of UML in this field. More precisely, we made an UML-profile, but its definition is not included in this chapter.

Publishing Unit Type, Single Publishing Unit

A publishing unit is the atomic element within the page structure. It is a set of information content shown to the user as presentation unit. All the contents of a publishing unit should be perceived by the user as a "consistent" portion of information (in a multimedia meaning) on the page.

Referring to a navigational model, a publishing unit can be defined using one of the following methods:

1. We derive the publishing unit from a whole node defined in the navigation model (according to the widespread Web application models, a node defines the *elementary granules* of information from/to which a user can navigate); the content of the node is "presented" to the user in one unit. This unit may inherit links and navigation features from the node from which it is derived.

2. We derive the publishing unit from a part of a node, defined in the navigation model; the content of the node can be "presented" to the user in more units organized in a *publishing cluster* (discussed later in this chapter). These units may inherit links and navigation features from the node from which they are derived, but they also may have *pure links* (discussed later in this chapter) that make the navigation across them possible.

3. The publishing unit does not derive from any node. In this case, it represents a special element of the page, such as site "logo" or copyright information.

The way we derive a publishing unit from a node or we pick up the information from a data base (or an other information model) is defined by a *mapping rule*.

A publishing unit is described by the following properties:

Name

It univocally identifies the publishing unit in the Publishing Model. In a publishing cluster and/or in a page section, different publishing units must have different names. If two publishing units have the same name, then the two units will be the same.

Graphics

It specifies the graphical properties of the publishing unit. A comment, and eventually sketches, can describe it.

Content

- It can specify the way through which the content of a publishing unit is derived from a node or picked up from a database or an information model (*mapping rule*).
- It can be a description of a pure publishing content, meaning a kind of content that does not derive from any information source, for example a logo of the society.
- Nothing. Some publishing units may not have content associated with them because they only act as link placeholders.

Based on the kind of information that the publishing unit models, we can have:

- **Publishing Unit Type:** it describes the common structure, properties, and features of a class of units; it is derived from a node type.
- **Single Publishing Unit:** it describes the structure, the properties, and the features of an individual unit. A single publishing unit is derived from a single node or it is not derived from any node; in the last case, it represents special content (logo, copyright information and so forth, or an index of high level collections).

In Figure 4 the publishing units contained in a page of our example site are shown.

For specifying the properties of the publishing units in the design document, the refer to the graphical set in Figure 5.

For each publishing unit, a table, shown in Figure 6, is used for specifying all the properties.

Publishing Cluster Type, Single Publishing Cluster

The publishing cluster represents the way to put together the information and the navigational features performed by a user during a task. It groups publishing units and links. The relationship between a publishing cluster and its publishing units is an aggregation. The designer has to define navigation across the publishing units within

Figure 4. Publishing Units in Meltin Pot's Page

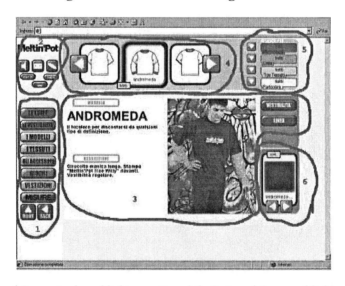

Note: 1,2 and 5 are single publishing units, while 3, 4 and 6 are publishing unit types.

Figure 5. Graphical Notation Used for Specifying the Single Publishing Unit and the Publishing Unit Type Primitives

Single Publishing Unit *Name*	Publishing Unit Type *Name*

the publishing cluster, and among publishing units belonging to different publishing clusters. Examples of publishing units belonging to the same publishing cluster could be a publishing unit representing a pictures index of a painter and a set of publishing units representing the pictures the shopping bag and its items, and so forth.

Through the publishing cluster, we perform the above-mentioned separation between contents and their visualisation aspects. For each publishing cluster of the section, we separately specify the contents, in terms of publishing units, and the possible visualisation configurations, in terms of subsets of the formerly defined publishing units. For understanding this key concept of the model, let us show an example. Consider the main section of the page of a product that includes only a publishing cluster (that can be omitted because of being the only one). Let us suppose that in this application the product is described by a general description and a technical description, and the designer decided to show these two parts of the overall product description one at a time. Conceptually we have only one page for a product with two publishing units (one for each product description) that is the *content*, but with two visualisation configurations—one with the publishing unit containing the general description, and the other one with the publishing unit containing the technical description. This second part represents the visualisation

Figure 6. Graphical Notation Used for Specifying the Properties of the Single Publishing Unit and Publishing Unit Type Primitives

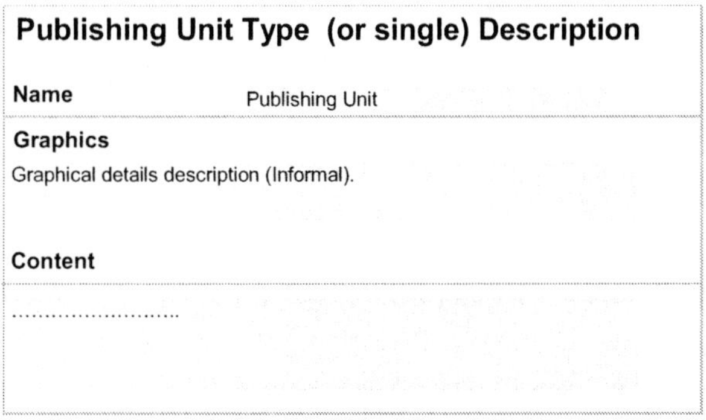

Publishing Unit Type (or single) Description
Name   Publishing Unit
Graphics Graphical details description (Informal).
Content ....

aspects of a page. To realise the advantages of the separation of these aspects, let us take into consideration the same page with the same content, but with a different visualisation strategy. Let us suppose that the designer wants to limit the overall number of application pages — for example, for reducing the number of the overall navigational clicks by the user. A suitable solution fulfilling the designer's goal is to have only a visualisation configuration containing both of the publishing units. This simple example shows as it is possible to specify several visualisation solutions starting from the same page's contents.

A publishing cluster is descried by the following properties:

- **Name:** It univocally identifies the publishing cluster in the Publishing Model. It is usually the name of the navigation element from which the publishing cluster is derived. In a Publishing Model, different clusters must have different names. If two clusters have the same name, then the two clusters will be the same.

- **Content:** It is specified in terms of the publishing units belonging to the publishing cluster.

- **Visualisation Configurations:** They specify the possible visualisation configurations of the publishing cluster. Each visualisation configuration is composed of a subset of the publishing units defining the publishing cluster content. Optionally, an order can be assigned to the publishing units within a visualisation configuration to show the importance rank in visualising them. Moreover, a default visualisation configuration has to be defined.

Based on the kind of publishing units belonging to the publishing cluster, we can have:

- **Publishing Cluster Type:** it has at least a publishing unit type.
- **Single Publishing Cluster:** it has only single publishing units.

In Figure 7, two publishing cluster types are shown. The first publishing cluster corresponds to the user task "to explore the collection," while the second one corresponds to the user task "to look at the details of a particular article."

For specifying the properties of the publishing cluster in the design document, the graphical set in Figure 8 is associated to the section.

For specifying the content in terms of publishing units, we put two possibilities at the designer's disposal. He can use an aggregation relationship between the publishing cluster and its publishing units in a graphical way, or specify the publishing units in the associated table as shown in Figure 9. The same notation can be used for both publishing cluster types and single publishing clusters.

Any additional comments can be added based on the designer's preferences.

Figure 7. Publishing Clusters in Meltin Pot's Page

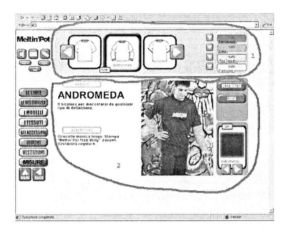

Section Type, Single Section

A section is a grouping of content, semantically correlated. It is defined in order to provide the pages of the application with a better organization. A section puts together publishing clusters that are semantically correlated. When a user goes from one cluster to another within the same section, he does not change his task, but he is changing context performing the same task.

A section is described by the following properties:

- **Name:** It univocally identifies the section in the overall publishing model of the application.
- **Graphics:** It specifies the graphical properties of the publishing section. It can be either described by a comment and eventually sketches or omitted because recursively defined by the graphical properties of the single publishing unit belonging to.
- **Content:** It specifies the content associated with the section. This content is expressed in terms of Publishing Cluster Types and/or Single Publishing Clusters.

Figure 8. Graphical Notation Used for Specifying the Publishing Cluster Type and the Single Publishing Cluster Primitives

Figure 9. Graphical Notation Used for Specifying the Properties of the Single Publishing Cluster and Publishing Cluster Type Primitives

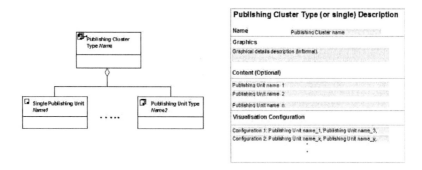

Based on the kind of publishing units belonging to the page section, we can have:

- **Page Section Type:** it has at least one publishing unit type.
- **Single Page Section:** it has only single publishing units.

In Figure 10, we show a page of our example application where there are three sections, two of which are Single Sections (Sections 1 and 2) while the third one, the main section, is a Section Type (Section 3). In this page each section has only one visualisation configuration, therefore section configurations do not have to be described.

For specifying the properties of the section in the design document, refer to the graphical set in Figure 11.

Figure 10. Page Sections in Meltin Pot's Page

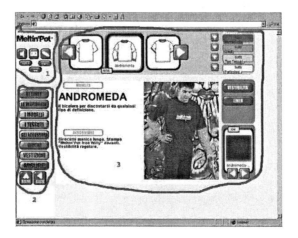

Figure 11. Graphical Notation Used for Specifying the Section Type and the Single Section Primitives

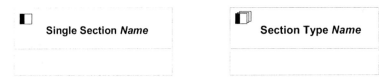

For specifying the content in terms of publishing clusters, we put two possibilities at the designer's disposal. He can use an aggregation relationship between the section and its publishing clusters in a graphical way or specify the publishing clusters in the associated table as shown in Figure 12. The same notation can be used for both Section Types and Single Sections. If the section contains only a Publishing Cluster, in the graphical representation, the publishing units of this cluster can be directly associated to the section.

Page Type, Single Page

A page represents what the user sees in a browser window. It is quite arduous defining precisely what a page is from the user's point of view. In particular, it could create confusion about what changing page means. To avoid possible confusion we use a semantic definition of a page. We assign a page to each semantic element of the application. We picked up these elements from the Information Model, meaning the following:

- **Entity:** is a "virtual object" of interest for the user. An entity, in general, makes more sense for the reader if it can be related to an object of the "real world." The entity "Raffaello," for example, is immediately understood as associated with a famous painter.
- **Semantic Association:** connects two different objects in the sense that it creates the "infrastructure" for a possible navigation path and it has a semantic

Figure 12. Graphical Notation Used for Specifying the Properties of the Single Section and Section Type Primitives

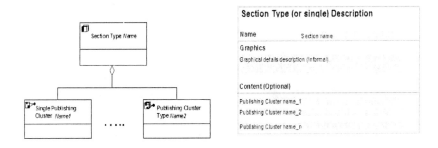

associated to it. The Semantic Association between Smith (an *Author*) and P121, P128 *(papers)* has a semantic meaning (authorship) and also provides a (possible) navigation path.

- **Collection:** is the basic element for building an access schema to the application contents. A collection, very shortly, is an organized set of objects, called members. A collection is created in order to assemble all the objects that, under certain circumstances, can be interesting for the user.

In Figure 13 we show two pages from our example application. The page on the left is for a dress article, while the other one is for the cloth choice.

The semantic definition of the Web page we have done appears independent from the device through which the application will be delivered. From the structural point of view, a page is a grouping of different sections whose contents could not be correlated semantically. The same sections may be used in more than one page. Generally, a page is composed by a main section dealing with the semantic element that gave rise to the page, and a number of secondary sections that allow the user to change the focus element. The different sections belonging to a page are very often completely unrelated from each other. Within a page, for example, may coexist a section showing a general menu (that never changes), a section showing specific objects, and a section listing auxiliary services. The three sections do not relate to each other, but for the fact that they are offered in the same page.

A page is described by the following properties:

- **Name:** It univocally identifies the page in the overall publishing model of the application.
- **Graphics:** It informally specifies the graphical properties of the page type. It can be either described by a comment or a sketch, or omitted because recursively defined by the graphical properties of the section types.
- **Content:** It specifies the content associated with the page. This content is expressed in terms of Publishing Section Types and/or Single Publishing Sections.

Figure 13. Page Examples from the Meltin Pot's Application

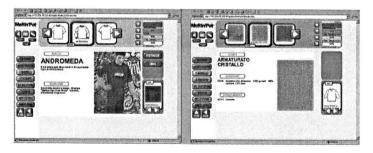

- **Main Topic Section:** It indicates the section containing the most important element of the page.

  A page can be either a *Single Page* or a *Page Type.*
- **Page Type:** it represents a set of pages that share some common properties. It defines a "category" of pages that a user can find in the application associated to the same conceptual element type.
- **Single Page:** it represents a specific page of the application that does not share its property with any other pages. Typical examples of this kind of page are the Home page, the Presentation page, etc.

For specifying the properties of the Page in the design document, the graphical set in Figure 14 is used.

For specifying the content in terms of sections, we put two possibilities at the designer's disposal. He can use an aggregation relationship between the page and its sections in a graphical way or specify the sections in the associated table as shown in Figure 15. The same notation can be used for both page types and single pages. In the following figures both the generic notation and its usage for specifying the page of the dress article are shown for a better understanding of the notation usage.

For each page (both single page and page type), a table is associated in order to describe the rest of its properties.

Any additional comments can be added based on the designer's preferences.

Depending on the designer's preferences, a layout sketch can be associated to the page. This sketch should express the designer's ideas about the section position within the page. Based on the former example (article page) a possible layout sketch may be what is illustrated in Figure 17.

Publishing Link

In order to model navigation at the publishing level, we redefine the notion of link in more general terms to denote a general user's interaction on a page. Most interactions are induced and constrained by the navigation design upon which

Figure 14. Graphical Notation Used for Specifying Page Type and Single Page Primitives

Figure 15.   Graphical Representation of a Page and its Sections: General Definition and Usage

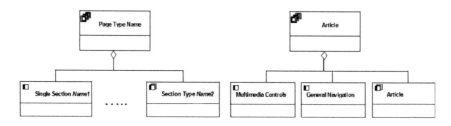

publishing design is built, but we also allow designers to introduce new interactions at this level for efficiency or usability reasons.

If the designer is using the model below a navigational model, we may distinguish between two kinds of links: *derived link* if it derives from a link defined in the navigation model, or *pure link* if it is not derived from any link. The pure links

Figure 16.   Graphical Table Associated to a Page: General Definition and Usage

Page Type (or single) Description

Name	Page name

Graphics

Graphical details description (Informal).

Content (Optional)

Section name_1
Section name_2

Section name_n

Main Topic

Section name

Page Type Description

Name	Article

Graphics

The page should be suitable for a 800 x 600 display mode. The main section.............

Content

Article
Multimedia Controls
General Navigation

Main Topic

Article

Figure 17. Layout Sketch for the Product Page

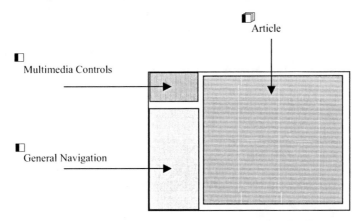

are introduced in the presentation to add further navigation possibilities, allowing movement of the focus of the page on a particular unit or to navigate towards a particular page.

The source of a publishing link is always either a publishing unit type or a single publishing unit; the kind of the target of a publishing link depends on the kind of the link.

The navigation dynamics, in presentation, lead to the following kinds of links:

1. **Focus Link:** a focus link allows movement of the focus of the page from a publishing unit (or publishing cluster) to another one maintaining the current content of the page at the same time. Following this kind of link, we navigate within the same page instance. The target of this kind of link can be one of the following publishing elements: publishing unit (single, type), publishing cluster (single, type), or page section (single, type).

2. **Intra-Page Link:** an intra-page link allows navigating across the instances of the same page type. Following this kind of link results in the change of the page content, but not the change of the page structure. This link may or may not involve a focus change. The target of this kind of link can be one of the following publishing elements: publishing unit (single, type), publishing cluster (single, type), or page section (single, type).

3. **Page Link:** a page link allows navigation across the instances of different page types. Following this kind of link results in the change of the page content and structure. The target of this kind of link can be one of the following publishing elements: single page or page type.

In this case, the focus may sometimes (but rarely) change determining an automatic page scroll on the screen.

A publishing link is described by the following properties:

- **Name:** It univocally identifies the link in the Publishing Model. It is usually the name of the relationship from which the link is derived. Given two publishing elements, if there are more links between them, each link must have its own name, different from the name of other links.
- **Link Placeholder:** It describes the placeholder of the link, that is, the point on the page where the user should "click" to follow the link. Examples could be: the name of the link label, the rule which the label is caught from the application data, some presentation aspects such as button, underlined writing, etc.
- **Population Criteria:** It specifies the population rule used to define the content of the target, e.g., the publishing unit type (or single publishing unit) content belonging to the target. If the conceptual page model has been made below a navigational model, it could easily specify the target content in terms of node. Moreover it specifies the visualisation configuration if the clusters of the destination page have more than one.
- **(Optional) Focus:** It specifies if the link involves a focus moving.
- **(Optional) Navigation Pattern:** It models the meaning of instantiating a link, since it concisely

In Figure 18, some link placeholders of the central section of the example page are shown.

For specifying the properties of the page in the design document, the graphical set in Figure 19 is shown.

Each link is linked to a publishing unit as shown in Figure 20, and is described by a graphical table, as shown next to the figure.

FUTURE WORK

The model will be completed at the end of this year. Now we are developing a specific application in a bank environment, both to verify the whole W2000 model and to open the issues needed to adapt the model from the developer's point of view.

The next step will be the development of a navigation engine independent from a specific application domain, similar to the former engine named JWEB that was described in the above sections.

At the same time we are working on the definition of a suite of metrics to estimate the effort needed to develop a Web application. Currently we have this

Figure 18. Some Link Placeholders

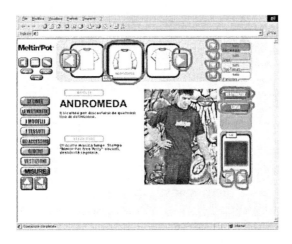

Figure 19. Graphical Notation Used for Specifying the Focus Link, Intra-Page Link and Page Link Primitives

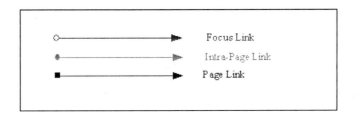

Figure 20. Graphical Notation Used for Attaching a Link to a Publishing Unit and for Describing the Link's Properties

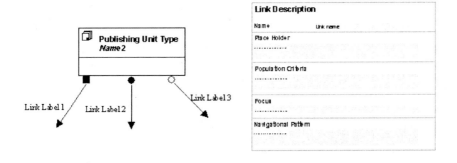

suite based on the methodology of W2000 and we are working to generalize this suite to estimate the effort to develop a Web application independently from the W2000 model.

CONCLUSIONS

When this research project is completed, we will have a complete environment to develop Web application using a structured approach similar to what happens for the traditional applications.

Our suite will supply the developers with a complete design methodology, a way to estimate the effort (and the cost) in the early design phase, and a set of tools that will aid the developers in their work. In addition, they will have also a navigation engine, which represents a significant part of the whole effort.

REFERENCES

Baresi, L., Garzotto, F., & Paolini, P. (2001). Extending UML for Modeling Web Applications. In *Proceedings of the 34th Hawaii International Conference on System Sciences, Decision Technologies For Management track, Unified Modeling Language: A Critical Review and Suggested Future Minitrack* (Vol. 3, p. 3055). Maui, HI.

Bochicchio, M.A., Paiano, R., Paolini, P. (1999). JWeb: An HDM Environment for fast development of Web Applications. *Proceedings of Multimedia Computing and Systems 1999 (IEEE ICMCS '99), vol. 2* (pp. 809-813). Florence, Italy.

Ceri, S., Fraternali, P., & Bongio, A. (2000, May 5). Web Modeling Language (WebML): a modeling language for designing Web sites. In *Proceedings Int. Conf. WWW9* (pp. 137-157). Amsterdam.

Conallen, J. (1999). Modelling Web Application Architectures with UML. *Communications of the ACM, 42*(10).

Garzotto, F., Mainetti, L., & Paolini, P. (1995). Hypermedia Application Design: a Structured Approach. In J.W. Schuler, N. Hannemann, & N. Streitz (Eds.), *Designing User Interfaces for Hypermedia*. Springer Verlag.

Garzotto, F., Mainetti, L., & Paolini, P. (1996). Information Reuse in Hypermedia Applications. *Hypertext 1996*, Washington DC, USA, 93-104.

Garzotto, F., Paolini, P., & Schwabe, D. (1993). HDM - A Model Based Approach to Hypermedia Application Design. *ACM Transactions on Information Systems, 11* (1), 1-26.

Perrone, V., Maritati, M., Paolini, P., Baresi, L., Garzotto, F. & Mainetti, L. (2000). *Hypermedia and Operation Design: Model, Notation and Tool Architecture.* Official Deliverable D7 of the European Project UWA IST2000-25131.

Schwabe, D., & Rossi, G. (2000). *An Object Oriented Approach to Web-Based Application Design.* Available on the World Wide Web at: http://www.telemidia.puc-rio.br/oohdm/oohdm.htm.

UWA (Ubiquitous Web Applications) Project. Available on the World Wide Web at: http://www.uwaproject.org.

Chapter XIII

LEZI: A Video Based Tool for Distance Learning

Mario A. Bochicchio
University of Lecce, Italy

Nicola Fiore
University of Lecce, Italy

ABSTRACT

In this chapter we present LEZI, an experimental software tool oriented to the production of indexed videos enriched with hypertextual and multimedia elements for distance learning applications.

LEZI is based on the assumption that in particular types of educational hypermedia productions, the quality of educational content may easily compensate for a user interface limited to the essentials or a reduced set of multimedia features. Production of this kind of hypermedia application can be high quality, even with short production cycles at very low cost.

The purpose of the chapter is to show how a traditional lesson or a conference can be effectively transformed into a powerful multimedia product based on a very simple and regular structure.

INTRODUCTION

Modern hypermedia applications are complex to conceive, and expensive to produce in terms of content and design (Bochicchio, Paiano & Paolini, 1999a; Bochicchio & Paolini, 1998). Attempting to reduce costs or to shorten production time may easily result in poor-quality products (Garzotto, Mainetti & Paolini, 1995).

Nevertheless, we are convinced that in some specific niches, good-quality multimedia contents can be easily created and transformed into video-based e-learning applications — in a short time and at a low cost.

Good teachers obtain and hold the attention of their students by speaking, by using images and slides, by showing objects, by writing on the blackboard, by using gestures, and so on. Therefore, good teachers can easily create good-quality content that can be video-recorded and used to produce hypermedia applications and to publish their work on CD/DVD or on the Web.

However, it is well known that long video sequences (e.g., one hour or more) are not compelling and not interactive. Moreover, usual linear cursors and VTR-like controls, as shown in Figure 1, are ineffective for navigating video sequences longer than a few minutes.

The idea discussed in the rest of the chapter is that, just as a book needs a hierarchical index to allow the reader to find a specific topic without reading the whole text, a video lesson needs a hierarchical index to enable the students to find each topic they are interested in without looking at the whole video.

Various commercial tools suitable to help teachers create indexed videos are analyzed in the in this chapter before introducing LEZI, an experimental tool oriented to the production of hierarchical indexes for long video sequences enriched with hypertexts and other multimedia elements (referred to hereafter as hypervideos).

The structure of the chapter is as follows: in the Background section, we define the position of our work in relation to the literature and the existing products. Further sections deal with the requirements, the conceptual modeling and the main implementation issues of the proposed tool. A description of the main features of

Figure 1. A Typical Linear Cursor to Navigate Video Sequences

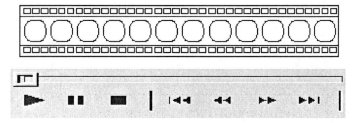

Figure 2. Video Sequence with Hierarchical Index

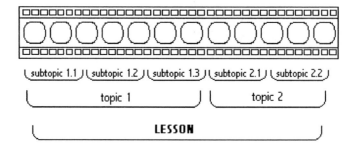

the tool is given in The LEZI II Prototype section, while two full-working examples of hypervideos, developed for real university classes, are given in the Applications section. Finally, we present our conclusions and we discuss future developments.

BACKGROUND

In recent years, international workgroups have defined standards (e.g., SMIL (SMIL, n.d.), HTML+Time, etc.) and developed tools to design, model, and produce interactive hypermedia applications, based on multimedia objects with temporal synchronization requirements (i.e., animation, video, etc.).

In our opinion, these tools, well defined from the theoretical point of view and very effective in terms of results, are often complex and unsuitable for people with low technical aptitude. Simplicity and user-friendliness are fundamental in the environment of teaching in order to enable teachers and scientists to publish educational material with limited economic resources and without specific technical skills.

An interesting example is GRINS (GRiNS, n.d.), an authoring product for creating and executing hypermedia SMIL documents. In general, GRINS needs a great amount of detailed information on the space-temporal aspects of the presentation; this increases the versatility and the flexibility of the tool, but requires technical skills and implementation abilities that the non-specialist may not have.

MTEACH (Montessoro & Caschi, 1999) is based on a different approach: it is an authoring methodology supported by a language and a compiler, which allows the authors of educational hypermedia products to work at high level. MTEACH aims to simplify the design and the development phases of educational applications by adopting predefined application templates. Nevertheless, it does not cover a number of interesting "authoring situations," as defined in the next section of the paper.

Figure 3. Video Madeus Execution View

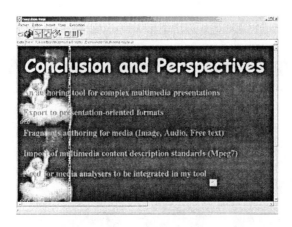

The Video Madeus authoring tool (Roisin, Tran-Thuong & Villard, 2000) is based on a model for the description of audio-visual information as shown in Figure 3.

Video Madeus focuses on the interaction of video elements (character, slot, scene, etc.) with other elements (text, sound, etc.) in a multimedia document. Figure 4 shows the timeline view, making it possible to visualise the structure and the temporal placement of media objects. In this window the author can modify the temporal placement of media objects directly. Whenever an act of editing is performed, the system ensures the continuous maintenance of all relations. The Video Madeus approach may be seen as data-driven rather than user-centered.

Real Presenter (RealPresenterPlus, 2001) is a commercial product, recently introduced by the well known RealNetwork company.

Figure 4. Video Madeus Timeline View

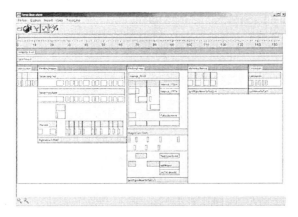

Figure 5. An Application Created with Real Presenter

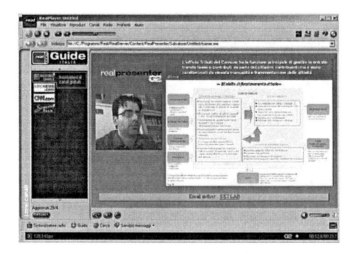

It is an authoring environment based on the RealOne platform for creating Web-based presentations. It enables the user to synchronize audio and video with PowerPoint presentations, and to deliver them over the Internet or in a corporate intranet (Figure 5).

With this tool the author of a PowerPoint presentation can produce a Web-based video without worrying about the constraints of time, distance, or size. Examples of users include teachers and professors, doctors demonstrating procedures, sales professionals, and corporate trainers.

Real Presenter approaches the ideal of "very easy content production," but it is limited to PowerPoint presentations, without considering that teachers, during their lesson, also need to use other resources (blackboards, gestures, etc.).

Figure 6. PowerPoint Presentation Structure

Figure 7. PowerPoint Presentation on the Web

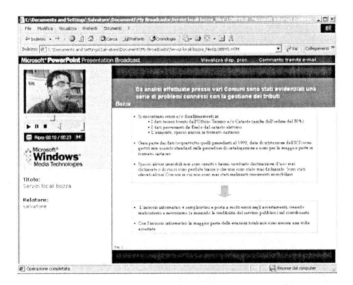

Also, the latest version of MS PowerPoint is able to publish its presentations on the Web as shown in Figure 7.

When a presentation is published on the Web or saved as a Web page, it automatically includes the following (Figure 6):

1. A navigation frame, containing the index of the slides
2. A slide frame
3. A button for showing or hiding the outline of the presentation
4. A button for showing or hiding the notes pane
5. A full-screen viewing option, which hides the browser controls and is similar to "slide show view" in Microsoft PowerPoint

This product also approaches the ideal of "very easy content production," but like the Real Presenter, it is limited to PowerPoint presentations. The navigation frame is very simple, but it does not describe the structure of the lesson at various levels of detail.

Microsoft Producer for PowerPoint version 2002 is an add-on tool to PowerPoint in Office XP, as shown in Figure 8. Built using Windows Media Technologies (Windows Media Technologies, 2002), it is designed to address the growing need among businesses and organizations using streaming media for easy ways to create dynamic internal and external streaming media communications.

By using the "Producer's Synchronize Wizard" as shown in Figure 9, users can synchronize the images, slides, and HTML pages that are displayed with the video

Figure 8. Microsoft Producer

and audio tracks. This is an especially powerful feature when synchronizing presenters' video and audio with the slides, images, and HTML pages they are referring to. Synchronization can take place during audio and video capture, or after video, audio and slides have been imported or captured into the project. Producer will automatically make adjustments in the timeline to ensure that the timing of all media is coordinated.

Producer automatically generates a TOC from the slide titles and image file names, making it easy for users to jump to different places in the presentation. The TOC entries can also be edited after they have been generated via the TOC tab by the presentation author. It is very simple to use; however, it is impossible to create structured indexes for long presentations.

In our opinion, each one of these tools tackles different aspects of the problem. An accurate analysis of both research and commercial tools has enabled us to

Figure 9. Synchronizing Audio, Video and Slides in Microsoft Producer

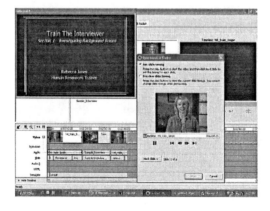

Figure 10. A Presentation Made with Microsoft Producer

extrapolate the essential requirements (discussed in the next section) of a good development environment based on indexed video.

Starting from these requirements, a LEZI prototype was developed, and a number of real lessons were produced and tested (Bochicchio, Paiano, Paolini, Andreassi & Montanaro, 2000). A project for a more complete prototype, called LEZI II, was then started at the SET-Lab of the University of Lecce, as part of a large research project focusing on the development of innovative educational tools and applications. The project comes at a moment of growing interest in educational video production in general, and WebTV in particular (Handler, Benavides, Morgan & Houghton, 2001; Abeshaus & Dickinson, 2001; Hochman & Marshall, 2001).

The first complete version of LEZI II, released in July 2001, performs very well in terms of ease of use, effectiveness, production costs and operating speed.

REQUIREMENTS

The fundamental requirement, for LEZI, is very high ease of use, so that it can be truly accessible even to users with very basic computer knowledge. This is essential for many scientists or teachers who have, in contrast, great communicative skills and could easily give high-quality conferences and lessons.

An even more important requirement is to keep production times down (ideally to about one hour of work, or less, for each hour of lesson). In some cases (e.g., conferences or special events) it may be important to apply this constraint up to the "real time production" limit (i.e., the indexed hypervideo of the event should be available on CD/DVD, and on-line, by the end of the event itself).

A third very important requirement is the ability to effectively support the most common "authoring situations," listed:

- a teacher presents his or her lesson in a classroom, possibly with a blackboard or slides
- a teacher presents his or her lesson outside the classroom, if this is appropriate for the topic concerned. For example, a lesson on archeology could be much more interesting if it is performed at an archeological dig
- a teacher uses gestures to "animate" some concept expressed by "static schema" (typically a slide), so that students need to simultaneously view the two different information sources (the teacher and the schema)
- a teacher uses his PC to explain how to use a specific computer program. The attention focus is on the display of the PC, on the voice of the teacher and, optionally, on a blackboard
- a teacher uses his PC to make a PowerPoint presentation. The attention focus is on the display of the PC and on the voice of the teacher.

The fourth requirement relates to finding the various topics and subtopics in the lesson. The user, in fact, needs a fast and effective way to find out the contents of the video lesson, so they can easily find and reach the subjects of interest without wasting time on uninteresting or already-known video sequences.

We maintain that the most common video players (Real Player, Microsoft Media Player and QuickTime player) in general do not offer an adequate solution to this problem. Indeed:
- they use a linear cursor to move forwards and backwards in the video. This system is usable and effective when the video duration does not exceed a few minutes. Very poor results are achieved, however, when the same system is applied to longer videos, such as a whole lesson (one hour or more)
- they do not provide a simple system for "describing" the overall structure of the lesson at various granularity levels, or for using this description to "navigate" within the lesson
- they are very slow to restart, while operating in streaming mode on the Internet, when the cursor is moved. It can be very frustrating to find on-line a specific subject in long video sequences.

The fifth requirement concerns the technical skills needed in the authoring phase; it is well known, for example, that a few hours of lesson can produce a very large amount of digital content (video, texts, audio, photos, etc.), which can be difficult to manage. This kind of problem requires a high-level authoring tool to simplify all technical tasks and to fully support teachers or lecturers, whatever technical knowledge they may have.

An additional requirement concerns the possibility of linking suitable comments, bibliographic references, and other teaching materials to the indexed hypervideo. The most common digital document formats (PDF, HTML, PPT, …) should be supported.

CONCEPTUAL MODELING

The W2000 (Baresi et al., 2001) methodology has been adopted to refine the informal description presented so far, to obtain a suitable conceptual model for LEZI II, and to derive from it the current LEZI II prototype.

W2000 is a user-centered methodology for conceiving and defining, at a conceptual level, hypermedia applications. It organizes the overall development process into a number of interdependent tasks. Each activity produces a model (UML uses the term "model" to identify a set of related diagrams), which describes some aspects of the hypermedia application, and is composed of a set of extended UML diagrams. The idea underlying W2000 is a requirements-driven, user-focused approach to design. It is crucial to start the design activity by considering requirements, and by setting user satisfaction as the crucial objective to be achieved (Finkelstein et al., 2001). In order to define requirements we need to identify the *stakeholders* (anyone having an interest in the application) and the *goals* (i.e., objectives that the application must satisfy in the stakeholder desires) and *situations of use*.

W2000 assumes that a hypermedia application must/can be seen at three different levels of abstraction:

- **Information level:** at this level, we describe only and all data the application will deal with. This level is based on the HDM2000 (Garzotto et al., 1991) modeling language. In a nutshell, the HDM methodology requires that after the requirements analysis, a schema of the application is defined. The schema is organized into two different parts: the hyperbase schema describes the basic navigational capabilities offered by the application, while the access schema describes the organization of the access structures (collections in the HDM terminology). A hyperbase schema is organized into entity types, defining the structure of the objects managed by the application, and link types, defining the basic navigation capabilities. An access schema, on the other hand, defines the basic indexes (possibly hierarchically organized), guided tours, etc., that allow the user to start browsing within the application. Both for the hyperbase schema and the access schema there is a sharp distinction between design in-the-large, where the general features of the design are defined, and design in-the-small, where the details are provided.

- **Navigation level:** at this level, we introduce navigation. This means that we should be able to reconcile entities, components, semantic associations, and collections in terms of *node*s, *link*s, and *cluster*s. Entities and components should be refactored freely. Needless to say, a tool could suggest a predefined rule; for example, all leaf components become nodes.
- **Presentation level:** at this level, nodes, links and clusters become *page*s, *sections* and *links* between pages (sections). It seems that different navigation models can be rendered using different presentations. It is not only a problem of the device used to view the pages, but also a choice of interaction paradigm and page structure.

Following the W2000 approach, a number of LEZI II variants have been identified; consequently, LEZI II has been classified as an *application family* (Bochicchio, Paiano & Paolini, 1999b).

In brief, for the main prototype we have identified the following roles:

- **Author:** manages his public or private lessons and related students; an example of an author might be a university teacher who publishes his or her courses on the Web; he or she can decide if the lessons are to be seen only by students of the class or if access is free.
- **Registered Student:** attends public or private lessons; can perform second-level authoring (co-authoring) operations (Garzotto et al., 1995). A registered student can customize the index of a lesson's topics to better study the topic and he can link suitable comments or bibliographic references.
- **Unregistered Student:** can only attend public lessons.
- **LEZI Manager:** manages the system.

It should be observed that the users of the LEZI II system are not rigidly associated with a single role. A registered student of a given lesson, for example, could be at the same time the author of a different lesson. Specifying roles is the best way to make user profiles explicit and to avoid duplicating functionalities and navigation paths for all users.

In Figure 11 the hyperbase diagram of LEZI II is outlined in terms of HDM2000 primitives (Garzotto, Mainetti & Paolini, 1993a, 1993b; Garzotto, Paolini & Schwabe, 1993).

The hyperbase schema is adopted to specify:

- the information structures needed by the various classes of users (information design)
- the navigation paths that allow users to find the piece of information suitable for their task (semantic navigation design)

Figure 11. LEZI II: Hyperbase in the Large

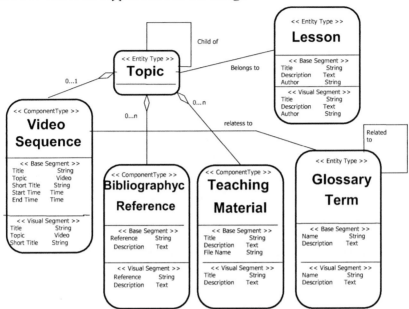

In Figure 12 we show the main functional use-case diagrams, in which the main functionalities are associated with the previously identified roles.

THE LEZI II PROTOTYPE

A prototype of the described application was released in July 2001 at the SET-Lab of the University of Lecce (http://mb.unile.it/Lezi).

Referring to the fourth requirement specified in Section 3, the access structure has been implemented as a tree, organized into topics and subtopics nodes. Each topic node corresponds to the sequence of the videos associated with its subtopics, and the root corresponds to the entire lesson. No more than four subtopic levels are allowed, and each leaf of the tree corresponds to two to five minutes of video. Each node (both topic and subtopic) of the tree contains a short textual description of the video associated to that node and the indication of its duration. This short description is very effective for finding the interesting topics and skipping the uninteresting (or the already-familiar) ones.

The tree-index acts as a hierarchical table of contents (TOC). It can be generated:

- manually, by marking the start and the end of each subtopic on the video in correspondence to a timeline measured during the lesson

Figure 12. W2000 Functional Use-Case Diagram of LEZI II

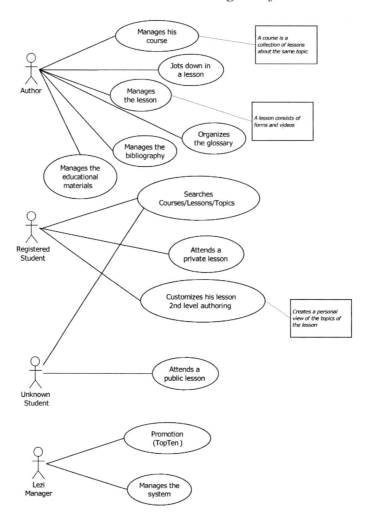

•   semi-automatically, by generating a set of nodes equally spaced in time. The authors of the lesson can then add to/delete/modify the text associated with each node, as well as its duration and its start/end time.

Multiple tree-indexes can be created for a given lesson, so that the same lesson can be easily readapted for different purposes and different users. Multiple tree-indexes can also be created by students for their own purposes, or to share with other students.

The prototype has two distinct parts: the authoring part, suitable for creating a new LEZI lesson, and the fruition part ("lesson player" hereafter), which may be used to navigate among existing lessons and to select and play the desired one.

Two versions of the prototype have been produced, with the same functions, for both on-line and disk-based operation. The disk-based version is suitable for creating and/or using stand-alone LEZI lessons, especially CD/DVD production, while the on-line version allows remote users on the Internet to create and/or play LEZI lessons. At any time it is possible to port stand-alone lessons to the Internet and vice versa.

From the technical point of view, the on-line LEZI environment requires, for the lesson server, a networked workstation equipped with RealServer (for the video streaming) and Internet Information Server, while the on-line LEZI client, suitable for both authoring and fruition, can be executed in any browser supporting JavaScript and equipped with the RealVideo plug-in. The disk-based version of the LEZI environment (both the authoring tool and the lesson player) is a standard MS Windows application including all necessary software components.

Different user interface styles (multi-skin), and a customizable set of interface objects (background, buttons, colors, fonts, etc.) are supported to better adapt each LEZI II lesson to the expected audience.

From the implementation point of view the on-line version is based on the MS-asp object model for server-side scripting and on JavaScript and DHTML to implement the visual interface for the client. A SMIL program (SMIL, n.d.) has been used to correctly synchronize the tree-index with the video streams; for the same purpose the JMF (JMF, n.d.) performed much worse in terms of speed and reliability. The logical structure is shown in Figure 13.

In comparison with the MS-ASF format, and the related set of tools for video production and streaming, the RealVideo format was more reliable and performed

Figure 13. LEZI: Logical Structure

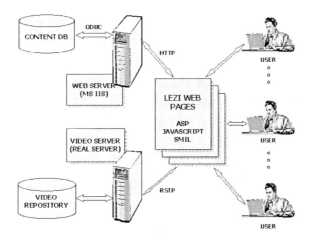

Figure 14. Recording System

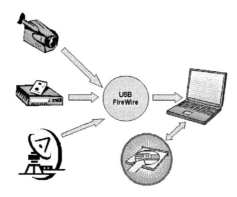

better. In particular, with RealVideo it was very simple and effective in producing video clips for multiple bandwidth targets, and able to automatically switch to lower/ higher bit-rates according to network conditions.

The first step in creating a lesson with the LEZI prototype is to produce the movie in Real-Video format.

The lesson can be recorded on a PC or on a notebook equipped with RealProducer by means of a video-camera and an USB video-converter (Figure 14).

For pre-recorded videos on videotape, or for live videos coming from other devices (satellite, decoder, etc.) the same system may be used; if they are already in digital format they will have to be converted into a RealProducer-compliant format before producing and using it in LEZI II.

Further steps to produce the lesson with LEZI II, are:

- At the end of the recording session, a tree index is created. Ten to 30 minutes are sufficient, in general, for each hour of lesson
- Teaching materials (if available as digital documents) and bibliographical references are added to the indexed video. Multiple document formats (doc, pdf, ppt, xml, html, etc.) are supported
- The LEZI II lesson is then generated (both for CD/DVD and for on-line use).

The prototypical use of the current version of LEZI II has shown the effectiveness of the LEZI approach for educational purposes. More extensive production of video lessons, and more accurate evaluation of the effectiveness of the approach are foreseen for the next academic year.

System Structure and Performance Considerations

A sample configuration to produce video is:

- a notebook Pentium® III processor 750 MHz-M with Microsoft Windows® XP
- RealProducer software
- a camcorder (like the smallest Sony DCR)
- an USB video-converter (like Belkin VideoBus) to connect the camcorder to the PC via a USB port.

The whole system is easy to set up and transport, and is inexpensive; the overall cost is about US$3,550.

A camcorder may also be used to directly record onto a DVD-R mini disc such as the Hitachi DZMV230A. In this case it will be necessary to convert the video into a RealProducer-compliant format before producing the movie in Real-Video format.

The described system also allows the user to record many hours of video even on normal hard disks or other storage devices; in multistream format about 70 MB are required for each hour of lesson.

The on-line version of LEZI requires a server equipped with:

- Real Server
- Windows 2000 Server with IIS installed
- a 100 Mb/s LAN or another access to network
- SQL SERVER DBMS

The overall cost is about US$13,000.

From the performance point of view, the number of concurrent users supported by the LEZI II server depends on RealServer, i.e., the video streaming server we adopted (RealServerGuide, n.d.).

Empirically, 10 users looking at various nodes of the same lesson (worst case test), or at different lessons, are very well supported by a server equipped with a Pentium III 800 processor, with 128MB Ram, on a 100 Mb/s LAN. Also, the connection of clients by ISDN line has shown excellent results. A more detailed and systematic test is planed for the future.

APPLICATIONS

The University of Lecce has produced many applications with LEZI II. In order to demonstrate the support to two different authoring situations, we briefly describe them in the following sections.

Figure 15.   In the Left Frame We See the Table of Contents. Once the "Definition of Hypermedia" Has Been Chosen, the Content Appears in the Right Frame

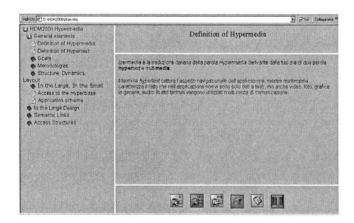

Computer Graphics Course

This application is based on the computer-graphics class given by Professor Paolo Paolini (Milano-Lecce-Como, 1999). The screen shots in Figures 15 and 16 are related to a group of lessons on the design/modeling methodology HDM 2000.

The class is given to students at the university level.

In order to provide an example of TOC, let us consider the topic "general content," which was structured in terms of the following subtopics: "definition of hypermedia," "definition of the hypertext," "purposes," "methodologies," "structure, dynamics, layout," "In-the-Large, In-the-Small." Each point is then structured into sub-sub-topics.

The user is free to "attend" the lesson starting from any point he prefers.

For instance, if the paragraph "methodologies" is chosen, it is not necessary to run the video at higher hierarchical levels, which can be skipped over to go directly to the selected node. The usual keys enable the user to go back, to advance rapidly (fast forward), to put the lesson in standby position, or stop it.

Metaponto

A second example, related to a different authoring situation, is "Metaponto," in which two teachers present their arguments outside the classroom in an archeological dig.

This application is centred on the history of Metaponto, one of the most important cities of the Magna Grecia, the part of southern Italy that was colonised by the ancient Greeks.

Figure 16. The Software Allows the User to Watch the Lesson they Choose, in This Case the "Definition of Hypermedia"

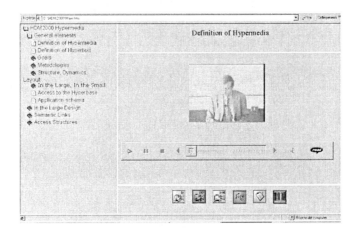

The authors of the lesson are two well-known scholars, Professor Francesco D'Andria archeological section and Professor Aldo Siciliano numismatics.

Figures 17 and 18 show some screenshots taken from the application.

The audience of the application is students doing various academic courses. Its content concerns the history and the growth of the city and surrounding territory, handicraft and production of ceramics, cultural and religious life, and the coinage, etc., in a general discussion of Magna Grecia, with specific attention given to Metaponto.

Figure 17. The Foundation of Metaponto

Figure 18. In-Depth Study and Bibliography — The Foundation of Metaponto

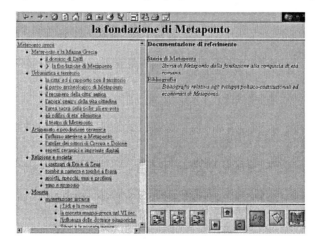

FUTURE TRENDS AND CONCLUSIONS

The idea described in the above sections is very simple: it is possible to publish good educational multimedia applications developed by academic staff with very little technical effort, in a short time, and with limited financial resources.

In our opinion, LEZI II enables teaching staff without specific technical preparation in multimedia production, but with valid content and good teaching skills, to easily prepare good multimedia interactive lessons, both for disk-based (CD/DVD) or on-line (Web) purposes.

More generally, the widespread use of LEZI II or other similar tools can effectively support the development and use of educational multimedia content in universities and schools.

Obviously, this kind of multimedia content is not intended to replace the publications of professional editors.

The next steps in the LEZI development at SET-Lab are:
- to complete the analysis of the authoring part of LEZI
- to implement a textual search among the nodes of all lessons available locally or on-line, based on a content-sharing model similar to NAPSTER, to support the re-use of existing LEZI lessons on the net
- to conduct a more detailed and systematic test
- to integrate the system with new video formats and channels (such as satellite and wireless), to better support the LEZI philosophy.

A free version of LEZI is available at http://mb.unile.it/Lezi. It can be also requested from mario.bochicchio@unile.it for experimental purposes.

We are convinced that many qualified teachers, especially those specialized in non-technical subjects, can easily use LEZI to create a wide range of first-rate educational multimedia materials, thus improving the effectiveness of teaching methods as well as cultural exchange between educational institutions.

ACKNOWLEDGMENTS

We acknowledge Professor Paolo Paolini for the original idea about LEZI and for the first implementation of the prototype, performed at the HOC-Lab of the Politecnico di Milano.

REFERENCES

Abeshaus, I., & Dickinson, R. (2001). Clay Animation How-To Video. *Proc. of SITE 2001*, Orlando, FL.

Baresi, L., Garzotto, F., & Paolini, P. (2001). Extending UML for Modeling Web Applications. *Proc. of 34th Hawaii International Conference on System Sciences (HICSS'01)*. Maui, HI, USA.

Bochicchio, M.A., & Paolini, P. (1998). An HDM Interpreter for On-Line Tutorials. In N. Magnenat-Thalmann & D. Thalman (Eds.), IEEE Computer Society *Proc. of MultiMedia Modeling 1998 (MMM '98)* (pp. 184-190). Los Alamitos, CA, USA.

Bochicchio, M.A., Paiano, R., & Paolini, P. (1999a). JWeb: An HDM Environment for Fast Development of Web Applications. *Proc. of Multimedia Computing and Systems* (IEEE ICMCS '99), 2, 809-813.

Bochicchio, M.A., Paiano, R., & Paolini, P. (1999b). JWeb: An Innovative Architecture for Web Applications. *Proc. of IEEE ICSC '99*. Hong Kong.

Bochicchio, M.A, Paiano, R., Paolini, P., Andreassi, E., & Montanaro, T. (2000). LEZI uno strumento per un facile sviluppo di video interattivi a scopo educativo. *Proc. of DIDAMATICA 2000* (pp. 72-78). Cesena, Italy.

Finkelstein, A. et al. (2001). Ubiquitous Web Application Development — A Framework for Understanding. 6th World Multiconference on Systemics, Cybernetics and Informatics. Orlando, FL, USA.

Garzotto, F., Mainetti, L., & Paolini, P. (1993a, January). Navigation Patterns in Hypermedia Data Base. *Proc. of 26th IEEE Int. Conf. On System Sciences*. Maui, HI, USA: IEEE Press.

Garzotto, F., Mainetti, L., & Paolini, P. (1993b, December). HDM2: Extending the E-R Approach to Hypermedia Application Design. *Proc. Of ER '93 —*

12th International Conference on the Entity-Relationship Approach. Arlington, VA, USA.

Garzotto, F., Mainetti, L., & Paolini, P. (1995). Hypermedia Application Design: A Structured Approach. In W. Chuler, J. Annemann, & N. Streitz (Eds.), *Designing User Interfaces for Hypermedia.* Heidelberg, Germany: Springer Verlag.

Garzotto, F., Paolini, P., & Schwabe, D. (1991, December). HDM – A Model for Design of Hypertext Applications. *Proc. ACM Hypertext '91.* San Antonio, TX, USA: ACM Press.

Garzotto, F., Paolini, P., & Schwabe, D. (1993). HDM – A Model-Based Approach to Hypertext Application Design. *TOIS,* 11(1), 1-26.

GRiNS. (n.d.). Retrieved August 2000 from the World Wide Web at http://www.oratrix.com/GRiNS.

Handler, M., Benavides, O., Morgan, K., & Houghton, R. (2001). iMovie and Educators: The Right Partnership for Making Digital Movies. *Proc. of SITE 2001,* Orlando, FL.

Heath, M., Dimock, K.V., & Burniske, J. (2001). Classrooms Under Construction: A Video Series. *Proc. of SITE 2001.*

Hochman, A. & Marshall, S. (2001). Camp Crystal Lake: A Wireless Network in the Wilderness Brings Video, Databases, and the Web to Elementary Students. *Proc. of SITE 2001,* Orlando, FL.

JMF. (n.d.). Retrieved August 2000 from the World Wide Web at http://www.javasoft.com/products/java-media/jmf/index.html.

Jourdan, M., Layaïda, N., Roisin, C., Sabry-Ismaïl, L., & Villard, L. (1998). Madeus, an Authoring Environment for Interactive Multimedia Documents. *ACM Multimedia 98 - Electronic Proceedings.*

Montessoro, P.L. & Caschi, S. (1999). MTEACH: Didactic Multimedia Production. *Proc. of Multimedia Computing and Systems 1999 (IEEE ICMCS '99),* 2, 1017-1019, Florence, Italy.

PresenterPlus. (n.d.). Retrieved August 2000 from the World Wide Web at http://www.realnetworks.com/products/presenterplus.

RealServer Guide. (n.d.). RealNetworks 1995-2000. Chapters 4 and 5.

Roisin, C., Tran-Thuong, T., & Villard, L. (2000). A proposal for a Video Modeling for Composing Multimedia Documents. *Proc of MMM2000.* Nagano, Japan.

SMIL. (n.d.). Retrieved August 2000 from the World Wide Web at http://www.w2.org/Audio/Video.

Windows Media Technologies. (n.d.). Retrieved June 2002 from the World Wide Web at http://www.microsoft.com/windows/windowsmedia/overview/default.asp.

Chapter XIV

Electronic Journalism in Peru

Antonio Díaz
Escuela de Administración de Negocios para Graduados, Peru

Martín Santana
Escuela de Administración de Negocios para Graduados, Peru

ABSTRACT

This chapter introduces electronic journalism as a new trend in the news services that have recently been boosted by Internet diffusion. It makes a presentation of electronic media pioneers in the world and the challenges they faced to deliver news to their traditional and Internet-based customers. Mainly, the chapter focuses on the description of the beginnings, evolution, strategies, and current state of Peruvian information media, focusing on Web-based journalism. Finally, the authors offer some conclusions about the approaches to develop Web news services adopted by traditional and virtual media, and suggest the need for future research in different countries in order to compare results and define the media trends in the Internet era.

BACKGROUND

Online journalism dates back to the end of the '70s when Knight-Ridder launched an initiative to develop a videotext service called *Viewtron,* which it later dropped in 1986 after realizing losses of US$50 million. Still, Knight-Ridder's interest in online information services remained unwavering and, in 1988, it made a decision to buy Dialog Information Services, Inc., a leader in information retrieval. Only a year later, the first signs of success already appeared (Díaz & Meso, 1998).

By the end of the '80s, Gannet — *USA Today's* publisher — launched a daily summary comprising 18 news pieces in text format it called *USA Today Decisionline.* Almost simultaneously, Dow Jones published *The Wall Street Journal* and *Barron's* on Prodigy, or directly on the Internet, with interactive multimedia features (Díaz & Meso, 1998).

In 1992, *The Chicago Tribune* became the world's first daily to launch an electronic version of its newspaper on America OnLine. In 1993, Knight-Ridder started publishing what would eventually become one of the paradigms of international electronic journalism, the *San Jose Mercury Center,* which was in fact something more than the *San Jose Mercury News* printed copy. By 1994, *The New York Times, The Washington Post, Los Angeles Times, USA Today* and *The Examiner,* among others, offered readers an online version, whether on the Internet, America OnLine, CompuServe, Prodigy, Interchange, Delphi, or their own networks (Díaz & Meso, 1998).

Although each type of medium — whether print, radio or television — publishes information in a different way responding to its specific characteristics and peculiarities, its respective approach, and the specific type of message receiver, (Romero, 2000), each one's Internet versions all seek new schemes to refresh the contents and reach audiences with new formats. Now, Internet-enabled readers can read newspapers, listen to the radio, and watch TV from anywhere in the world (McClung, 2001).

After defining journalism as the job of compiling and disseminating information (Gargurevich, 1999), electronic journalism stands out for four features: it uses multimedia resources (text, image, audio, databases, and executable programs), it breaks down the sequence of information because it uses hypertext and hypermedia, it breaks down periodicity because it allows access to information at any time without need to wait until the next edition, and it is interactive, allowing users to access information of their interest (Díaz & Meso, 1998). Thus, electronic journalism uses every Internet resource to disseminate information and taps into this medium's unlimited capacity to hold contents and to provide ongoing updates. Moreover, the Internet is the first truly global-reach channel making it possible to disseminate information to the remotest corners of the earth without greater distribution costs (Singer, 2001).

The arrival of the Internet has had a major impact on the way that journalists do journalism. Just like radio and television were milestones in journalism that displaced daily newspapers and led to the closing of some evening newspaper editions (Burnham, 2000), at present the Web is becoming a medium that, through its interactivity, allows readers to disagree with the publishers or contribute to the writers' work by incorporating readers' opinions (Giles, 2000). This is the true journalistic potential of the Internet. Additionally, the Internet makes it possible to deliver news on a permanent basis, so editors must constantly determine how much information to gather (Maynard, 2000).

The arrival of the Internet confronted the printed media with a dual challenge. On the one hand, there was a risk of disappearing because users now find it easier to access information on the Web. On the other hand, this new channel provides them with an opportunity to broaden their readership (Boynton, 2000). Compared to a radio listener or television viewer, readers are individuals with a heightened interest in accessing information they look for through the medium that best suits their specific interests (Romero, 2000). They may therefore wonder if being present on the Internet may translate into larger readership for the printed media thanks to a "cross-sales" mechanism. For instance, Boston's *The Christian Science Monitor* sells through its Web page as many subscriptions for the printed version as through other conventional channels. Remarkably enough, though, Web subscriber retention rates are double those from other sources (Regan, 2000). Although one-fourth of respondents to a US survey performed by Kaye (as cited in McClung, 2001) on reasons to surf the Internet declared they spend less time watching TV, listening to the radio, or reading newspapers and magazines since they found out about the Web, a later study concluded that the obvious drop in the use of those media cannot be attributed to the Internet's becoming a mass medium in the U.S. (Stempel, Hargrove & Bernt, 2000).

Many sites relating to printed media have evolved from pages that initially were but word-for-word copies of the printed version to become a dynamic environment that can be constantly updated (Pack, 2001). In this sense, Internet journalism ethics should not be different from that governing traditional channels to the extent that, until now, online journalists' experience and values are born from the former. The Web only gives them an expanded way of displaying information (McNamara, 2000). Digital-era journalists must find the way to reach a global audience without compromising the principles of truthfulness, of reliable sources, independence (Pavlik, 2000) and their originality. However, to the extent journalism moves to the

Internet, there is an increased risk of contents' plagiarism given the enormous size of the information files that are being put together (Wier, 2000).

Journalism on the Internet poses a number of challenges. On the one hand, news pieces for the printed media are discussed before they are broadcast, while, on the Internet, as on radio, journalists are compelled to make very quick decisions, almost in real time (Kansas, 2001). On the other hand, the Internet opens the doors to new, purely virtual media, although they must still walk a long way before they gain enough credibility and overcome the stigma that "anybody can publish on the Web." Additionally, they must rise to the challenge of a huge infrastructure that has already been put in place by consolidated news groups and overcome limited access to capital (Giles, 2000; Uy, 2001). Some think that, at least in the first decade of the Web, the printed media have overpowered electronic journalism because they are specialized on preparing reports, likely thanks to their large-scale journalistic infrastructure ("Internet Won't," 2001), which they use to their own advantage.

On the other hand, as access to the Internet increases and the public gets used to obtaining their information through the Web, probably evening news show will have to create new ways of presenting information. Otherwise, they would blunder if they repeat information the public is already aware of (Brown, 2000). Webmasters of some news media have already identified increased traffic in the early afternoon hours, presumably when office workers are back at their desks after the lunch break (Rainie, 2000).

Given the phenomenon of ethnocentricity—manifest, for instance, in a local medium's Web page written by locals for locals who find in the information contents sufficient elements for understanding the news piece (Priess, 2000)—publishers may find it convenient to specialize on reporting about a reality that is best known to them, i.e., local reality (Singer, 2001). Although the cost of preparing a news feature has remained almost unaltered, and although presenting news in a multimedia format (Fulton, 2000) may slightly increase costs, it is clearly cheaper to prepare a page and make it available to millions of people around the world over the Internet than to distribute it on a printed format (Small, 2000).

When deciding to move to the Internet world, information media must carefully analyze their project's feasibility, a particularly critical step for those initiatives that lack a prior base in the real world. The collapse of Taiwan's virtual *Tomorrow Times* information medium — despite 1.8 million daily page visits — poses a question about the viability of sustaining the high cost of generating news that must be updated on a permanent basis (Ling & Guyot, 2001), when no journalistic infrastructure has been developed in the physical world. We must remember that the Internet has made people used to obtaining free information while revenue-generation models based on advertising have shown to be unsustainable.

Peruvian information media are no strangers to Web journalism. Lima's main dailies publishing on the Internet are *Correo* (www.correoperu.com.pe), *El Comercio* (www.elcomercioperu.com.pe), *El Peruano*[1] (www.elperuano.com.pe), *Expreso* (www.expreso.com.pe), *Gestión* (www.gestion.com.pe), *La República* (www.larepublica.com.pe), *Ojo* (www.ojo.com.pe), and *Síntesis* (www.sintesis.com.pe).

Two of Lima's radio broadcasters send their news programming over the Internet. They are Radioprogramas del Perú and Cadena Peruana de Noticias, (www.rpp.com.pe and www.cpnradio.com.pe). Television networks on the Web are Frecuencia Latina, (www.frecuencialatina.com.pe), América Televisión (www.americatv.com.pe), Panamericana Televisión (www.pantel.com.pe) and Televisión Nacional del Perú (www.tnp.com.pe). Exclusively virtual information media are www.peru.com, www.primerapagina.com.pe and www.gatoencerrado.terra.com.pe.

Internet penetration in Peru — a country with a little over 25 million people — is low. Only 33% of Peruvians have heard about the Internet or used it at all (Chaparro, 2001). In the first quarter of 2000, 130,000 users accessed the Internet through a commuted line while 390,000 used dedicated lines (Araoz & van Ginhoven, 2001). To June 2001, the total figures exceeded 800,000 (Cifras y datos, 2001). A 2000 survey on technological innovation among 8,976 Peruvian companies showed that only 38% had an Internet connection, 36% effectively used the Internet, and 4.5% were planning to get a connection in the next 12 months (Instituto Nacional de Estadística e Informática, 2001).

The above figures clearly point to a hurdle for further developing successful news media on the Web targeting a Peruvian audience. However, there exists a potential foreign market. Non-official figures show that Peruvian expatriates — who have greater Internet access and typically show a strong community feeling and are deeply attached to their roots (Altamirano, 2000) — may reach two million.

ELECTRONIC JOURNALISM IN PERU

For this study, the media chosen, in addition to being published on the Internet, also showed some special features that are described below.

The following printed media were chosen:
- Lima's best recalled and most widely read daily, *El Comercio*, also has a reputation for being the most truthful, entertaining, and the best at covering

> local political news events (Actitudes hacia la prensa escrita, 2001). It is read by an average of 574,700 people in Lima (Instituto Cuánto, 2001).

- *Gestión* was Peru's first written medium to produce an online version. Its printed edition, targeting the business community, reaches an average 27,500 readers in Lima (Instituto Cuánto, 2001).
- *La República* was Peru's second printed medium to publish an electronic version. It is regarded as the second most truthful and also mentioned as the second most reliable daily in providing local political news coverage (Actitudes hacia la prensa escrita, 2001). It is read by an average of 171,300 readers in Lima (Instituto Cuánto, 2001).

Radio broadcasters in this survey comprise those that broadcast over the Web but focus on news programming:

- *Radioprogramas del Perú*, *RPP Noticias,* enjoys a spontaneous recall rate of 27% among all radio broadcasters and 62% among news radio broadcasters. It is the most widely-heard radio broadcaster (23% of listeners) (Radio, 2001). Its annual average half-hour audience in Lima reaches 95,100 listeners (Insituto Cuánto, 2001).
- *CPN Radio,* Radio Cadena Peruana de Noticias, is spontaneously recalled by 6% of listeners of all radio stations (Radio, 2001) and has an annual average half-hour audience of 22,900 listeners in Lima (Insituto Cuánto, 2001).

Rather than displaying full and updated information, Peruvian television networks on the Web underscore programming information. Their Web sites are closer to an institutional page than to an information page. They were not included in this study.

Of the three Peruvian information media lacking a print, radio, or television matching part, only www.peru.com and www.primerapagina.com.pe participated in this study; www.gatoencerrado.terra.com.pe did not answer.

In all cases, in-depth interviews were conducted on relevant topics for this study with their electronic publishing officials. They were asked to narrate their areas' operations and work style when preparing news pieces. As a complement, each medium's Web site is described and analyzed.

El Comercio

Founded in Lima in 1839, *El Comercio* has been in publication for 162 years and is the doyen of Peruvian dailies. It is presently owned by Empresa Editora El Comercio S.A. and a member of Grupo de Diarios de América.[2] In 1996, it published the company's institutional page on the Internet and in 1997 it started publishing the www.elcomercioperu.com.pe electronic daily. In May 2001, it organized an independent area charged with the daily's electronic publication. This division comprises 33 staff, of which nine are journalists, 10 are technical experts, and the rest manage the daily's portal.

The electronic version is almost completely dependent on the printed version for its contents. News is updated on the Web using information provided by the daily's reporters and input from news agencies. The editing company's television operations through *Canal N* cable broadcaster and *Radio Canal N* radio station help in updating news contents. The site www.elcomercioperu.com.pe publishes not only the news of the day, but also *Canal N's* fresh headlines. News is tracked through other information media as it evolves. Occasionally, www.elcomercioperu.com.pe publishes reports prepared by other *El Comercio* newspapers and supplements. The contents and site design editor is ultimately responsible for all Internet publications.

The site www.elcomercioperu.com.pe gets an average of three millions monthly hits, mostly from Peruvian residents in the United States, followed by expatriates residing in Japan. Hits originating in Peru rank third. Both the daily and its electronic version's target audience is found in the top two income groups, comprised of professionals, students, and members of the Armed Forces. Other subscribers to *El Comercio* include a number of foreign universities and organizations, and Peruvian embassies abroad. No "cannibalization" seems to take place between the printed and virtual media.

Information sections in the daily's electronic version include national, city, and world affairs. Business, politics, communities, entertainment, technology, special sports reports, and graphic sections, as well as access to past editions are the other options. Its most widely read pages are the front page and local soccer news. In December 2001, the Internet publication of a report prepared by *Somos* magazine[3] featuring photographs of young Peruvian actresses who had acted in a soap opera; only shortly after its airing the electronic newspaper received a record number of visits.

The site www.elcomercioperu.com.pe's revenues come from advertising by some announcers. Nevertheless, this revenue generation model fails to pay for the virtual daily's operating costs. Another revenue stream originates in the sale of news to the TIM telephone operator who distributes the news to its cellular telephone customers. Additionally, www.elcomercioperu.com.pe has prepared private circulation newsletters for Profuturo pension fund manager's staff and the JobShark employment agency.

As yet another alternative source of revenues and an attempt to turn the daily's electronic version into a profitable venture, it has created a portal providing, among other services, the www.ec-store.com.pe virtual shop that reached sales worth

US$3 million in 2000. Other portal services include an electronic job hunting agency, postal office boxes in the United States, health and university student counseling, a veterinarian's online office, a debate forum, PC World in Spanish for Peru, a public interest services page, a leisure and entertainment feature, a virtual corporate directory, Internet access and a virtual cards site, and a link to www.batanga.com virtual radio broadcast.

As a means to increase traffic to www.ec-store.com.pe and thus enlarge sales, there is a project to put in place Internet public kiosks. However, most purchases through www.ec-store.com.pe do not originate in users who access Internet from a public kiosk, but rather from surfers who reach the Web from their homes or offices. The www.elcomercioperu.com.pe site publishes the small ads regularly found on the daily's print version. This same site has an option to write and pay for small ads. Additionally, *El Comercio* also offers a free e-mail news service.

El Comercio's management has made a decision to make the newspaper a Latin American leader. Comprised in their strategy to reach their goal is the effort to provide Internet-based news services, an irreversible and final decision despite the fact that news electronic publishing in itself may not yield acceptable financial results.

Gestión

An economics, finance, and business newspaper, *Gestión* first circulated in 1990 and is owned by Corporación Gestión, a company that seeks to become Peru's information leader by providing a "constant flow of impartial, plural and independent information."

Gestión's economic and business reporting goes hand in hand with information about political events and ongoing debate on business and government proposals and plans. Daily issues include sections on politics, the economy, editorial opinion, business and finance, the stock exchange, databases, and world affairs. Other sections include the latest business comments and other information. Guest writers fill *Gestión*'s pages on industry, taxes, marketing, and foreign and international trade. Major Peruvian and international consultants provide opinion on economics, taxes, real estate and other issues. In 1995, *Gestión* joined the Ibero-American Financial Dailies' Network[4].

Gestión was Peru's first daily to publish on the Internet when it launched its electronic site www.gestion.com.pe in September 1996 to spread Peru's economic, financial and political news, and become a channel for communication among its readers. Its site includes the same sections as the printed publication and also provides links to the other members of the Ibero-American Financial Dailies'

Network, as well as links to online versions of various international specialized daily publications[5]. From www.gestion.com.pe it is possible to access other media run by the corporation, including *CPN Radio* www.cpnradio.com.pe information broadcast station and its *Gestión Médica*[6] (www.gestion.com.pe/GM) weekly health publication.

Gestión readership comprises mainly members of the business community, government officials, and students and faculty from higher learning organizations. It is also the site of choice for economic and financial references for other media. Although it can be found at newsstands, a high percentage of its circulation is by subscription. Although *Gestión*'s circulation has not grown as expected, its presence on the Internet cannot be blamed. Most www.gestion.com.pe visitors are businessmen from the U.S., Spain, Argentina, Chile, and Japan who have business and interests in Peru. Ever since www.gestion.com.pe started publishing, Peruvian embassies abroad have cancelled their subscriptions. Articles on political issues are the most frequently visited, followed by economic reports. *Gestión*'s contents are prepared with materials and interviews gathered by its reporters, together with news from news agencies. Information in www.gestión.com.pe is posted on the Web by *CPN Radio* personnel that work the late-night shift. *CPN Radio* updates the news during the day. *Gestión* also offers a free e-mail news service called *Gestión Mail* that distributes economic, political, financial and business news before 7 a.m., with an update at 3 p.m. on the main news events until that time.

La República

Founded in Lima in 1981, *La República* has as its objective to inform and become an opinion maker for the Peruvian public. Initially, it underscored police reports, but later became an overseer for government action. It describes itself as an opinion-making daily rather than an impartial and objective medium. Its slogan "our opinion makes news" reflects its style in displaying information.

This newspaper has always been characterized by its technological innovations. Since 1995, it has been using satellites to publish local editions in other cities around Peru[7]. Driven by its commitment to innovation, in October 1996 it launched an electronic version called www.larepublica.com.pe at an investment of US$10,000, without expecting any economic benefit from it. However, the photo reporting of the abduction of a number of personalities who attended a reception at the Japanese ambassador's residency in Lima in December that year brought large windfall revenues when a Japanese newspaper showed interest in buying the photographs published in www.larepublica.com.pe. The sale of that material amounted to several times the investment made to materialize the newspaper's Internet initiative.

However, and although *La República* later tried to sell the photographs of various reports to finance its electronic publication, this was possible only intermittently and to a small scale. The project to launch a simultaneous version of *La República* in New Jersey [8] via satellite emerged through contacts with a Peruvian businessman who sells a printed version of www.larepublica.com.pe in Patterson, to which he attaches his own business advertising.

Although there is a banner area in the site www.larepublica.com.pe, its existence is not conditioned to its stand-alone capacity to create a stream of revenues because it is understood that the electronic version can reach anywhere in the world where there are people interested in its contents. An important consideration for *La República* managers is interaction with its readers. The Internet has strengthened this feature. Since its launching, the number of opinion letters it gets through e-mails from readers outside Peru has grown steadily. Some visitors at www.larepublica.com.pe have become the newspaper's foreign correspondents and they "add a Peruvian flavor" to international reports. Foreign readers account for 70% of the electronic edition's readership.

All of *La República*, including its supplements, is published on www.larepublica.com.pe. The newspaper includes sections on politics, editorial opinion, local news, cultural, economic, police, and entertainment, as well as opinion columns, besides sports, comic strips, and horse racing pages. Its electronic version includes links to the *Líbero* sports newspaper, owned by the same publishing company, and a section called Latinoticias that publishes articles from Argentina's *La Prensa*. Among all these sections, the most visited cover current political affairs and sports. A discussion forum where readers shared their views on Peru's deep political crisis at that moment and the large corruption network within government operated for four months at the end of 2000. A discussion forum has not been totally discarded as a future option.

Information published on www.larepublica.com.pe comes from articles written by the daily's reporters and from writers of both the printed edition and news agencies. News is not updated throughout the day. Two people are charged with summarizing and entering *La República* contents on the Internet. The electronic version is published daily around 3 a.m., i.e., it is published before the printed edition. At one point, this difference in publication times for the two versions was an issue for *La República*'s regular circulation. Given its critical stand towards President Fujimori in the last year of his administration, the government intelligence agencies decided to purchase large numbers of newspaper copies to prevent investigative reporting about corruption from reaching the public. State security agents would read at the beginning of the day www.larepublica.com.pe and, depending on the articles' contents, decide whether or not to purchase *La*

República. The up-side of this operation for the newspaper was that on those particular days the newspaper was sold out.

At present, the *La República* publishing group has shown interest in buying an open (non-cable) television channel to reach its corporate goals through operations in various media channels.

Cadena Peruana de Noticias – CPN Radio

A news radio chain owned by Corporación Gestión, *CPN Radio* broadcasts from Lima throughout Peru on both the FM and AM bands through a satellite link to Panamsat. *CPN Radio* first broadcast in 1996. It was purchased by Corporación Gestión in 1998, when it renewed its programming and significantly expanded coverage. *CPN Radio* and *Gestión* newspaper share their general information sources, including reporters and news agencies. Highly specialized economics, finance, and business information are published only by the newspaper.

In June 2000, through an agreement between *CPN Radio* and Terra Networks and at an investment of US$20,000, the www.terra.com.pe/cpn site was launched to give the broadcaster Internet access to the www.terra.com.pe/cpn portal. In September 2001, a new page was launched at the www.cpnradio.com.pe site although it still provided information to Terra. The reason to move into the virtual medium was the radio's interest in positioning itself and creating an image before the public vis-à-vis Radioprogramas del Perú, *CPN Radio*'s direct competitor. *CPN Radio*'s Internet participation is ensured independently of its economic results. To date, it has not yet become a source of corporate revenues.

To launch the www.cpnradio.com.pe project, professional journalists within the organization were reassigned. Also a network technical expert was hired. At present, two editors alternate shifts until midnight and are responsible for updating headlines along the day. To refresh their news, they rely not only on material supplied by *CPN Radio* and *Gestión* but also on news from other media.

"Information on the spot" is *CPN Radio*'s slogan for its www.cpnradio.com.pe site. Audiences reaching the broadcaster are mostly adults who want to stay abreast of current affairs. Between 60% and 70% of visitors to www.cpnradio.com.pe originate in Peru, half of which come from Lima, while the remaining 30% to 40% come from abroad. Political features are most often followed, with the economy coming next. Visitors can also listen to radio programming in real time. In its publication, www.cpnradio.com.pe includes headlines with photographs, and the political, economic, financial, business, local affairs, national affairs, world affairs, showbusiness, sports, and culture sections. It also has a "last minute news" flash section, complete radio programming, and links to articles written by the broadcaster's columnists.

Radioprogramas del Perú – *RPP Noticias*

Initially conceived in 1963 as an entertainment radio broadcaster, in 1979 Radioprogramas del Perú became a round-the-clock news broadcaster when it created *RPP Noticias,* building on the concepts of immediacy, objectivity and plurality. At present, it reaches 97% of Peruvians through a network of FM and AM affiliates. *RPP Noticias* seeks to become a Latin American and world telecommunications leader. In 1992, it expanded its broadcasting throughout the region by establishing the Latin American Broadcasting Association[9].

RPP Internet launched its institutional Web page in 1996. At the end of 1999 the www.rpp.com.pe site was added to the original product with a view at "making radio broadcast's immediacy and volatile contents a more permanent product, by transforming it into a written medium that would target audiences interested in more exhaustive information without loosing the interactivity characterizing radio broadcasts, "a strategy to globalize information through the Internet." After creating www.rpp.com.pe, the RPP Group can call itself a generator of contents that can be encapsulated in various formats[10]. Although *RPP Noticias* provides support in journalistic coverage for information broadcast through www.rpp.com.pe, which saves on content preparation, the Internet area staffs its own four writers, an economics-specialized reporter, and another one to cover sports. It also relies on two audio broadcast specialists for Internet news broadcasting.

While *RPP Noticias* focuses on audiences above 18 years of age throughout the socio-economic spectrum, www.rpp.com.pe targets Peruvians of both sexes living in Peru, aged between 23 and 45, and belonging to the middle and high-income groups. These readers have Internet access at their work places, universities, or Internet public kiosks and they are interested in staying abreast of events. It also targets Peruvians of both sexes living abroad, between 25 and 50 years old and belonging to an intermediate income level. They resort to www.rpp.com.pe as their means to be informed about, communicated with, and linked to Peru. At the end of 2001, *RPP Internet* got an average 3 million monthly visits and hit 4.8 million visits during the Peruvian elections. About 40% of visits to www.rpp.com.pe originate in Peru, closely followed by visitors from the U.S., Argentina, and Japan. Its most visited pages covered the political, sports, local affairs, entertainment, and financial sections.

RPP Internet's information is supplied in both audio and text format, although photographs are attached to the main news features. At www.rpp.com.pe, visitors find the latest news in the "news by the minute" section, as well as local affairs, political, sports, world affairs, finance, cultural, entertainment, and special reports sections. There is also the option to participate in opinion surveys. Through the audio on demand service, the comedy,[11] gastronomy, interviews,[12] and the labor, medical, veterinarian, geriatric and sexuality questions-and-answers sections can be reached. There is also a discussion forum around current affairs. Likewise, the direct *RPP Noticias* audio broadcast can be heard on www.rpp.com.pe. Users can also join the regular chat sessions. Parallel consumption has not been slighted. In the near future, radio announcers may answer telephone calls from both *RPP Noticias* listeners and answer questions from www.rpp.com.pe users.

A new market has opened thanks to www.rpp.com.pe and an effort is underway to increase the number of single-service users and visits to create a stream of revenues from advertising and contents sales. *RPP Internet* announcers can sponsor Web-format radio programs and with their banners lure clients to their own Web sites. If they do not own a Web site, they can design an area providing their own information and piggyback on www.rpp.com.pe's structure. Content sales can be arranged through windows where www.rpp.com.pe contents are shown on clients' windows or by creating direct links to the client's site in the headlines newsletters that are distributed every day on text or HTML format. Additionally, *RPP Internet* provides contents to the CNN, BBC and www.elarea.com networks and it sells CD-ROMs including a summary of the main events of 2001. WAP technology enables Nextel and Telefónica telephone operators' clients to access *RPP Noticias*, while Bellsouth's clients get headlines on their short-messaging service.

Although to date *RPP Internet* revenues are below expenses, the www.rpp.com.pe is here to stay. It is widely held that launching this service has had a positive influence on RPP Group's image-building by creating among both listeners and announcers a perception of leadership, while strengthening the Group's competitive standing in terms of its capacity to reach a wider target audience that comprises both radio listeners and Web users.

www.peru.com

The www.peru.com site is owned by Interlatin Corporation, a Peruvian company that owns several domains (www.colombia.com, www.bolivia.com and www.futbolargentino.com). They seek to develop portals throughout Latin American countries that provide information and specific services adapted to individual countries.

Although www.peru.com has been operational since 1998, this domain was already registered in 1995 and became the company's main tool in luring traffic towards its site. It is totally dedicated to delivering information about and covering topics relating to Peru. The site targets Peruvian expatriates based on the principle that Peruvian residents have a choice of alternative ways to get information. In November 2001, the site got 11 million visits, mostly from the United States (over 50% of the total), followed by visitors from Japan and Spain.

The site www.peru.com seeks to differentiate its contents through quick publication of information gathered by an in-house team of journalists and wire-fed news. A company policy requires reporters to generate information that is clearly different from what may be available on other media. For this reason interviews about current affairs are avoided while aiming, rather, for the "exclusive" interview. News must be original and it is the company's perception that this has helped in building credibility among visitors. After being edited, information is published in text, audio, image and/or video formats as soon as possible. Updated headlines based on ongoing reporting appear in the "last minute section." Journalists at www.peru.com recognize they do not have all of the journalistic infrastructure available to traditional media and, therefore, resort to their own inventiveness in finding and publishing the most recent information.

Its press area comprises the soccer and sports section covered by eight reporters, a current political affairs section covered by six journalists, and a show business department covered by three reporters. A project is currently being evaluated to recruit senior journalism students to work as correspondents in cities around Peru. Emphasis is placed on current political affairs, although the soccer page is the most visited of all sections. A weekly chat session is available covering soccer and show business and, exceptionally, political issues.

Besides its news coverage, www.peru.com contents include travel services, a browser, chat rooms, free e-mail addresses, job searches, a Lima city street finder (www.idonde.com), a communication media directory, messaging to cellular telephones, a community of Peruvian expatriates around the world, access to music radio broadcasts, electronic postcards and a virtual shop (www.iquiero.com). It also includes sections on automobiles, jokes, movies, finance, gastronomy, the horoscope, pets, music, and others. Other sections are special reports, the weekly survey, raffles, the day's video, and special culture-oriented articles. Exclusive features are summarized in English.

Interlatin Corporation's sources of revenues are diverse and balanced. Its www.iquiero.com virtual shop has recorded growing sales in recent months. Products sold range from pastries and cakes to toys, electric household appliances, alcoholic beverages, clothes, books, perfume, music, jewelry and others. Its travel agency, www.peru.com/travel, also contributes to income generation. In a pessimistic scenario, Interlatin management foresees reaching their break-even point in June 2003. In the meantime, they continue to generate traffic towards www.peru.com

by tapping the site's attractions, in particular news, jokes, and e-mail services. Additionally, www.peru.com accepts advertising and provides Web page design services. Through agreements with TIM Peru and Nextel, www.peru.com sells news to these telephone operators who then distribute them among their users. Occasionally, they prepare special event reports, which are an additional source of income.

Becoming an Internet news leader is www.peru.com's goal. Different from reporters from other news media that operate through various channels, www.peru.com's journalists focus on the Internet and try to provide "an additional information step." They have even proposed purchasing a fly-away to broadcast directly on the Web. Although they recognize their experimental approach in a totally different environment where nothing is yet final, they are also persuaded that the Internet cannot be stopped and is here to stay.

www.primerapagina.com.pe

Owned by Chile's iLatinHoldings, which also developed several business pages including www.elarea.com, www.areasalud.com, www.elgolpe.com, www.planetaviajes.com, www.areafinanzas.com, www.viajuridica.com in Latin America, the www.primerapagina.com.pe site provided local contents specifically from Peru. A shareholder restructuring at iLatinHoldings in August 2000 hurt the launching of the site when the marketing budget allowance was cancelled together with the planned promotional initiative. Still, the site appeared in September 2000 as an online news service with a "last minute" news updating section. Initially, news was provided on video and audio format, as well as text plus photographs.

News was gathered from international agencies and the site director's personal contacts, plus some information was gathered from broadcasts by two television channels. In its initial months, www.primerapagina.com.pe counted on a team of 22 writers and four editors, one each for the sections on political and financial affairs, current affairs, sports, and entertainment. The site covered the main events of the day, national and world affairs, infographs, specials, opinion columns, and surveys on current issues. Hits to www.primerapagina.com.pe bordered 150,000 every month, 60% of which originated in Peru and another 40% abroad.

Their business plan was based on good, quality writing, aimed at luring traffic to the site and persuading strategic partners to join the venture and sell advertising. However, the publicity-based revenues generation scheme did not bear fruit while the attempt to sell www.primerapagina.com.pe to US CNN chain stalled, as did arrangements with Lycos and Yahoo. After investments of one million dollars and returns of scarcely US$10,000, by mid-2001 iLatinHoldings decided to sell its specialized Peruvian sites. All of the staff was laid off in August that year, while the site's head kept a 30% share; only four freelance reporters were in charge of writing.

The director has been given a free hand to negotiate the best rescue formula for www.primerapagina.com.pe. Until November 2001, the site prepared an in-house newsletter for TIM Peru, a telephone operator. Additionally, an option was under study to distribute publications by installments together with a Peruvian publishing group; these installments would provide links to www.primerapagina.com.pe. Another project considered preparing a television program in cooperation with *Televisión Nacional del Perú* and www.trabajando.com[13] to cover labor issues. At the present time, although the link to the site is still active, the "front page" news is not updated; it corresponds to February 21, 2002. The site just provides links to similar Web pages in Argentina, Chile, and Colombia, as well as with all other iLatinHolding sites.

FUTURE TRENDS

Only a few years have passed since some Peruvians media that had already an established presence in other channels decided to enter the Internet, while others were organized exclusively to serve this channel. Although the last word has not yet been said about electronic journalism, the experiences so far allow us to draw some lessons.

Although the approaches to develop the Internet with a print or radio media basis have moved along different roads, some seem more clearly determined to explore new options to increase their revenues and earnings while others simply wish to expand their readership or number of listeners by drawing international audiences. However, they all seem persuaded that there is no turning back and that they have entered the Web, never to escape from it. The same thing cannot be said about the new media. Those who do not have a traditional media foundation have no choice but to yield satisfactory economic results that will allow them to survive. News pieces and reports prepared for traditional media are the raw material for the articles published by conventional media on the Web. To attain the above goal, special staff has been recruited. Exclusively virtual media had to draw a press team out of the blue and have made them responsible for researching news and then publishing their reports.

Likewise, increasing participation of Peruvian information groups in various channels —including the Web — opens the possibility for them not just to strengthen their own image, but also to reach a larger number of users and thus develop new businesses in the field of information. To do so, only rigorous environment and trend surveying can contribute to sound decision-making regarding the path to follow. A valid approach is to take into account the option to increase Internet involvement while acknowledging the restrictions that apply to the Internet in Peru, and thus help develop traditional channels.

Finally, Internet reporting display formats combine the advantages of radio, television, and printed channels. When easy-to-use, flexible, and portable devices are sufficiently developed and widespread (all featuring multimedia capabilities), newsmen will have to be ready to meet the ever-faster pace of information needs in modern societies. In the meantime, the number of Peruvians that go to the Internet to stay abreast of events increases constantly. It should be especially interesting to make similar researches in different countries in order to compare results and define the media trends in the Internet era.

CONCLUSION

A common feature among all studied media — independent of their origin, editorial line or its visitors' place of origin — is that the most visited sections are the Peruvian political current affairs and sports pages, thus leading us to think that Peruvians looking for international news visit other media, most likely foreign ones. Although the media provide international news contents, they do so from a Peruvian perspective. In almost all media, most visits come from abroad, which may be explained by two facts. The first is low Internet penetration in Peru; second, the strong family, cultural and social ties of almost two million Peruvians living abroad and who have better conditions to access the Web. So, most of the advertising, as a source of revenue for those media, should be oriented for Peruvians living abroad.

Initial plans had to be modified as Internet media identified difficulties and opportunities along the way. Table 1 shows that the medium's reputation has an impact on traffic generated to its site, as is the case of *RPP Noticias* and *El Comercio,* which are the two media with the highest number of listeners and readers in Peru, respectively. The large volume of traffic through www.peru.com may be attributed, in the first place, to its domain name — the first one to pop up on Internet browsers when the word "Peru" is typed in. It is also attributable to the varied and interesting range of content options offered by the site, without disdain for the substantial effort put in by its team of journalists. However, it is clear that advertising, no matter how high traffic through the site, does not constitute in itself a sufficiently sound source of revenues to cover operating costs.

All the media rely on text and photograph formats. Radio broadcasting sites www.cpnradio.com.pe and www.rpp.com.pe provide audio for their whole programming, while the latter also provides an option to access some of its already

Table 1. Traffic by Site

	Approximate Number of Monthly Visits
www.elcomercioperu.com.pe	3.000.000
www.gestion.com.pe	n/a*
www.larepublica.com.pe	n/a
www.cpnradio.com.pe	n/a*
www.rpp.com.pe	3.500.000
www.peru.com	11.000.000

One million monthly hits planned for 2002.

Table 2. Multimedia Resources Used in Deploying Information

	Text	Video	Direct Audio	Audio on Demand	Photo graphs
www.elcomercioperu.com.pe	x				x
www.gestion.com.pe	x				x
www.larepublica.com.pe	x				x
www.cpnradio.com.pe	x		x		x
www.rpp.com.pe	x		x	x	x
www.peru.com	x	x	x*		x

Only some programs are broadcast directly over the Web

Table 3. Service Offerings

	News Updating	e-mail Headlines	Chatting	Discussion Fora
www.elcomercioperu.com.pe	x	x		x
www.gestion.com.pe	x	x		
www.larepublica.com.pe				x*
www.cpnradio.com.pe	x	x		
www.rpp.com.pe	x	x	x	x
www.peru.com	x		x	x

Discussion Fora provided towards year end 2000

broadcast programs through an audio-on-demand option. The site www.peru.com's efforts to provide video over the Web are also remarkable as this is the only Peruvian medium to do so. Table 2 shows how multimedia resources are used.

Peruvian Internet media offer a wide range of services. Outstanding among them is www.rpp.com.pe with its news updates, e-mail headlines, chatrooms and discussions fora, as shown in Table 3. *La República* newspaper does not provide other services beyond information, but e-mail may have led to a perceived increased interaction with its readers.

Purely virtual Peruvian media are hard put to make any short-term inroads into traditional channels. Instead, they must try to develop business lines that can sustain the work of their news teams. Using Internet resources to create virtual communities that may be served with alternative products is an option deserving consideration.

ENDNOTES

1   Peru's oficial gazet.

2   *La Nación* from Argentina, *O Globo* and *Zero Hora* from Brazil, *El Mercurio* from Chile, *El Tiempo* from Colombia, *El Comercio* from Ecuador, *El Universal* from Mexico, *El Nuevo Diario* from Puerto Rico, *El País* from Uruguay and *El Nacional* from Venezuela, on top of *El Comercio* from Peru.

3   Weekly magazine included in *El Comercio's* Saturday edition. The most widely read in Peru.

4   *El Cronista* from Argentina, *La Razón* from Bolivia, *Gazeta Mercantil* from Brazil, *El Diario* from Chile, *La República* from Colombia, *Hoy* from Ecuador, *Prensa Libre* from Guatemala, *El Economista* from Mexico, *El Observador* from Uruguay, *Expansión* from Spain and *Diario Económico* from Portugal, on top of Peru's *Gestión*.

5   *The Wall Street Journal*, the *New York Times* and *Washington Post* from the US; *Financial Times* and *The Economist* from England; and *Nikkei Business News* from Japan.

6   A free, nationwide tabloid published since 1996.

7   The newspaper includes local contents for its Piura, Chiclayo, Trujillo, Arequipa and Iquitos editions.

8   This US state is home to the largest community of Peruvian expatriates.

9   A chain comprising *Radio Mitre* from Argentina, *Radio Panamericana* from Boliva, *RCN* from Colombia, *Radio Quito* from Ecuador, *Radio RPP Noticias* from Peru and *Caracas Radio* from Venezuela. This broadcasting network reaches 106 million listeners.

10   At present, RPP Group broadcasts news on cable TV.

11   The radio leader in Peru.

12   Only audio broadcasts of the day's news are available free of charge. Interviews from previous days are sold at request.

13   Chile's online job bourse.

REFERENCES

Actitudes hacia la prensa escrita. (2001, April). Retrieved December 3, 2001, from the World Wide Web at: http://www.apoyo.com/infor_util/inv_mercados/igm_prensa_042001.html.

Altamirano, T. (2000). *Liderazgo y organizaciones de peruanos en el exterior: Culturas transnacionales e imaginarios sobre el desarrollo*. Lima, Peru: Fondo Editorial PUCP y PromPerú.

Araoz, M. & van Ginhoven, S. (2001). *Preparación de los países andinos para integrar las redes de tecnologías de la información: El caso de Perú*. Lima, Peru: Centro de Investigación de la Universidad del Pacífico.

Boynton, R. (2000). New media may be old media's savior. *Columbia Journalism Review, 39*(2), 29-34.

Brown, M. (2000, October 2). Bringing people closer to the news. *Adweek, 41*(40), IQ26.

Burnham, A. (2000). Journalism.com. *The Virginia Quarterly Review, 76*(2), 203-213.

Chaparro, H. (2001, December 16). Investigación exploratoria en el mundo digital. *Semana Económica, 17*(801), 10.

Cifras y datos. (2001, August). Retrieved November 15, 2001, from the World Wide Web at: http://www.osiptel.gob.pe/cifydat/frames/fr4.html.

Díaz, J. & Meso, K. (1998). Desarrollo del periodismo electrónico. *El profesional de la información, 7*(12), 4-11.

Fulton, K. (2000). News isn't always journalism. *Columbia Journalism Review, 39*(2), 30-35.

Gargurevich, J. (1999). *Los periodistas: Historia del gremio en el Perú*. Lima: Ediciones La Voz.

Giles, B. (2000). Journalism in the era of the web. *Nieman Reports, 54*(4), 3.

Instituto Cuánto. (2001, September). *Anuario estadístico: Perú en números 2001*. Lima: Author.

Instituto Nacional de Estadística e Informática. (2001). *Impactos de las tecnologías de información y comunicación en el Perú*. Lima, Peru.

Internet won't eliminate print media. (2001, August). *USA Today, 130*(2675), 15-16.

Kansas, D. (2001, July 16). A dot-com editor sheds his five-year 'cocoon', and looks at how journalism has changed in the age of the Internet. *New York Times*, C-5.

Ling, C. & Guyot, E. (2001, February 23). Taiwan newspaper closes web edition, cites funding woes. *Wall Street Journal*.

Maynard, N. H. (2000). Digitization and the news. *Nieman Report, 54*(4), 11-13.

McClung, S. (2001). College radio station web sites: Perceptions of value and use. *Journalism & Mass Communication Educator, 56*(1), 62-73.

McNamara, T. (2000). Defining the blurry line between commerce and content. *Columbia Journalism Review, 39*(2), 31-35.

Pack, T. (2001, September - October). All the news that's fit to digitally print. *Link-up, 18*(5), 16.

Pavlik, J. (2000). The journalist: A disappearing species in the online world? *The UNESCO Courier, 53*(2), 34.

Priess, F. (2000). Los medios de comunicación en los conflictos armados. In A. Cacua & F. Priess (Eds.), *Ética y responsabilidad: reflexiones para periodistas.* Bogotá: Editora Guadalupe.

Radio. (2001, February). Retrieved December 4, 2001, from the World Wide Web at: http://www.apoyo.com/infor_util/inv_mercados/igm/igm_2001_2.html.

Rainie, L. (2000). Why the Internet is (mostly) good for news. *Nieman Reports, 54*(4), 17-18.

Regan, T. (2000). Technology is changing journalism. *Nieman Reports, 54*(4), 6-9.

Romero, G. (2000). Autocontrol de la información. In A. Cacua & F. Priess (Eds.), *Ética y responsabilidad: reflexiones para periodistas.* Bogotá: Editora Guadalupe.

Singer, J. B. (2001). The metro wide web: Changes in newspapers's gatekeeping role online. *Journalism and Mass Communication Quarterly, 78*(1), 65-80.

Small, J. (2000). Economics 101 of Internet news. *Nieman Reports, 54*(4), 41-42.

Stempel, G., Hargrove, T. & Bernt, J. (2000). Relation of growth of use of the Internet to changes in media use from 1995 to 1999. *Journalism and Mass Communication Quarterly, 77*(1), 71-79.

Uy, E. (2001). Reporters on superhighway meet roadblocks. *News Media and the Law, 25*(3), 49-50.

Wier, D. (2000). Web journalism crosses many traditional lines. *Nieman Reports, 54*(4), 35-37.

Chapter XV

An Integrated Network Management Framework Using CORBA, Mobile Agents and Web-Based Technologies

Dongming Cui
The University of Auckland, New Zealand

Jairo A. Gutiérrez
The University of Auckland, New Zealand

ABSTRACT

Today's network management is still dominated by the platform-centered paradigm based on client/server technologies. This centralized approach has drawbacks in scalability, reliability, efficiency and flexibility, and is unsuitable for large and heterogenous networks. Modern networks require an open management architecture, which can provide standard interfaces for information sharing among management systems, has extensibility for handling change quickly, and has means to manage large networks. Emerging technologies such as Web-, CORBA-, and Mobile Agent-based technologies represent an excellent opportunity to solve these problems. In this chapter a new Web-based network management framework is proposed, which combines the strengths of these novel ways of managing networks and the results of a prototype implementation are discussed. Our preliminary results indicate that the integration of Web-, CORBA-, and Mobile Agent-based technologies within an Integrated Network Management System framework can dramatically improve the performance of the networked environment.

BACKGROUND

Global competition has led to a greater reliance on information processing systems. Networks are required to extend beyond physical boundaries to support virtual corporations, virtual LANs, inter-enterprise systems, inter-networking, outsourcing and electronic commerce. Despite the fact that networks are becoming larger and more complex, today's network management is still dominated by the platform-centered paradigm based on client/server (C/S) technologies (e.g., SNMP). This centralized approach has drawbacks in scalability, reliability, efficiency and flexibility, and is unsuitable for large and heterogeneous networks (Goldszmidt & Yemini, 1998; Lazar, Saracco & Stadler, 1997; Yemini, 1993).

Numerous studies have shown that new technologies such as Mobile Agents (MA), CORBA and Web technologies have individually solved some of the problems associated with network management (Baek, Ha & Park, 1998; Baldi, Gai & Picco, 1997; Bieszczad, Pagurek & White, 1998; Cheikhrouhou, Conti, Labetoulle & Marcus, 1999; Deri & Ban, 1997; Goldszmidt & Yemini, 1998; Haggerty & Seethapaman, 1998; He & Shayman, 2000; Hegering, Abeck & Neumair, 1999; Liotta, Pavlou & Knight, 2002; Luo, Confrey & Trivedi, 1999; Terplan, 1999; Wren & Gutiérrez, 1999). However, few studies have looked into the impact of combining the strengths of these new technologies on an integrated network management system (INMS). Integrated management of a networked system involves several disciplines and different levels of managed objects. In recent years, the emphasis in network management has moved from managing machines to managing functionalities and the performance of these functionalities. On the other hand, there are no widely established methods today for dealing with large numbers of network elements. Managing large enterprise networks requires powerful abstractions that capture the essentials of the state of the network rather than the details.

THE CONCEPTUAL MODEL

The conceptual framework presented in this chapter was derived from a rigorous compilation of the agent-, CORBA- and Web-based network management literature. The goals in designing a scalable INMS with the help of these new technologies include:

- To improve accessibility and ease-of-use
- To solve the problems of scalability, extensibility, and interoperability
- To solve current efficiency and flexibility problems
- To solve the legacy interoperability problem

The proposed framework (Figure 1) was designed with those goals in mind.
The conceptual model follows a completely distributed architecture with the following components:

- Web browsers act as accessible, easy-to-use, portable user interfaces
- A CORBA Object Request Broker (ORB) acts as the scalable, extensible, interoperable middleware with support for legacy Network Management (NM) applications, MA-based NM applications as well as CORBA-based NM applications
- Mobile agents support efficient, reliable and interoperable executions; extend the functionalities of CORBA, and support legacy integrations such as with SNMP services

Figure 1. The Conceptual Model of the Proposed Scalable INMS Framework

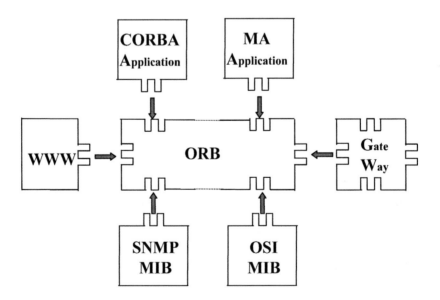

- Optionally, network management gateways support legacy systems interoperability

Each component and various factors that affect each component will be described in more detail in the following section.

THE PROPOSED FRAMEWORK

In the proposed framework, a dynamic binding mechanism is used for linking a manager to the platform. The mechanism is realized by implementing interfaces using CORBA's Interface Definition Language (IDL). Additionally, the integration of CORBA and the Web enables users to access CORBA-based information resources through a Web browser. The implementation method for this integration is through CORBA IDL-to-Java mappings. A Java applet is treated as a CORBA client and a CORBA server is located in the HTTP server side. This method may overcome the bottlenecks associated with the use of CGI.

Basic Network Management Operations

There are two types of network management operations in this management system: a manager's operation to an agent and an agent's operation to a manager. A manager of the proposed platform can be a legacy SNMP Manager, a CORBA application, or a MA-based application. The manager sends a request to an agent or receives event notifications from agents using network management service primitives, IDLs, or MAs respectively. Each manager provides basic functions used:
- To get values of Managed Objects (MOs) in an agent
- To set values of MOs in an agent
- To perform an action to an MO in an agent
- To create a new MO
- To delete an MO in an agent
- To be notified of certain events

Usually, SNMP is used to provide the network management service primitives to support the above functions. CMIP and other proprietary network management protocols may also be allowed to provide their management service primitives.

In the case of CORBA-based applications, it is necessary to map CORBA operations to SNMP messages or SNMP messages to CORBA operations for the exchange of management information. The way in which the CORBA operations are mapped to SNMP's message PDU is dependent on the specific implementation. It is possible, for example, to use the conversion procedures described by the Joint Inter-Domain Management (JIDM) specifications for the mapping of CORBA IDL to SNMP messages, and vice-versa (OMG, 2002).

The proposed framework follows a three-tier architecture: Web browser, CORBA and MA-based management platform with built-in Web server, and managed network resources such as agents and agencies. The environment in which the agents are executed is called a Distributed Agent Environment (DAE) or Agent Execution Environment (AEE) (see Figure 2). It consists of a set of agent systems called agencies, representing the runtime environments for MAs. Each agency comprises one or more places, each providing a set of resources, like a certain amount of memory, access to a file system, and SNMP services. Agencies can be grouped into regions or domains in order to facilitate management operations. For instance, a region can be associated with a single authority, providing certain security policies for each member agency.

The proposed MA-based platform was built on top of an ORB, and Java (JDK1.2) was used as the development language. The CORBA components of the AdventNet SNMP API (http://www.adventnet.com/) package were used to integrate the CORBA middleware with SNMP. Java enables distributed Web-enabled applications to transparently invoke operations on remote network services using the industry-standard Object Management Group (OMG) (http://www.omg.org) IDL and the Internet Inter-ORB protocol defined also by the OMG. The agent transport and further interactions between DAEs and non-DAE components are performed via CORBA mechanisms. In this way, standard

Figure 2. The DAE of the Proposed Framework

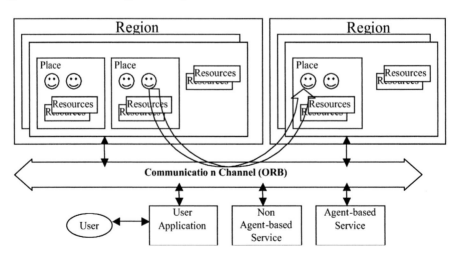

services such as CORBA trading, naming, or event services can be used to enhance the platform functionality in a very comfortable manner.

INTEGRATED NETWORK MANAGEMENT

Management information in a large network today is usually distributed between the MIBs of network elements and, as a consequence, represents small aspects of the configuration or operation of those elements rather than of the network as a whole. At the same time, more demanding management applications require access to a much higher level of management information and services.

The framework proposed is an object-oriented information model, where the value of an object's attribute can be defined as an arbitrary computation (i.e., by a MA) over other attribute values (i.e., SNMP MIB parameters). The latter can be information residing inside element management agents (i.e., SNMP agents) or other computed attributes (i.e., results produced by MAs). Figure 3 shows the data structures and different levels of access.

With this OO information model, network managers can define and interact with MOs that represent a "computed view" (Anerousis, 1999) of management information. Computed views can represent a summary of lower level configuration and performance information. The objects representing computed views of management information could be regarded as implementing a MA with "middleware management services." These middleware management services are carried by MAs that move around the network, extracting information from local managed elements using a standards-based management protocol such as SNMP, processing this information according to the specification of the computed view, and making it available to management applications through a distributed computing environment (i.e., CORBA or Java) (see Figure 4). This higher-level management information improves the efficiency of the INMS. Network managers, hence, do not need to interact with and interpret raw management data. In our prototype we used a Grasshopper (IKV, 1999) MA with an AdventNet SNMP API.

Figure 3. Data Structure and Levels of Access

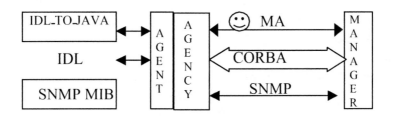

Figure 4.   Three-Level Architecture for Generating Computed Views of Management Information

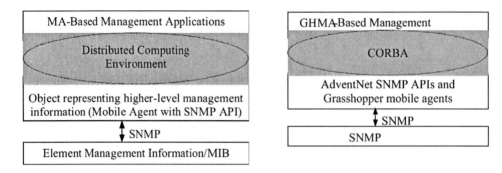

The SNMP data-handling services included a set of Java classes for high-level representation of SNMP data types and Protocol Data Units. A set of Java-based ASN.1/BER encoding methods is also available to be used by other SNMP services.

The SNMP manager service selected by the proposed framework allows MAs to interact with SNMP agents using a third-party SNMP stack integrated in the agents' code — to query SNMP agents — and includes a Trap Listener that receives SNMP traps and redirects them to the interested MAs.

The prototyping for the proposed INMS framework included a scenario of Web-SNMP integration, a scenario of CORBA-SNMP integration, and a scenario of MA-SNMP integration. Full details of the complete prototype system and proof-of-concept experiments can be found in Cui (2000).

The INMS consists of a HTTP Web server, Java applets and the management platform, which performs network management operations. The web server that allows for remote access and control from standard Web browsers brings ease-of-use and accessibility to NM development. Additionally, the lower cost of Web and Java technologies improves the cost/benefit ratio of these enhanced systems. A dynamic binding mechanism, which is realized by implementing interfaces using CORBA IDL, is used for linking a manager (either legacy or MA-based applications) to the platform. The resources of a managed network are thus modeled with abstractions (i.e., service names). This makes the management operation efficient and consistent and also improves the extensibility and interoperability of the INMS.

In summary, the presence of Web technology decouples user interfaces from traditional NM consoles, supports Web-based management and, therefore, improves the user friendliness and the user accessibility of the INMS. The use of

CORBA technology as the INMS infrastructure increases the system's capability for handling new features without requiring significant redesign and coding, adds the capability of handling large numbers of objects without inflicting performance or resource constraints, and adds the capability of interacting with other external components to request or offer services and facilities. This improves the extensibility, scalability, and interoperability of the INMS. Finally, the implementation of MA-based technologies introduces a higher-level abstraction of management information; reduces data collected; allows faster, and often preventative, maintenance as opposed to slow, and often reactive, maintenance; and, hence, improves the efficiency of the INMS.

PROOF-OF-CONCEPT IMPLEMENTATION

The implementation was carried out in a networking laboratory using three Cisco routers (2500 series), two Cisco Catalyst 1900 switches, an Allied Telesyn 3600 series hub and 10 Windows 95 workstations. The following applications and systems were used to develop the prototype:
- Operating systems: Windows NT Server 4.0 and Windows 95
- Browser: Internet Explorer (IE) 5.0
- MIB: WINNT SNMP services
- Web server: Jetty Web server
- ORB: JDK 1.2/1.2.2 ORB and IONA's OrbixWeb 3.0
- MA: Grasshopper toolkit
- SUN's JDF 1.2/1.2.2 Java — used to design and map SNMP/Java/CORBA
- AdventNet API — used to design SNMP NM applications and to provide SNMP access to Web, CORBA, and MA-based applications.

We used the independent variable "use of MA technology" to test the theory that an improvement of NM efficiency is caused by the application of MA-based technologies. We measured the response time of completing certain pre-defined SNMP operations. The measured time was an average measurement over a high number of executions.

The experimental results shown in Figure 5 indicate that the performance management MA has a shorter response time than equivalent SNMP operations as the number of NEs increases. In other words, once the MA service has been established, the speed of response from SNMP operations is faster than from non-MA SNMP operations when handling a large number of objects.

Figure 5. Comparison of TonyHopperAgents and Non-MA SNMP Operations

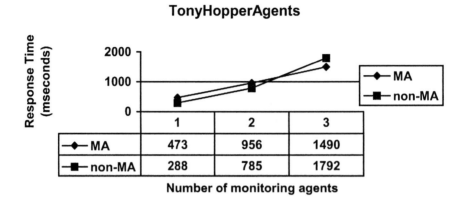

Figure 6 shows the experimental results of the comparison of response times in the non-JVM NE performance management MA and the related controlled non-MA scenarios. These figures show the total time (in msec) to complete the task in a network composed of several domains, each with several Ethernet-connected workstations.

The results indicate that the speed of completing the performance management tasks with agents is slightly slower than with equivalent SNMP operations. Although the prototype has proved the feasibility of managing non-JVM NE by using MAs, it is clear that proxy-based operations introduce significant overheads.

Figure 7 shows the experimental results of the comparison of response times using a policy-driven configuration management MA and the controlled non-MA scenarios.

The results indicate that the speed of completing the policy-driven configuration tasks with agents is faster than with equivalent SNMP operations.

Figure 6. The Comparison of TonyHubGhAgent and the Non-MA SNMP Operations

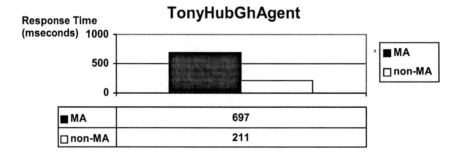

Figure 7. Results of the Comparison Between TonyIfSetAgent and Non-MA SNMP Operations

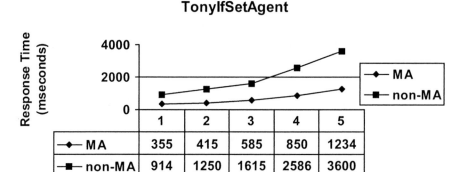

TonyIfSetAgent

	1	2	3	4	5
◆ MA	355	415	585	850	1234
■ non-MA	914	1250	1615	2586	3600

Number of monitoring agents

Our preliminary results show that MAs can offer a solution more suitable than traditional solutions for dealing with computed views of management information or dealing with "what if" applications.

CONCLUSIONS

The proposed MA-based INMS framework has been compared with non-MA-based SNMP management operations. SNMP management applications have been implemented as control models. The experimental results showed that the MA-based prototype improved the efficiency of network management operators.

During the lab experiments, other characteristics of the proposed INMS have also been observed. For instance, it was observed that the MA approach for network management is able to avoid any centralization point and provides better scalability and flexibility than centralized client/server schemes. Several administrators can be concurrently active and even cooperate to obtain a single administrative goal. It is easy to generate or destroy agents and to replicate them in the case of a large number of nodes in the subnetwork. In the prototyped applications, agents act on behalf of administrators and fulfill administration needs by moving and executing on different nodes. Furthermore, it is easy to tailor new agents to meet new administration needs and/or to delegate the automation of new management tasks.

In summary, the proposed framework can be used to delegate management activities to agents as well as to add Web and CORBA advantages to the INMS.

The implementation of the Grasshopper management environment has shown that MA solutions can also be convenient from a performance point of view.

Currently the INMS is implemented at a homogeneous configuration. It is desirable that the concepts of the proposed framework are tested in a heterogeneous environment, which is more common in a real network. The ideas described in this chapter have broad applications for distributed computing services. The current WBEM, JMX, and even Microsoft's COM/DCOM platforms may provide other ways for integrating CORBA, the Web, and MA-based technologies into an INMS.

REFERENCES

Anerousis, N. (1999). An Architecture for Building Scalable, Web-based Management Services. *Journal of Network and Systems Management, 7*(1), 73-104.

Baek, J.-W., Ha, T.-J. & Park, J.-T. (1998, February 15-20). ATM Customer Network Management Using WWW and CORBA Technologies. *Proceedings of the IEEE/IFIP Network Operations and Management Symposium* (NOMS'98). New Orleans, LA.

Baldi, M., Gai, S., & Picco, G.P. (1997). Exporting Code Mobility in Decentralized and Flexible Network Management. In K. Rothermel & R. Popescu-Zeletin (Eds.), *Mobile Agents, Lecture Notes in Computer Science Series*, vol. 1219 (pp. 13-26). Berlin, Germany: Springer-Verlag.

Bieszczad, A., Pagurek, B. & White, T. (1999). *Mobile Agents for Network Management. IEEE Communications Surveys*. Retrieved on November 15, 1999, from the World Wide Web: http://www.comsoc.org/pubs/surveys/4q98issue/bies.html.

Cheikhrouhou, M., Conti, P., Labetoulle, J., & Marcus, K. (1999). Intelligent Agents for Network Management: a Fault Detection Experiment. In M. Sloman, S. M., & E. Lupu, (Eds.), *Integrated Network Management, VI,* (pp. 595-609). Boston, MA: Chapman & Hall.

Cui, D. (2000, December). *Integrated Network Management using Web-, CORBA-, and Mobile Agent-based Technologies*. MCom thesis. The University of Auckland, Aukland, New Zealand.

Deri, L. & Ban, B. (1997). *Static vs. Dynamic CMIP/SNMP Network Management Using CORBA*. IBM Zurich Research Laboratory. Retrieved on October 7, 1999, from the World Wide Web: http://www.misa.ch/public/papers/deri97w.html.

Goldszmidt, G. & Yemini, Y. (1998, March). Delegated Agents for Network Management. *IEEE Communications Magazine, 36*(3), 66-70.

Haggerty, P. & Seethapaman, K. (1998). The Benefits of CORBA-based Network Management. *Communications of the ACM, 41*(10), 73-79.

He, Q. & Shayman, M. A. (2000). Using Reinforcement Learning for Proactive Network Fault Management. *IEEE Computer, 33*(9), 515-521.

Hegering, H.-G., Abeck, S. & Neumair, B. (1999). *Integrated Management of Networked Systems: Concepts, Architectures, and their Operational Application.* San Francisco, CA: Morgan Kaufmann Publishers.

IKV. (1999). *IKV's Grasshopper MA Platform. Grasshopper Programmer's Guide.* Retrieved on September 21, 1999, from the World Wide Web: http://www.grasshopper.de.

Lazar, A., Saracco, R., and Stadler, R. (Eds.). (1997). *Proceedings of the Fifth IFIP/IEEE International Symposium on Integrated Network Management.* San Diego, CA: Chapman & Hall.

Liotta, A., Pavlou, G. & Knight, G. (2002). Exploiting Agent Mobility for Large-Scale Network Monitoring. *IEEE Network, 16*(3), 7-15.

Luo, T., Confrey, T. & Trivedi, K. S. (1999). A Reliable CORBA-based Network Management System. *Proceedings of the IEEE International Conference on Communications, ICC'99,* (pp. 1374-1387). Tokyo, Japan.

Object Management Group (OMG). (2002). Retrieved on June 14, 2002, from the World Wide Web: http://www.omg.org.

Terplan, K. (1999). *Web-based systems and network management.* Boca Raton, FL: CRC Press.

Wren, M.J. & Gutiérrez, J. A. (1999). Agent and Web-based Technologies in Network Management. *Proceedings of the IEEE Global Telecommunications Conference (GLOBECOM'99),* (pp. 1877-1881). Rio de Janeiro, Brazil.

Yemini, Y. (1993, May). The OSI Network Management Model. *IEEE Communications Magazine,* 20-29.

About the Authors

George Ditsa is a lecturer in information systems in the School of Economics and Information Systems, Faculty of Commerce, University of Wollongong, Australia. Mr. Ditsa holds a B.Sc. (Hons) degree in Computer Science from the University Science and Technology, Kumasi, Ghana and an M.B.A. (IS) degree from the University of Wollongong. Mr. Ditsa worked for many years in the IS area as a programmer/analyst and project team leader in various organizations before taking up the lectureship position. His current research interests include strategic IS management, project management, user satisfaction of IS, cultural issues in IS management and, knowledge management and knowledge management systems. Mr. Ditsa has published numerous articles in conference proceedings and academic journals and he is about to complete his Ph.D. on the topic, "Executive Information Systems Use in Organisational Contexts: An Explanatory User Behaviour Testing."

*   *   *

Bruce H. Andrews is a professor of management science and director of the Center for Business and Economic Research in the School of Business at the University of Southern Maine, USA. He earned his doctorate in operations research at Polytechnic University. His research and consulting activities are primarily focused on applied, quantitatively-based decision-making in complex environments where standard modeling tools and perspectives fall short. Dr. Andrews has published extensively in applied management science journals, particularly *INTERFACES*, where his award-winning work with L.L. Bean was included as part of the Edelman International Competition for Best Successful Practice of Management Science.

Tamara Babaian is currently an assistant professor at the Computer Information Systems Department of Bentley College, Waltham, MA, USA. She has received her B.S./M.S. in Applied Mathematics from Yerevan State University of Armenia in 1994, and a Ph.D. in Computer Science from Tufts University, Medford, MA, in 2000. She spent a year at Harvard University as a postdoctoral fellow doing research in the area of collaborative interfaces. Her research interests include both theoretical and practical aspects of artificial intelligence. In particular, she has studied the topics of knowledge representation, reasoning and planning in the presence of incomplete information, and applied the developed methods to the problem of collaborative human-computer problem solving.

Mario A. Bochicchio is head of the Software Engineering and Telemedia Lab (SET-Lab) (Innovation Engineering Department—University of Lecce, Italy). He has more than 10 years of teaching experience (hypermedia design, database applications, educational technologies, etc.) in various Italian universities. Currently he is involved in various national and European projects about ubiquitous Web applications, educational technologies, and IC technologies for cultural heritage.

Fiona Y. Chan received her B.Sc. degree in Computing Studies, Information Systems from Hong Kong Baptist University in 2001. She is currently working as a research assistant in the Department of Computer Science at the same university. Her research interests include systems approach, agent technology, and recommender systems.

Larry Y.C. Cheung is currently studying for a Ph.D. at Loughborough University, UK, in the area of workflow management.

William K. Cheung received his B.Sc. and M.Phil. degrees both in Electronic Engineering from the Chinese University of Hong Kong, and his Ph.D. degree in Computer Science from the Hong Kong University of Science and Technology. He was the recipient of the Croucher Foundation Studentship and the Edward Youde Memorial Scholarship in 1991 and 1993 respectively. He is currently an assistant professor in the Department of Computer Science, Hong Kong Baptist University. His current research interests include pattern recognition, machine learning, and intelligent agents with applications to multimedia retrieval, Web mining, and e-commerce.

Paul W.H. Chung is a professor of computer science at Loughborough University, UK, since 1999. Prior to that he was a British Gas-Royal Academy of Engineering senior research fellow in Computer-aided Safe Plant Design. His research interests include adaptive workflow and automated risk assessment. He received his B.Sc. in Computing Science from Imperial College in 1981 and Ph.D. in artificial intelligence from the University of Edinburgh in 1986.

John Coombes received his M.Sc. in Information Systems at the University of Sheffield in 1999 and is currently a Ph.D. candidate at the City University of Hong Kong. His focus of study is idea convergence using electronic group support systems. His fields of interest span e-commerce, m-commerce, systems analysis and design, online education, and human-computer interaction. His long-term plan is the study of group support systems, virtual organizations, IT-enabled learning, information management, and information systems implementation.

Dongming Cui completed his Master of Commerce degree (2001) in the Department of Management Science and Information Systems of the University of Auckland in New Zealand. He is a consultant with Pioneer Computers (Australia) and his research interests include scalable network management systems and the use of mobile agents-based technologies in computer networking.

Ray J. Dawson obtained a bachelor's degree in Mathematics with Engineering and a master's degree in Engineering from Nottingham University before entering the industry with Plessey Telecommunications in 1977. While working at the company, he developed an interest in the working methods for software development as practiced in industry. This became a research interest when he joined Loughborough University, UK, as a lecturer in 1987. Other research interests are information systems and knowledge management, which he now combines with his interest in industrial working practices to work with companies to improve their information and knowledge management systems. Ray Dawson is now a senior lecturer in Computer Science at Loughborough University, as well as a chartered engineer and member of the British Computer Society.

Antonio Díaz is an assistant professor of information systems at the Escuela de Administración de Negocios para Graduados (ESAN) in Lima, Peru. He holds an M.B.A. with specialization in information systems from ESAN and a B.S. degree in Aeronautical Engineering from Escuela de Ingeniería Aeronáutica (Argentina). His research interests include electronic business and impact of information technology on economic and social issues.

Brian Dobing is an assistant professor in Information Systems at the University of Lethbridge, Canada. He received his M.B.A. and M.Sc. in Computational Science from the University of Saskatchewan, and his Ph.D. from the University of Minnesota. His research focuses on issues in user-analyst relationships and object-oriented analysis. He has recently published articles in the *Journal of Database Management, Internet Research*, and the *Journal of Computing Information Systems*.

Nicola Fiore is a Ph.D. student in information engineering at the Department of Innovation Engineering, University of Lecce, Italy. His research activity concerns modeling methodologies and their formalisation (HDM, W2000 and UWA) for hypermedia applications, and the design and development of tools for rapid prototyping.

Jairo A. Gutiérrez is a senior lecturer in Information Systems at the University of Auckland, New Zealand. Previously, he worked as an R&D manager, systems integration consultant, and information systems manager. He also conducted seminars on LAN/WAN technologies. He teaches data communications and computer networking. His current research interests include network management systems, programmable networks, and high-speed computer networking. He received a Systems and Computer Engineering degree from The University of The Andes (Colombia, 1983), a master's degree in Computer Science from Texas A&M University (1985), and a Ph.D. (1997) in Information Systems from The University of Auckland (New Zealand).

Thomas A. Horan, Ph.D., is executive director of the Claremont Information and Technology Institute and Associate Professor in the School of Information Science at the Claremont Graduate University, USA. His research focuses on the planning and assessment of advanced technology systems, including telecommunications and transportation. Dr. Horan has published widely in urban transportation and information science journals. His recent book, *Digital Places: Building Our City Of Bits* (ULI, 2000) synthesized this research into a broader vision of technology deployment. Over the last decade, Dr. Horan has also held visiting positions at UCLA, University of Minnesota, Harvard University, and MIT. Prior to joining Claremont Graduate University, Dr. Horan spent seven years in the Washington, D.C. area. From 1992-94, Dr. Horan was a senior fellow at George Mason University and from 1988-1992, he was a senior analyst at the U.S. General Accounting Office (GAO). Dr. Horan has both his master's and doctorate degrees from the Claremont Graduate University.

Mohamed Khalifa received his M.A. and Ph.D. in Information Systems from the Wharton Business School of the University of Pennsylvania. He is currently associate professor at the Information Systems Department of City University of Hong Kong, where he also serves as program leader for the Master of Arts in Electronic Business and as director for the Asia Center for Electronic Business (jointly managed with Peking University).

Moez Limayem is an associate professor and the BBA electronic commerce program coordinator of the Information Systems at City University of Hong Kong. Until recently, he was the chair of the Management Information Systems department at Laval University in Canada. He holds an M.B.A. and a Ph.D. in MIS from the University of Minnesota. His current research interests include business process reengineering, CRM, and electronic commerce. He has had several articles published in many journals, such as *Management Science, Information Systems Research, IEEE Transactions, Accounting, Management & Information Technologies, Group Decision and Negotiation*, and *Small Group Research*. He has been invited to present his research in many countries in North America, Europe, Africa, Asia, and in the Middle East. He won the best MIS paper award at the *ASAC* conference in 1998. Dr. Limayem also acts as a consultant for the UNESCO and several private and public companies. In 1994, Professor Limayem won the prestigious *HERMES* award for excellence in teaching. In 1995 and 1998, he won the award for the best MIS teacher in the Faculty of Business Administration at Laval University, and he recently received the 3M award for the best teacher in Canada. In November 2001, he won the Teaching Excellence Award at City University of Hong Kong.

Leonardo Mangia received the Dr.Eng. degree in Computer Science Engineering from the University of Lecce, Italy, and so far he has been working both as consultant and researcher in various projects in the Web application fields. Since 1998 he has been at the Department of Engineering, University of Lecce, where he is now a Ph.D. in Computer Science Engineering. His research interests include information systems and the methodology of Web application design and sizing.

Erik Molenaar received his German Diploma (M.Sc. equivalent) in Computer Science at the University of Technology in Aachen, Germany, based on his work on application-sharing solutions for multi-party scenarios, based on the event-sharing paradigm. As a graduate student with the University of Technology in Aachen, Erik has been working on implementation issues for conferencing control protocols and middleware solutions such as CORBA.

Roberto Paiano received the Dr.Eng. degree in Electronic Engineering from the University of Bologna, Italy. He worked at IBM in Italy until 1996. Since 1997 he has been at the Department of Engineering, University of Lecce, Italy, where he is an assistant professor. His research interests include information systems and the methodology of Web application design and sizing. He is a member of the IEEE and the IEEE Computer Society.

Vito Perrone is a Ph.D. student in Computer Science in the Department of Electronics and Information at the Politecnico di Milano, Italy, since 2001. His research interests span Web technology and Web-site design, tools for designing and prototyping of Web applications, Web application usability, and conceptual and logical modeling. He received a degree in Computer Science Engineering from the University of Lecce in 2001, and so far he has been working both as consultant and researcher in various projects in the Web application fields.

Martín Santana is an associate professor of information technology at the Escuela de Administración de Negocios para Graduados (ESAN) in Lima, Peru. He holds a Ph.D. in Business Administration from Florida International University and an M.S. in Information Systems from the École des Hautes Études Commerciales in Montreal. His research interests include electronic business, systems development approaches, and conflict management in the development process. He has published in the areas of the use of global applications of information technology, the management of the systems development process, and the consequences of information technology in organizations.

Dirk Trossen is a senior research engineer at Nokia Research Center, USA. Dirk received his M.Sc. in Mathematics and a Ph.D. in Computer Science at the University of Technology in Aachen, Germany, based on his work on scalable group communication, streaming, and conference control protocols. His research work also includes modeling of group communication systems for performance evaluation. At Nokia Research Center, Dirk focuses on 3G services, SIP-based service creation, protocol functionality for inter-technology networking, and seamless user experience across heterogeneous networks. He has been an active contributor to industry standards (such as the Internet Engineering Task Force). Dirk has published more than 30 papers in international conferences and journals.

Steven Walczak is an associate professor of information systems and of health administration in the Business School at the University of Colorado at Denver, USA. He received his Ph.D. from the University of Florida's Computer and

Information Sciences program. Dr. Walczak's research interests are in the fields of artificial intelligence (AI), knowledge management, and object-oriented systems design. His AI research is centered on empirical studies and applications of AI methods to novel problems, particularly in financial and medical domains. Dr. Walczak has more than 70 refereed publications in academic and practitioner journals, conference proceedings, and book chapters.

Li Yao is an associate professor of the Department of Management Science and Engineering at National University of Defense Technology, China. She received a B.S. in Software of Computer Science from NanKai University in 1985, an M.S. in Artificial Intelligence from National University of Defense Technology in 1990, and a Ph.D. in Information System Engineering from National University of Defense Technology in 1995. Her research interests are intelligent information systems, intelligent decisions, and knowledge management. She has published more than 50 scholarly articles in journals and conferences. Her work has published in the *Journal of Software, Journal of Computer Research & Development, Journal of Management Sciences in China* (in Chinese), and so on.

Irena Yegorova is a doctoral student in finance at Baruch College and Graduate School and University Center, City University of New York, USA. She earned her undergraduate and M.B.A. degrees from the University of Southern Maine. She is interested in applied research that is motivated by complex problems facing financial decision makers. Her current research interests include credit risk management, credit scoring and default prediction modeling, and artificial intelligence applications in finance. Irena has co-authored several articles and research presentations related to credit scoring model development.

Sajjad Zahir is a professor of management in the area of Decision Sciences and Information Systems at the University of Lethbridge, Alberta, Canada. He received his doctorate degree from the University of Oregon, Eugene, USA. His current research interests are in multicriteria decision models, decision support systems and intelligent systems and Internet technologies. He has published in the *European Journal of Operational Research*, the *Canadian Journal of Administrative Sciences*, the *Journal of the Operational Research Society*, the *Journal of American Society for Information Science*, the *International Journal of Information Technology and Decision Making, Internet Research: Electronic Networking Applications and Policy*, the *Journal of Computer and Information Systems*, the *International Journal of Operations and Quantitative Management, INFOR*, and also in several physics journals.

Weiming Zhang is a professor of the School of Humanities and Management at National University of Defense Technology, China. He received a B.S. in Information System Engineering from National University of Defense Technology in 1984, an M.S. in Information System Engineering from National University of Defense Technology in 1995, and a Ph.D. in Information System Engineering from National University of Defense Technology in 2001. He has published many articles in journals and conferences. His research interests are management information systems and decision support systems.

Index